The Politics Within

The Politics Within

A Primer in Political Attitudes and Behavior

SECOND EDITION

Jarol B. Manheim
*Virginia Polytechnic Institute
and State University*

Longman
New York & London

THE POLITICS WITHIN
A Primer in Political Attitudes and Behavior
SECOND EDITION

Longman Inc., 19 West 44th Street,
New York, N.Y. 10036
Associated companies, branches, and representatives
throughout the world.

Developmental Editor: Irving E. Rockwood
Editorial and Design Supervisor: Joan Matthews
Manufacturing and Production Supervisor: Ann Musso

Library of Congress Cataloging in Publication Data

Manheim, Jarol B., 1946–
   The politics within.

   Includes bibliographies and index.
   1. Political psychology. 2. Political sociology.
3. Attitude (Psychology) I. Title.
JA74.5.M35   1982   306'.2   81-12320
ISBN 0-582-28284-5   AACR2
ISBN 0-582-28283-7 (pbk.)

Manufactured in the United States of America
9 8 7 6 5 4 3 2 1

To
Katherine Ann Hinckley
Teacher

Contents

Preface to the Second Edition

As is frequently the case, the second edition of this book is longer than the first, a phenomenon potentially attributable to one or more of three factors. First, I may simply have become more verbose with age at the rate of five to ten pages per year. If that is true, the book has grown in size only, and a second edition is unwarranted. Since had I believed this to be the case I should hardly have mentioned it, let us assume otherwise. (It is also possible, of course, that my new publisher, borrowing a page from the era of Dickens, has agreed to pay me by the word, but this, I assure you, is not the case.)

Second, I may have grown intellectually since last setting down my thoughts on the subject so that the presentation here reflects my own more thorough understanding of the material at hand. This I find a more flattering image, and I commend it to your attention. Here, too, however, there is a rival hypothesis, namely that I have merely moved from one level of banality to another, or have simply become more thoroughly banal. Modesty prevents me from refuting this charge, but we all realize that it is wholly lacking in validity.

Finally, all else may have been held constant for seven years while the study of political behavior has itself matured. Here I find the evidence somewhat mixed. In some ways, the development of theory and research in this area has stagnated or at least slowed. Interesting work is being done, publications are issuing forth albeit at a reduced rate, and our understanding of political phenomena is advancing. But somehow the journals have been less challenging, the thinking less seminal in the aggregate, during the last seven years than in the period just before in those areas of political science, sociology, and psychology that have *traditionally* contributed to the study of political behavior. At the same time, during this period the very definition of political behavior has been broadened, and exciting new fields of inquiry have been staked out. A case in point is the life sciences approach to political behavior with its challenging methodological quandaries and its occasionally controversial theoretical propositions with which political scientists are only now beginning to come to terms.

In truth, there is a little of each of these three factors in this new edition. I have been teaching seven years longer now and in that time have no doubt learned to spend more words on the same bill of goods, so some degree of verbal inflation is probably inevitable. In addition, I like to think I have grown intellectually during these same years. For example, I made a conscious decision in the first edition to exclude any real discussion of personality and politics because I was not satisfied that I understood what of significance the theories really told us. I have included such a chapter in the present edition, whether because I finally figured out what the theories were saying or because I decided that the problem must lie with them rather than with me. (That judgment I leave to you.) And finally, the intellectual sophistication of the material has grown as well. This is reflected in the chapter on physiological bases of political behavior, which was anticipated in the first edition but simply could not be written at that time, and in the wealth of recent material added elsewhere in the text.

In undertaking this revision I have been assisted by W. Lance Bennett of the University of Washington, John Wahlke of the University of Arizona, and an anonymous referee, each of whom read the manuscript and offered helpful suggestions. I gratefully acknowledge their help, which substantially enriched the final product, though the ultimate choices, and the responsibility for their consequences, remain my own. I also wish to thank my editor at Longman, Irv Rockwood, who rescued this book from the remaindering bins of an Englewood Cliffs, New Jersey, publisher who shall remain anonymous; Joan Matthews, Anne Musso, and Irene Glynn for their able and incredibly expeditious production and editorial assistance; and Wally Littman, whose artistic ability has contributed so much to both editions of this book. And finally, I thank my wife, Amy, and daughter, Laura, for their patience while I scratched and scrawled, cut and pasted, rejoiced and cursed. And, of course, Cookie, who continues to endure.

Jarol B. Manheim

Preface to the First Edition

In our efforts to introduce students to the study of political behavior, we often seem to require of them what amounts to a quantum leap from the comparatively pastoral reflections of Plato and the Philosopher King to the more rigorous and technologically oriented analyses of the Survey Research Center and the American Voter. We ask them to trade Aristotle for Angus Campbell, Rousseau for Robert Dahl, and perhaps even Thoreau for B. F. Skinner. Yet relatively few efforts have been made in the literature of political behavior to bridge this gap in a more gentle fashion, to coax the student into behavioral kinds of concerns without overwhelming him with tables, scatter diagrams, and various forms of correlational rejoicing. As a result, relatively few students are able—or perhaps more precisely, few are willing—to grasp the subject matter of and to develop an interest in the behavioral study of politics. To the contrary, many define behavioral political analysis as sterile or irrelevant.

One way in which we might respond to this circumstance would be to present an analysis of political behavior in a manner that permitted the student consciously to relate what he reads to his own perceptions of political reality. That is, if we were able to establish not so much the relevance but the explanatory power of techniques of political analysis in contemporary life, we might attract not only the attention but the intellectual curiosity of the student. In this way we could use the intuitive appeal of our subject matter to provide the student with a highly personalized psychological linkage with the study of political behavior. The present book is an attempt in this direction.

The problem in such an undertaking is twofold. To begin with, one must create for the student a series of clearly discernible connections between his own personal experiences and the substance of behavioral analysis, for such connections provide a critical basis for understanding more general theoretical premises. At the same time, however, one must take care to provide the student with a set of theoretical premises sufficient to give substantive meaning both to what he learns in the classroom and reads, and to what he later observes on his own. Fortunately, there exist in the political sphere a number of topics (symbolic politics, political socialization, elections and campaigning, and the like) that appear to provide precisely the kinds of foci to which students do in fact relate on a personalized basis. Once elucidated, these phenomena tend to be clearly identifiable in the student's own experience, and in many instances they appear to have elicited considerable amounts of independent thinking. Thus it seems reasonable to expect that these topics could provide the desired linkage between a student's own political existence, on the one hand, and analytical approaches to the study of political behavior on the other.

Moreover, these particular topics have the added virtue of themselves being capable of presentation as manifestations of a more or less unified body of theory pertaining to the structure and dynamics of political attitudes. Indeed, by emphasizing the development, structure, modification, and implementation of political attitudes, we are able to provide a common framework for the analysis of these and other aspects of political behavior. We can speak of the growth of attitudes (political socialization), the sharing of attitudes (political culture), the manipulation of attitudes (political campaigning), the application of attitudes (voting behavior and other forms of participation), and so forth. And each of these elements of political life can be traced back to basic notions in attitude theory.

It is the purpose of the present book, then, first to provide the student with enough substantive information about attitude theory to constitute a useful analytical tool, and subsequently to help him to employ this analytical perspective in evaluating and understanding his own political environment. At the same time, we must recognize that the student is not yet a professional social scientist, and must often be coaxed with rather than overwhelmed by theoretical formulations. With this in mind, I shall offer a variety of relatively complex theoretical schema in rather simplified form and shall endeavor throughout to make the essence of each concept more readily understandable for the student by presenting a limited number of variations. I fully realize that any such undertaking entails considerable risk, and I accept full responsibility for any anomalies that may result. Nevertheless, I ask the indulgence of the more sophisticated reader for any reasonable limitations of the text that may arise from this choice of approach.

Finally, consistent with the expressed goal of nurturing student interest in the concepts under consideration, I have appended to each chapter a brief annotated bibliography to assist in further exploration of topics covered in that chapter. My purpose here has not been to suggest to the reader the entire breadth of available research on the points in question, but rather, to point out one or two anthologies that I believe best capture the thrust of that research, a classic treatment of the issues in question, an especially readable analysis of related topics, or perhaps simply an interesting book that has some bearing on the matters under discussion. Thus the recommended readings are intended only to offer an immediate second step for the student whose appetite has been whetted by a particular element in the presentation.

I wish to express my gratitude to Professors Judson L. James of Virginia Polytechnic Institute and State University and Dan Nimmo of the University of Tennessee, both of whose erudite comments and suggestions have proven of immeasurable value in the distillation of a final manuscript; to Melanie Wallace and Helena Zengara for their assistance in the preparation of early drafts of the manuscript; to Gilbert Jardine and Milton McGowen for their faith and encouragement; to Ann Torbert for her generally tactful and always able editorial assistance; and to my wife Amy and our cat Cookie for their endurance.

The Politics Within

1

Some Introductory Comments

A few years ago a number of college students were asked to describe their images of politics and of political science. They reported viewing politics as, among other things, active, strong, practical, and important, yet at the same time cruel, impersonal, and dirty. Political science was seen as realistic, philosophical, theoretical, beneficial, interesting, important, and practical, yet also as inartistic and unromantic. Finally, in the same study, both students and faculty members were asked to specify terms that they might use to define politics. In general, the students tended to emphasize such structural factors as government, law, and system, whereas their professors opted for such process terms as power, conflict, persuasion, and strategy. At the least, we may conclude from these results that students view politics and its study with some ambivalence and that their images of the subject differ significantly from the images held by faculty members.[1]

If this finding is accurate, it reflects a state of affairs that may derive in large measure from the apparent inability of political scientists themselves to arrive at a concise, enduring, and generally accepted definition of their own field. After all, if political scientists cannot agree on a definition of politics, how then could anyone else be expected to agree on one? This definitional problem has plagued the discipline since its inception, and it is no less significant today. Perhaps some comments on the nature of contemporary political science will help to make this clear.

One of the more evident trends in political science in recent years has been the willingness of its practitioners to transcend traditional disciplinary boundaries, to blur the lines that set off political analysis from other forms of social inquiry. Theories of political behavior have thus come to have more and more in common with the analytical frameworks developed by those in other areas. In point of fact, the situation has become such that we political scientists have, in effect, become a profession of borrowers and imitators. From mathematics, for example, we have borrowed a taste for precision instrumentation and rigorous inquiry, and with it have created a "science" of politics replete with mathematical models, statistical significances, and the ubiquitous computer error. From engineering and cybernetics we have borrowed the concept of systems analysis, and with it have created a powerful heuristic tool which aids us in explaining the processes of political interaction among men and their institutions. From economics we have borrowed the model of the rationally behaving individual, and with it have come to view politics as the operation of hierarchies of personal preference. And similarly, from the various other social sciences we have borrowed those notions of psychological and social process that have enabled us to fill in requisite details of our manifold political formulations. Indeed, it might appear to the casual observer that those of us who style ourselves political scientists are either too lazy or too ignorant to come up with our own original lines of inquiry, or too clever to waste our time doing so when we can so easily borrow from other disciplines that which we desire—namely, a satisfactory conceptualization of political activity.

But while this academic kleptomania has been pursued with renewed vigor in recent years, it is hardly a latter-day phenomenon. To the contrary, the borrowing of conceptual frameworks by students of politics has fairly deep historical roots, and can in fact be traced back at least as far as Aristotle, who, in first referring to man as a "political animal," contributed to the rather lengthy development of a very powerful biological analogy in politics. Over the years, this particular analogy has been reflected in attempts to apply to political analysis such frameworks as the circulation of the blood (by James Herrington), Lamarckian heredity (by Auguste Comte), the life cycle (by Thomas Hobbes), and the Darwinian notion of survival of the fittest (by Herbert Spencer). While each of these models proved rather compelling at the time of its presentation, however, reflective as each was of contemporaneous scientific advances, all have proven in the long run to be rather short-lived.

I raise this point not to heap ridicule upon the learned proponents of these various conceptualizations, for in fact it is my belief that they have performed a vital service for those who would "understand" politics. Indeed, by evaluating these analogies and identifying both the strengths and the weaknesses of each, by distilling the essence of politics from the potpourri of social activity, these pioneers of political analysis have helped us over time to increase our knowledge of the fundamental processes of political life. To belittle such an accomplishment would reflect badly not only upon one's sense of gratitude but upon one's humility as well.

Rather, I emphasize this collective touch of larceny so common among important political theorists because it illustrates something quite significant not only about political science but about politics itself. For above all, this frequently felt compulsion to encroach upon the explanatory models of other disciplines suggests that political activity is, in the final analysis, not an especially unique activity and that the political process is not an especially unique process. Politics is instead a special combination of common activities and common processes as they are applied to a unique set of objects. And the study of politics is thus by necessity an exercise in integrating and synthesizing the techniques and the accumulated wisdom of other, more specialized fields of inquiry.

Because thinking about politics (for example) is just like thinking about anything else, the knowledge and perspective of the psychologist become relevant to political analysis. Similarly, because the political aspects of a culture and a social system are but a subset of the culture and system as wholes, anthropological and sociological insights can also shed light on the nature of politics. Even the old biological analogy (*"head* of government," *"long arm* of the law," *"body* politic") can be used to great benefit because it helps us formulate in our own minds a more precise interpretation of a concept which we hope to communicate. In each instance, it is neither the tools of analysis nor the observed process itself that is inherently the stuff of politics. It is instead the often loosely defined set of objects of analysis (the government, influence relationships, control of resources, or whatever) that identifies any particular phenomenon as being essentially "political." It is the substance and not the procedure that is unique. Thus we may conceive of politics as encompassing all thoughts, actions, attitudes, or events that relate in some way to objects perceived—either by those directly involved or by outside observers—to have political meaning, and we may conceive of political science as that area of inquiry which attempts to impose conceptual unity upon this diversity of human endeavor.

The present book makes no pretense of pushing forward the boundaries of political science inch by grudging inch by calling forth some grand new analogy that will outperform all the preceding weaponry of political analysis. Such is, after all, not the purpose of a primer. What I do hope to accomplish is to illustrate by a variety of devices the ways in which students of politics can apply to good advantage the collective wisdom of other social science disciplines in the continuing search for an understanding of political phenomena. In particular, in considering the implications of attitude structure and attitude dynamics for individual political behavior I shall focus attention on matters usually reserved for the social psychologist. By investigating these psychological processes in a political context, I hope to develop useful insights into the nature and foundations of political activity.

This emphasis on political psychology is easily justified when one realizes that political activity takes place on two distinct yet closely interrelated levels which may be termed the *concrete* and the *symbolic*. At the concrete level, politics involves control of or influence over the distribution of physical goods and services through a society. Thus the allocation among competing individuals and interests of such items as roads and mass transit, school facilities, jobs, parks, police protection, money, and the like involves the operation of concrete politics. Indeed, almost every activity that we regard as political in nature is somehow related to deciding—or to attempting to influence those who decide—who is going to get how much of what from whom under what circumstances. And since the results of such decisions can have a significant impact upon the lives and well-being of those individuals who submit to them, the stakes of concrete politics are quite high.

At the same time, however, political decisions and activities serve to distribute throughout a society a set of less tangible goods and services, a set of symbols, which can have an equally significant impact. For not only are various manifestations of physical wealth conveyed through the political process, but such psychological staples as hope, faith, certainty, trust, understanding, and support, objects that are nothing more than mere states of mind, are given, withheld, or even withdrawn as well. These intangibles, these meanings that attach to virtually every decision regarding the distribution of physical goods and services, are the stock in trade of the second order of political activity, that of symbolic politics.

When, for example, we learn that war has been made less likely by the decisions of our national leaders, not only do we retain as a consequence physical control over assets ranging from tax dollars to our very lives, but we acquire as well a certain positive psychological orientation which structures our subsequent political perception and activity. We become optimistic; we feel a sense of security. Conversely, when we learn that war has been made more likely by the decisions of our national leaders, not only are we faced with loss of life or property, but we acquire a certain negative psychological orientation, perhaps fear or anger, which can structure our outlook in rather different directions. And more generally, every political act, whether it be undertaken by the individual or by others in the political system, has the potential both to give and to take away not only the physical resources of the society but the psychological appurtenances as well. And because what people think and know about politics influences their political behavior, these psychological distributions may have great importance for both the individual and society.

When we study the behavior of people in politics, then, we must be aware not only of the generally apparent events of concrete politics, but of the underlying and equally important manifestations of symbolic politics as well. We must look behind the facade of politics as a process by which physical resources are allocated throughout a society to discover the dynamics of individual psychology that sustain the process. Politics is a self-balancing equation with both physical and psychological components, and only when we understand the relationship between the two can we hope fully to comprehend the equation itself. With such an understanding as a goal, the following chapters seek to clarify the role played by attitudes, beliefs, and other psychological states in helping to structure political life.

The pages that follow attempt to bring together many diverse yet closely related phenomena by investigating, first, the psychological conditions and processes that influence political behavior, and subsequently that behavior itself. Chapter 2 starts us out by defining some rather basic constructs, outlining some important characteristics of political attitudes, and establishing a conceptual base for a consideration of the relationship between the individual and political reality. Chapter 3 extends this framework to include personality. Chapter 4 places the individual and his or her attitudes into a social environment by investigating the links that bind not only individuals to their cultures but cultures to their individual members. Once it has been established that such cultural bonds exist and that individuals become formally and effectively integrated into sociopolitical systems, the discussion focuses, in Chapter 5, on the process-es by which individuals in fact become acculturated—in other words, the processes of political learning. Here both the quality and the substance of lessons learned by individuals through politi-cal experience will be considered, as well as the sources from which those lessons are derived. In Chapter 6 it is suggested that the ex-istence of political learning necessarily implies the existence of a dynamic psychological process by which attitudes may be acquired, modified, or even changed. This chapter presents several theories of attitude change and considers their implications both for the in-dividual in question and for would-be persuaders. Chapter 7 dem-onstrates the real-world application of our theories of attitude structure and development in the area of political campaigning, while Chapter 8 deals more generally with the relationship be-tween political attitudes and political behavior by developing an admittedly speculative conceptualization of political activity in which I identify a number of underlying psychological dimensions. Chapter 9 examines the physiological characteristics of the indi-vidual in a search for the roots of attitudes, personality, and a variety of related psychological phenomena.

SUGGESTIONS FOR FURTHER READING

Any of a number of books representative of the various borrowings of political scientists might be recommended, but high on any such list would surely be the following: Hayward R. Alker, Jr., *Mathema-tics and Politics* (New York: Macmillan, 1965), a discussion of math-ematical modeling and its applications to political analysis; David Easton's important contribution of a systems theory of political activity in *A Systems Analysis of Political Life* (New York: John Wiley, 1965); and Anthony Downs's analysis of rational political behavior in *An Economic Theory of Democracy* (New York: Harper, 1957). An important application of the biological model to politics is in Thom-as L. Thorson's *Biopolitics* (New York: Holt, Rinehart and Win-ston, 1970).

The importance of symbolic action in politics is perhaps best summarized in Murray Edelman's *The Symbolic Uses of Politics* (Urbana: University of Illinois Press, 1964). This book is rather sophisticated and at times difficult to read, but it will prove re-warding to anyone interested in the topic. A related analysis of political images may be found in Dan D. Nimmo, *Popular Images of Politics* (Englewood Cliffs, N.J.: Prentice-Hall, 1974). Treating many of the same questions but at a somewhat less sophisticated level is the classic by Harold Lasswell, *Politics: Who Gets What, When, How* (New York: McGraw-Hill, 1936).

NOTES

1. Dan Klassen and Charles Mundale, "The Student's Image of Politics and Political Science," *Teaching Political Science* 1, no. 1 (October 1973): 35–46.

2

Political Attitudes

The Building Blocks
of Political Behavior

This book begins from the premise that much of what we generally refer to as "political behavior" can best be understood in the context of certain attitudes that people hold. In a very real sense, these attitudes are the building blocks of political activity. In the political edifice that is any particular individual, they may be relatively numerous or relatively scarce. They may be combined with infinite variety, and each may differ widely in scope and substance from the next. Indeed, no two people are likely to share a full set of identical political attitudes. But whatever their number or their content, and in whatever combination they may occur in any individual, there exist in the structures and functions of all these attitudes certain regularities that provide a basis for a broader, systematic analysis. Let us therefore begin our discussion by examining rather closely these common structural and functional characteristics.

WHAT IS AN ATTITUDE?

We can define an *attitude* as a predisposition to respond to a particular stimulus in a particular manner.[1] In other words, an attitude represents a greater likelihood that a person will react to a given experience or communication one particular way rather than in some other way. An example from physiology may clarify this point.

When you visit the doctor for a physical examination, one of the rituals that is always performed is the testing of reflexes. You sit on the edge of the examination table, the doctor taps with his little hammer just below your knee, and, assuming that your reflexes are healthy, your leg swings forward involuntarily. The tap of the hammer below your knee provides a *stimulus* to your body— most simply, a new force that calls for some kind of reaction, or *response*. The response is provided when your leg kicks forward involuntarily. Tap, kick. Tap, kick. As long as your leg is relaxed— that is, as long as your guard is down—there is a direct channel operating between the stimulus and the response.

But suppose you tense up the muscles in your leg so that the stimulus is blocked or modified. Then you can *decide* whether and how you *want* to kick in response to the tapping of the doctor's hammer. You can hold your leg still, you can kick extra hard, you can move your leg sideways, and so forth. A third element has been introduced, the element of personal preference. What is it that you as an individual *prefer* to do in this particular circumstance? The stimulus must now be filtered through a sort of psychological analysis before a response is delivered, and this is where attitudes come in. Attitudes serve to delineate the criteria according to which this analysis is performed. And the response that ensues may, as we have noted, be quite different from the initial response when the filter was not in place.

As any physician or psychologist will tell you, this example is somewhat oversimplified, but it does help illustrate the point. An attitude is basically a set of psychological conditions that makes any particular response to a given situation more or less likely than any other response in accordance with the wishes and beliefs of the individual in question. An attitude *intervenes* between the stimulus and the response.

We can see this intervention at work in politics as well. When we are exposed to campaign advertising for one or another candidate, for example, we consider that advertising *in the context* of our own personal needs and preferences. When we learn of conflict or cooperation among nations, we interpret that conflict or cooperation *in the context* of our own hopes and fears. When we make decisions about our own role in politics, about our willingness to participate, we do so *in the context* of our feelings about the political system, about the value of participation, about the likelihood of success. In each instance we respond to political stimuli not in a void but in terms of a particular and highly individualized context, in terms of something inside each of us that helps give meaning to the political options that have been presented. That intervening something, that context, is what we mean when we refer to an "attitude."

What we are saying, then, is that attitudes play a vital role in the process known as communication, in the bringing of individuals into contact with new stimuli from the world around them. Communication is the meeting at the skin of one's inner sensations with the essence of any outside object or organism. It is the touch of the doctor's hammer against the nerve endings of the knee, the impact of light waves from a printed page upon the receptors in the eye, the clash of ideas and experiences with thought and expectation. And in those instances where communication requires understanding, interpretation, or evaluation of newly arrived information, it is attitudes that provide the individual with the necessary bridge between past and present, between a stimulus and its meaning. Attitudes act as a screen through which an individual's perceptions of reality must be filtered. Attitudes intervene, in a special and highly constructive manner, between a message or stimulus as it has been issued and the individual who receives and "understands" that message. And as a result, the nature of the message itself may be changed, and its meaning may become highly individualized.[2]

As a matter of fact, you are at this very moment engaged in precisely the kind of process we have been describing, as illustrated in Figure 2.1. Somewhere out there—it matters not where—an ivory-tower intellectual has issued a message to you in the

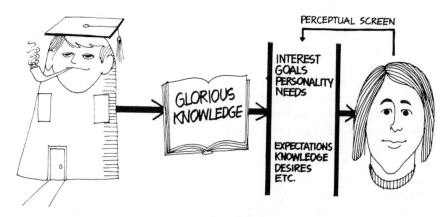

FIGURE 2.1   Attitudes as a Perceptual Screen.

form of this book. For your part, you could have read the book or not, read it carefully or skimmed it, read all of it or only certain sections, or perhaps spent the time more fruitfully enjoying the Sunday comics. If you have in fact chosen to read the book, which at this point would appear to be a safe assumption, you might choose to reread certain sections that you find particularly enlightening while skipping others that you find especially tedious. You might agree with certain gems of wisdom and file them away in your memory to be called up to impress your friends at some appropriate future moment; or you might disagree with other ideas and reject them out of hand. You might be able to relate part of what you read here to your own experience, while not really seeing the relevance of some other part. In other words, a message has reached you in the standardized form of this book, but by the time you have digested it, it has taken on your own individual stamp. The message represented by this book has been filtered by your own knowledge, needs, and expectations—by your own attitudes. *In the process of receiving the message, you have interpreted it.* You have in effect redesigned the message and its meaning to fit your own circumstances. It is this process of interpreting, of individualizing the message within the context of existing attitudes, that we have termed intervention.

This same sort of thing happens regarding politics many times every day. You might not read a book about politics every day, but chances are you watch a news report on television, or read a newspaper, or at the least overhear someone discussing some political issue or personality. Whatever information you take in from such encounters you register in much the same way we have been discussing. You use your attitudes to help you understand the various messages you have received. Indeed, as we shall see in a later chapter, you may even use your attitudes to help select the messages to which you are likely to be exposed in the first place. So the process we are describing is one that takes place with great frequency. The issuer of a political message need not be the author of this (or any other) book; it might be a friend with whom you are conversing, a candidate making a political speech, the President of the United States, or just about anyone. The message itself can range from written or oral expression to such symbolic acts as blowing up a building or assassinating a public figure. But no matter who the source or what the message, the ultimate meaning of whatever information you receive is yours alone to assign. And whatever meaning you assign will derive from your own attitudes, from your own predispositions, from your own personalized understanding of events: Your attitudes will intervene between you as an individual and the reality you experience.

THE FUNCTIONS OF ATTITUDES

Without such intervention on the part of our attitudes, we would be hopelessly adrift amid millions of seemingly random events. For only in the context of our existing storehouse of beliefs and values can any new experience, any new information that we encounter while communicating with the world, take on meaning. Only on the basis of our existing wants, needs, knowledge, and expectations can we hope to interpret and understand our most recent perceptions of reality. It is our attitudes that in large measure provide the necessary mechanism for linking "then" with "now." It is our attitudes that serve as a combination map-guidebook-dictionary, telling us what to expect, what to avoid, and what to make of it all.

As individuals we make use of our attitudes in a variety of ways, some of which are worth pointing out here. For example, we often employ our attitudes to create for ourselves a sense of our own personal worth.[3] In very much the same way that demonstrating an ability to play the guitar might enhance a young man's image of himself, might give him more pride or comfort, holding a particular set of attitudes that is consistent with some chosen political philosophy or party preference can serve to bolster one's self-esteem. I am a LIBERAL, and I believe in peace and brotherhood and social equality. I am a DEMOCRAT, and I think we have a really great bunch of candidates this year who will solve all the nation's problems. By holding such "appropriate" or desirable attitudes, each of us senses that we are in fact precisely the sort of person we would most like to be, and each of us presumably derives a certain satisfaction from this knowledge. Thus we can use our attitudes, and our political attitudes in particular, for bolstering our appraisal of ourselves.

A second function of our attitudes, and one that we have really suggested already, is to offer us a structured way of using and acquiring knowledge, a rather sophisticated filing system that helps us anchor ourselves psychologically by giving to our perceptions the appearance of stability and consistency.[4] In other words, we use our attitudes to place current events into the context of past experiences, and in the process we in effect reassure ourselves that the world is not disintegrating one random bit at a time, but rather that things are fairly stable and can in fact be understood. We use our attitudes to order the political universe, and the resulting sense of stability helps us to maintain a state of social or political equilibrium. We remain at ease because our attitudes help us understand our surroundings.

A third way in which we use our attitudes is to help us cope with situations that are of clear personal significance but are nevertheless effectively beyond our control.[5] Examples of such situations range from wars and other forms of national crisis to much more mundane aspects of our everyday lives, things that affect us but that we decide we can only "make the best of." Here we rely on our attitudes to protect us from the proverbial slings and arrows of outrageous fortune. We defend ourselves against adversity by absorbing its blows with the figurative sponge of our attitudes while protecting our deeper sense of personal well-being. In essence, we use our attitudes in such instances to change the rules of the game, to modify our notions of what constitutes personal well-being so as to cushion our adjustment to circumstances that are probably unavoidable.

Yet another way in which we use our attitudes is for outright protection, whether it be of our self-image proper or of the various attitudes that derive from that self-image.[6] For just as our attitudes help us cope with unavoidable circumstance, they can also help us construct psychological defenses against unfavorable or nonrelevant contacts with reality. They can help us defend ourselves against unwanted observations, against unsolicited attempts at influence, and against various other unnecessary or unpleasant encounters with the outside world. We protect ourselves and our existing attitudes by using those attitudes to restrict the flow of incoming information in such a manner as to preserve our psychological status quo. We shall investigate this final use of attitudes at considerable greater length several chapters hence.

Each of these various functions of our attitudes may come into play many times a day in many different circumstances, sometimes at the level of awareness, but more often below it. Each function enhances the importance of individual predispositions, whether of a political or nonpolitical nature. And since humans are, on balance, social animals, since they feel the need to seek out encounters with social and political reality, it is reasonable to expect that their attitudes, those mental states that are so vital to their definition and understanding of their environment, will play a critical role in governing their responses to the social and political stimuli that impinge on their consciousness as a result. Or to put it more simply: People's attitudes help determine their behavior. By accounting for the multiple pressures acting upon an individual's psychological state at a particular point in time (wants, needs, expectations), attitudes provide the individual with a basis upon which to internalize incoming stimuli and to formulate any response or behavior that ensues. Attitudes come between reality and reaction.

But what exactly, you have surely asked yourself by now, are these things called attitudes? What can we say of them other than to suggest vaguely that they are "predispositions" of some sort? What do attitudes look like? As a matter of fact, the answers to these questions are implicit in much that we have said already, for we suggested above that attitudes concern such things as wishes, beliefs, and responses or behaviors. Indeed, it is these three elements that, subject to certain clarifications, constitute the most basic components of the phenomenon we have labeled "attitude," and that as a consequence merit further scrutiny.[7] Let us therefore investigate each in turn.

EVALUATION: THE AFFECTIVE COMPONENT

The first principal element of an attitude that we shall consider is generally referred to as the *affective component*, or simply *affect*. Affect refers to the personal evaluations—either wishes or preferences—that are integrated with our thought processes.[8] If we are indeed more likely to act (respond) in one particular manner or another, this is probably due in large measure to these wishes and preferences. I *like* the color green; I *dislike* the color purple; therefore, I am more likely to respond favorably to objects (campaign posters, for example) that are green than to those that are purple. I *favor* the Republican party; I *oppose* the Democratic party; therefore, I am more likely to respond favorably to candidates who identify with the Republican party than to those who identify as Democrats. And similarly; I think that we *should* try to improve our relations with all the countries of the world; I think that we *should not* try to mold the world in our own image; therefore (again), I am more likely to respond favorably to certain kinds of appeals, or stimuli, and less likely to respond favorably to others. Like-Dislike, Favor-Oppose, Should-Should Not, Agree-Disagree, Approve-Disapprove, Good-Bad, and so forth. Each of these dichotomies represents the application of personal values to a given situation, and the particular set of such evaluations called to mind by that situation constitutes the first principal component of an attitude.

The examples mentioned above also illustrate one important characteristic of the affective, or evaluative, component. For it is this component that gives to an attitude a quality we can call *direction*.[9] Individuals respond to various objects or events either positively or negatively: Again, we *like* or we *dislike*, we *agree* or we *disagree*, and so on. The direction of a particular attitude is important because it helps determine the nature of the response that an individual will make. For example, if as above we assume a favorable attitude toward Republicans, and if a Republican candidate appeals to us to donate time or money to his campaign, he is *more likely* to receive our assistance than would be a Democrat making the same appeal. This is the case simply because we are in general more favorably disposed toward Republicans than toward Democrats. But—and this is important—because we may hold a *variety* of attitudes relevant to this decision (our views of the candidate or of making political contributions in general, for example), and because some of these attitudes may discourage the very response that others support, it does *not* necessarily follow that we will *certainly* give to the Republican cause, but only that we are *somewhat more likely* to do so than to give to the Democrats. Individual attitudes do represent predispositions, but they do not represent predeterminations of behavior.

Somewhat more likely. But *how much* more likely? Here we come to a second important characteristic of the affective component, one we can term *intensity*. If we are to understand the relationship between attitudes and behavior, it is not sufficient to know only the direction of an individual's preferences. It is not enough to know "which way" an individual feels. We must also know "how much." I admire Candidate Smith and I would probably vote for him except that I like Candidate Jones *so much more*. I believe in the freedom of expression; or, I believe *strongly* in the freedom of expression as protected by the First Amendment, and I would be willing to go to great lengths to defend that freedom. The United States should not consider forming an alliance with the People's Republic of China; or, *under absolutely no circumstances* should the United States consider forming an alliance with those red devils in Peking. Each instance illustrates the fact that in evaluating a given object or situation, an individual not only assumes a positive or negative orientation, but is more or less intense in personal preferences as well.[10] This intensity can take many forms, some more obvious than others; but as we shall see, regardless of its form, it is at least as important as the direction of preference in determining the behavioral implications of a given attitude.

The first principal element of an attitude, then, is the so-called affective component, the set of personal feelings or preferences that the individual manifests with regard to the object or situation about which the attitude in question is held.[11] These evaluations of attitude objects are important both in terms of their direction—either a positive or a negative (or even a neutral) inclination toward the object—and in terms of their degree of intensity.

BELIEFS: THE COGNITIVE COMPONENT

Generally speaking, when people try to define their attitudes, it is the affective component that most frequently comes to mind. "What are my attitudes? Well, I like this and I dislike that. I favor this, and I really agree with so-and-so." But affect is really only a part of the overall picture, for evaluations have to be based on something: They have to be based on certain special items of knowledge called *beliefs*. And it is these beliefs that constitute the second principal component of an attitude, one that is usually referred to as the *cognitive component*.

Beliefs—or *cognitions*, as they are often called (hence the term *cognitive component*)—are observations of fact or reality.[12] It is important to realize that *beliefs are not necessarily the same as reality, but rather they represent the way in which a particular individual sees reality.* Beliefs represent an individual's own description of his physical and social environment, the way he perceives the context in which he lives his life. Put most simply, beliefs are those perceptions of the state of the world about which value judgments are made. What characteristics of a particular object lead us to like it or to dislike it, to approve or to disapprove? What observations have we made of this object? What facts do we "know" about the object?

There can be at least two different kinds of beliefs. The first is a belief *in* something, the second a belief *about* something. The principal difference between the two is that beliefs in something, such as a belief in God or a belief in the national destiny of the American people, can be neither proven nor disproven by observation, at least in the short run. There is no physical way to measure either a deity or a destiny, although many people *believe* that either or both exist, and this belief influences their behavior.

Beliefs about something, on the other hand, are constantly subject to testing. I believe that John has blue eyes. I believe that the Democrats offer more progressive legislation than do the Republicans. I believe that space exploration has brought many changes in technology that have altered our everyday lives. Each of these beliefs can be tested every time I see John, every time the Democrats and Republicans squabble over legislation, and every time new technological or astronautical events take place. Each belief of this type can be judged against observable facts and evaluated on its merit empirically.[13]

But although there are significant differences between these two kinds of beliefs, they do have one important element in common: Basically, both kinds of beliefs serve to describe an individual's view of reality. Sometimes these beliefs are accurate, sometimes inaccurate. Sometimes they are testable by observation, sometimes not. Regardless, the views about the world that an individual holds will serve as a sort of roadmap that can be used to help the individual decide both where he or she is (in a social sense) at a given point in life, and in which direction to move in order to reach future goals. This map of reality, this set of beliefs about the world—and in our case about politics in particular—makes up what we have termed the cognitive component of an attitude.

Political beliefs and values tend to be organized to a greater or lesser extent into what are often termed *belief systems*. A belief system is a set of related judgments and perceptions about politics or political objects at a relatively general level that can be used by the individual who holds them to give meaning to the more specific things he or she experiences, and can be used as well by an observer (such as you or I) to describe the general characteristics of that individual's preferences. Ideology is a case in point. An ideology is a set of beliefs and values that people use to understand their political environment and guide their interactions with it. To be democratic and a capitalist is genuinely to perceive the nature of humankind, the proper role of government and its relations with citizens, and the desirability of a given style of economic organization from a particular and consistent perspective. To be a Marxist and a socialist is just as genuinely and just as consistently to see these phenomena in rather different terms. Where the ideology is truly held, neither set of perceptions is a facade or an intellectual fabrication; each is a distinctive, systematic, and orderly world view in which the various components are believed by the individual to be interrelated. This interrelatedness gives meaning to the notion of a belief *system*.

Not all belief systems, of course, are fully developed, their components fully integrated; nor is it necessary from an observer's standpoint that an individual recognize an organized belief system for what it is. People may favor a series of policies that is by some contemporary definition "liberal" without regarding themselves as liberals, or for that matter without noting any linkage among their preferences whatsoever. Such sets of preferences may be considered belief systems for the simple reason that they evidence the existence of some underlying collection of beliefs and values that gives consistent direction to people's expressed opinions and behavior.[14]

COGNITIVE MAPPING: THE PICTURES IN OUR HEADS

Before we move to a discussion of the third and final component of an attitude, let us try to visualize what we have said so far in terms of what we might call *cognitive space*.[15] Cognitive space is basically nothing more than a kind of pencil-and-paper representation of what happens between a person's ears.

Suppose for the sake of argument that a blank piece of paper represents a small portion of your best friend's brain, and suppose that we want to get some idea of what an attitude "looks like" wandering around in all that gray matter. So far we have said that there are two things we should be on the lookout for in analyzing an attitude: beliefs, and evaluations of those beliefs. Using our picture-map of your friend's brain, we can graphically represent his beliefs as signposts that will help us locate just where the attitude in question is situated. This is true in the sense that beliefs tell us which perceptions of reality any particular attitude is going to make use of.

Perhaps we can make this a bit clearer by analyzing your friend's attitude, based on his particular set of beliefs, toward, say, Edward M. Kennedy. On our blank paper we can locate a whole series of perceptions that your friend might have about Edward M. Kennedy. For example, over there in the top right-hand corner near the ear is a perception that says: "Edward M. Kennedy—Corruption Fighter." A little farther down and toward the center is another, which proclaims: "Edward M. Kennedy—Sex Symbol." Several more such points can be located as illustrated in Figure 2.2. Note that each of these points is simply an association of the attitude object—Edward M. Kennedy—with one observation of fact, either accurate or inaccurate. No value judgment has yet been made about any of these perceptions. Each dot ("signpost") simply represents a particular location in your friend's mind where we can find some belief, some bit of information, about Edward M. Kennedy.

The common thread in all of these beliefs is, of course, Edward

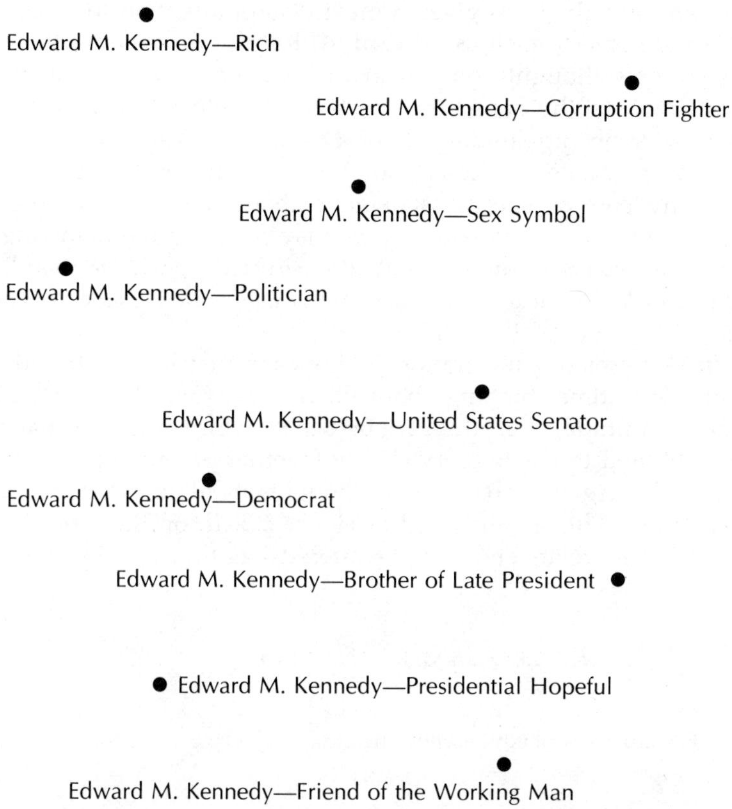

●
Edward M. Kennedy—Rich

●
Edward M. Kennedy—Corruption Fighter

●
Edward M. Kennedy—Sex Symbol

●
Edward M. Kennedy—Politician

●
Edward M. Kennedy—United States Senator

●
Edward M. Kennedy—Democrat

Edward M. Kennedy—Brother of Late President ●

● Edward M. Kennedy—Presidential Hopeful

●
Edward M. Kennedy—Friend of the Working Man

FIGURE 2.2   Beliefs about Edward M. Kennedy Located in Cognitive Space.

M. Kennedy; and it is by invoking his name that your friend is able to call up all of the various associated cognitions. Were he to contemplate a different attitude object, we would be concerned with an entirely different set of belief locations. And the more beliefs your friend had concerning any particular attitude object (such as Edward M. Kennedy), the greater the number of cognitive signposts that would be called to mind by mention of that object.

But just how much has your friend really thought about Edward M. Kennedy lately? How much has he really weighed all these beliefs? Do these points we have located represent a coherent pattern of thought about the attitude object, or only a scattering of random, seldom-used perceptions? We can use the notion of cognitive space to answer here as well. Essentially the argument would run as follows.

If an individual has given a great deal of attention to a particular attitude object, such as Edward M. Kennedy, we could then expect that his thoughts on the matter will have become relatively "organized" in the sense that he has probably worked out some formal relationship among all of Edward M. Kennedy's various attributes.[16] While we could not hope in the present context to make any sort of specific statement about how any two beliefs might be related to one another, we may conclude the following: *In general, the more a person thinks about a particular object, the more likely it is that each element of the attitude formed will be closely associated with all the other elements of that attitude.*

In terms of our illustration, this means that if your friend has spent a long time thinking about Edward M. Kennedy and formulating an attitude, then the various beliefs which underlie that attitude will tend to cluster very closely together on our cognitive map simply because they have been thought about in relationship to one another. This is illustrated in Figure 2.3. If, on the other hand, the beliefs are relatively widely scattered—as they are, by compari-

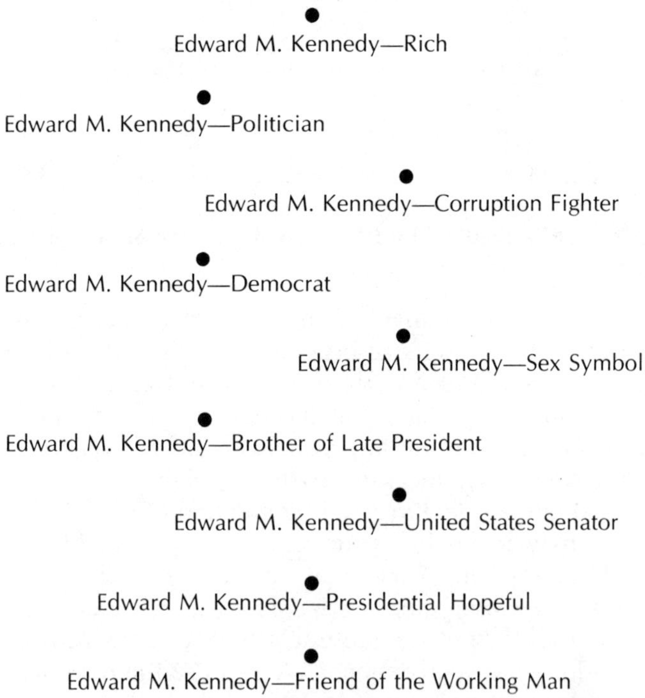

●
Edward M. Kennedy—Rich

●
Edward M. Kennedy—Politician

●
Edward M. Kennedy—Corruption Fighter

●
Edward M. Kennedy—Democrat

●
Edward M. Kennedy—Sex Symbol

●
Edward M. Kennedy—Brother of Late President

●
Edward M. Kennedy—United States Senator

●
Edward M. Kennedy—Presidential Hopeful

●
Edward M. Kennedy—Friend of the Working Man

FIGURE 2.3 Tightly Organized Beliefs about Edward M. Kennedy.

son, in Figure 2.2—then we have an indication that your friend probably hasn't given much thought to Edward M. Kennedy and has not bothered to integrate all these widely scattered beliefs into any sort of coherent, unified perception. As we shall see later, this kind of information is useful if we are trying to influence your friend to *change* his attitudes toward Edward M. Kennedy.

So far, then, we have a picture of your friend's hypothetical beliefs about Edward M. Kennedy. We know what they are, where they are located, and how closely related they are to one another. The next step is somehow to attach to each of these beliefs the appropriate value judgment or preference that your friend has concerning it. Remember that in doing so we have to take into account both the direction and the intensity of the evaluation.

Probably the best way to conduct this evaluation is with a special kind of symbol used by mathematicians called a *vector*. A vector is simply a line with an arrow at one end that represents both the direction and magnitude of a given force. The magnitude of the force is represented by the relative length of the line, and its direction by the way the arrow is pointing. Thus vector *A* below represents a force that is greater than that represented by vector *B* (because the line is longer) and that is moving in the opposite direction.

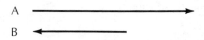

Suppose now that we label these directions. Let us say, for example, that movement toward the left of the page represents movement in the "negative" direction and that movement toward the right is movement in the "positive" direction. Movement in either direction now represents an evaluation: Vector *A* thus represents a positive evaluation (like, favor, agree, approve, etc.), while vector *B* represents a negative evaluation (dislike, oppose, disagree, disapprove, etc.). Furthermore, note that vector *A* is clearly longer than vector *B*. Indeed, it is roughly twice as long. And we said above that the length of a vector indicates the magnitude of a given force moving in a particular direction. As you have probably guessed by now, for our purposes we are defining that force as the degree of intensity associated with a particular evaluation. If you favor something strongly, you favor it with more force than if you favor it weakly. If you like something very much, you like it with more force than if you like it somewhat. The greater the emphasis you place on a particular preference, the greater is the potential impact of that preference on your overall attitude. We can represent this emphasis factor in terms of the relative lengths of the evaluative vectors associated with an individual's beliefs. Let us now apply this technique to our picture of the cognitive space representing your friend's brain so that we can see how attitudes are constructed.

Figure 2.4 illustrates the addition of evaluation vectors to the beliefs we located earlier. As above, any arrow pointing to the left represents a negative evaluation, while arrows pointing to the right represent generally positive views. Thus your friend's most intensely negative association is with Edward M. Kennedy as United States Senator, while his other negative evaluations are of Edward M. Kennedy as rich, politician, brother of the late President, and presidential hopeful. His positive evaluations, which in this hypothetical instance tend to be roughly coequal in intensity, are of Edward M. Kennedy as corruption fighter, Democrat, sex symbol, and friend of the working man.

What we have essentially in Figure 2.4 is a graphic representa-

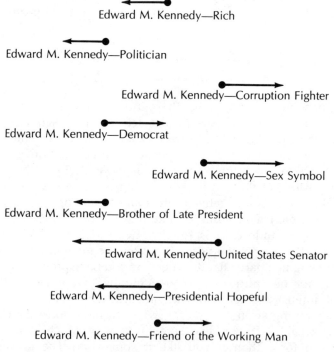

FIGURE 2.4   Evaluations of Edward M. Kennedy in Cognitive Space.

tion of the whole set of beliefs and evaluations that go to make up your friend's view of the attitude object Edward M. Kennedy. How, then, do we describe your friend's attitude itself? In one sense, we already have. For if an attitude consists of affects and beliefs, then each point-vector combination in Figure 2.4 represents one attitude. Thus your friend's attitude toward "Edward M. Kennedy—United States Senator" is negative and located at a particular point in this imaginary cognitive space. His or her attitude toward "Edward M. Kennedy—Corruption Fighter" is positive and located at another point in cognitive space. And so forth. Each of these combinations of belief and evaluation is in fact a full-fledged attitude.

But when we ask, "What is your attitude toward Edward M. Kennedy?" we are really requiring that all these lesser attitudes, which may have in common no more than the fact that they all happen to refer to Edward M. Kennedy, be somehow related to one another. We are asking the individual to draw together all these various beliefs and evaluations into an organized body, to match them against one another, and to arrive at one overall atti-

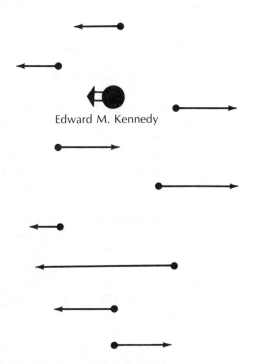

Edward M. Kennedy

FIGURE 2.5   Formation of an Attitude Cluster.

tude. We call this larger collection of several lesser attitudes an *attitude cluster*.[17] The formation of such clusters can take place at higher and higher levels. For example, after we gather together and sort out your friend's attitudes regarding Edward M. Kennedy, we could combine them with his attitudes about Hubert Humphrey, Walter Mondale, Edmund Muskie, Richard Daley, Thomas P. O'Neill, Jay Rockefeller, and others until we arrive at a cluster we could label "attitude toward leaders of the national Democratic party past and present." We could then continue the process yet again and again.

Figure 2.5 illustrates the process of collecting your friend's attitudes about Edward M. Kennedy into a larger, more general attitude cluster. This is easily accomplished by combining the various vectors mathematically to obtain a net evaluative vector for the attitude cluster. In this particular case, we find a slightly negative evaluation. More generally, it should be obvious that *the more that individual attitudes are aligned in the same direction and the more intensely they are felt, the more predictable and intense will be the resulting attitude cluster*; and conversely (as in the case of your friend), *if the attitudes comprising an individual's attitude cluster are inconsistent in direction and/or minimal in intensity, the cluster will tend to be less predictable and intense*.[18]

COSTS AND BENEFITS: THE CONATIVE COMPONENT

Up to this point we have devoted a good deal of attention to the importance of affects and beliefs in the cognitive (thought) processes of the individual. For while terminology may vary from one social psychologist to the next, most of them generally agree that affects and beliefs are in fact principal components of those phenomena we have termed attitudes. But on the third element there is substantially less agreement—regarding not whether this factor exists, but whether it may properly be considered a component of an attitude or is instead a full-fledged attitude in its own right. This third element is the so-called *conative component*, or *conation*.

Conation, it is argued, is that part of a given attitude (or attitude cluster) which links that attitude to actual behavior.[19] Remember that we began by defining an attitude as a predisposition to respond to a particular stimulus in a specified manner, as a condition that makes certain kinds of behavior more or less likely than others. Conation is that component of an attitude that makes the final association with behavior. But it is important to recognize that conation does not refer to the actual behavior itself. Conation *precedes* behavior, and refers to the beliefs of the individual about different kinds of responses to a particular situation.[20] The conative component asks these questions: How does any particular act on my part relate to my beliefs and to my value preferences? and Would this or that particular act be instrumental in furthering the attainment of my goals, and if so, to what extent? Thus conation is not the same as the behavior itself, but rather it is an *evaluation of the potential consequences or the potential impact of the behavior*.

It is at this point that the greatest disagreement tends to arise among social psychologists. If conation is an evaluation of potential behavior in the context of one's perceptions and values, is it then an integral part of the interaction of those perceptions and values—that is, is it truly a basic component of an attitude—or is it simply yet another lesser attitude (similar, for example, to "Edward M. Kennedy—Democrat" in our earlier illustration) that comes into consideration when we are building and applying attitude clusters? We need not overly concern ourselves with this here, but it at least deserves mention because it raises for the second time a most important point to which we shall return repeatedly.

Particularly as the focus of our discussion shifts from attitudes to behavior, it is essential to keep in mind that there is not generally a one-to-one correspondence between holding a particular attitude and undertaking a particular behavior. Being liberal or conservative may *incline* one to vote a particular way, but it does not *assure* such a vote. Being concerned with the rights of women or minorities may *incline* one to certain actions, but it does not *assure* that those actions will indeed be taken. Behavior cannot be predicted solely on the basis of a single attitude or attitude cluster. It is instead the result of a much more complex interaction of different attitudes and considerations, principal among which *may* be an evaluation of the potential effects of various alternative behaviors in terms of their costs and their benefits to the individual.[21] As we shall see later, these costs and benefits are as likely to be psychological as social or physical.

THE IMPORTANCE OF AN ATTITUDE: SALIENCE AND CENTRALITY

Before we conclude our analysis of attitude structure, we should look briefly at two characteristics of attitudes that will become important later in our discussion. The first of these we may term *sa-*

lience. Salience refers to the intrinsic importance of a particular attitude or attitude cluster to the individual who holds it.[22] Going back
to earlier examples, we might like the color green very much, but
still our attitude about the whole matter of color may be insufficiently important to make us feel any deep commitment to our
preference. Our evaluation of Edward M. Kennedy, on the other
hand, may be of very great personal importance, a matter in which
we have invested a considerable amount of personal interest. Because there is something inherent in this attitude or its object that
leads us to attach to it a high degree of personal significance, because we perceive it as being relatively important in its own right,
we would say that our attitude toward Edward M. Kennedy is
more *salient* to us than is our attitude toward the color green.

In general, there tends to be a rather close association between
the extremity of an individual's attitudes and the salience of those
attitudes. That is, those people who hold comparatively extreme
(noncentrist) views tend to be among the people most deeply committed to their preferences.[23] Analytically, there is some difference
between extremity and salience as attitude characteristics, but the
fact that the two tend to be highly correlated (mutually associated to
a high degree) will be of interest at a later stage of our discussion.

The second important characteristic of attitudes that deserves
mention can be labeled *centrality.* Centrality refers to the importance attached to a particular attitude, not because of some intrinsic
quality it possesses, but rather because of the position occupied by
that attitude in a larger system of values. Presumably, each of us
has a set of values that we hold dear and that serve to govern in
an overall sense the kinds of positive and negative feelings we
associate with particular attitude objects.[24] We can think of these
critical values as comprising a sort of central nervous system out of
which develop various lesser attitudes and value orientations.
These numerous attitudes branch out from the system of central
values in a treelike fashion, growing ever less critical as they get
farther and farther away from the central structure.

Figure 2.6 provides a simplified illustration of this concept. The
figure pictures four politicians occupying various positions in a
hypothetical tree (a member of the birch family): Politician 1 is
standing securely upon the trunk of the tree; politician 2 is resting
upon a bough; politician 3 is out on a limb; and politician 4 is pre-
cariously balanced upon a twig. For purposes of illustration, suppose that each politician represents an attitude or a set of attitudes
that is more or less central to your system of values as represented
by the tree itself. Politician 1, for example, might represent your

FIGURE 2.6   The Centrality of Attitudes.

strong favorable orientation toward the ultimate desirability of democratic rule. Position 2, then, might represent your support for our present form of government as being a reasonable approximation of democratic rule. Politician 3 might represent your conviction that the Republican party is best suited to operate that government. And politician 4 might represent your feeling that John Smith is a fine representative of the Republican party and is deserving of your support. Each attitude represented is thus a subsidiary of the preceding attitude all the way back to the central value structure.

But suppose now that some of these attitudes come under challenge. Suppose, for example, you discover that John Smith is a crooked politician. You are thus forced to make some adjustment in your attitude toward Mr. Smith. This can be accomplished in the figure by chopping off the twig upon which politician 4 is perched. But as you do so, note that the rest of the tree remains unchanged. A twig can be removed without causing further damage. And more generally, the farther away one moves from the central value system—the farther into the outer extremes of the hypothetical tree one gets—the easier it is to challenge any particular attitude without threatening the basic underlying structure of values.

There is, in other words, relatively little personal psychological cost in changing your mind when the attitude in question is not very *central*.

But suppose instead you discover that our present government does not really represent democratic forms. In becoming convinced of this fact, you essentially wield the axe on the bough supporting politician 2. And in doing so you also eliminate all the limbs and twigs that emanate from that bough. If the government is not inherently democratic and should be altered, then support of the party best suited to operate that government—and, in turn, of the individuals who operate that party—must fall by the wayside as well. When a distant attitude is challenged or threatened, the stakes involved in modifying that attitude are relatively low. But when an attitude that lies much closer to the basic values of the individual comes under challenge, not only is the changing of that attitude more difficult to engineer, as we shall see in a later chapter, but the potential consequences of that challenge are commensurately greater as well.[25]

IN SUMMARY

In this chapter we have emphasized what might be described as the mechanical aspects of political attitudes, the common structural and functional characteristics which help to determine the role of attitudes in converting political stimuli into political behavior. We have discussed those elements common to all attitudes—regardless of the particular objects, observations, or preferences which they represent—that contribute to their impact upon the political life of the individual. We have, in short, seen in the most general of terms what attitudes are and how they work.

Yet while the structure and functions of people's attitudes are relatively uniform, the substance of those attitudes—their focus and content—may vary widely. Indeed, as we suggested at the outset, it is most unlikely that any two people hold all of the same political attitudes. So if we are fully to understand the workings of political attitudes, we must begin to seek out those factors which contribute to their substantive content. We must begin to explore the sources of similarity and of difference in the particular attitudes of particular individuals. It is to this task that we turn in the following chapters.

SUGGESTIONS FOR FURTHER READING

If anyone writes with less lucidity than political scientists, it must surely be social psychologists. And thus, while much has been written on the topic of attitude structure, the problem of recommending suitable readings for beginners is a difficult one. Fortunately, an economist by the name of Kenneth Boulding has made the task somewhat easier with his extremely readable and sympathetic treatment of attitudes in *The Image: Knowledge in Life and Society* (Ann Arbor: University of Michigan Press, 1956). Additionally, Robert E. Lane and David O. Sears provide a rather less impressionistic analysis of many of the points discussed in the present chapter in *Public Opinion* (Englewood Cliffs, N.J.: Prentice-Hall, 1964). Thomas C. Schelling offers an entertaining and enlightening examination of the effects of conation in a collective context in *Micromotives and Macrobehavior* (New York: W. W. Norton, 1978).

NOTES

1. Richard V. Wagner, "The Study of Attitude Change: An Introduction," in *The Study of Attitude Change*, ed. Richard V. Wagner and John J. Sherwood (Belmont, Calif.: Brooks/Cole, 1969), p. 2. The conceptual limitations of this and other definitions of attitudes are suggested by Charles A. Kiesler, Barry E. Collins, and Norman Miller in *Attitude Change: A Critical Analysis of Theoretical Approaches* (New York: John Wiley, 1969), pp. 1–5.
2. David Krech and Richard S. Crutchfield, "Perceiving the World," in *The Process and Effects of Mass Communication*, ed. Wilbur Schramm and Donald F. Roberts (rev. ed.; Urbana: University of Illinois Press, 1971), pp. 235–64.
3. Daniel Katz, "The Functional Approach to the Study of Attitudes," *Public Opinion Quarterly* 24 (1960) 173–75.
4. Ibid., pp. 175 f.
5. Ibid., pp. 170 f.
6. Ibid., pp. 172 f.
7. Wagner, "The Study of Attitude Change," p. 3.
8. Chester A. Insko and John Schopler, "Triadic Consistency: A Statement of Affective-Cognitive-Conative Consistency," *Psychological Review* 74 (1967): 361 f.
9. Theodore M. Newcomb, Ralph H. Turner, and Philip E. Converse, *Social Psychology* (New York: Holt, Rinehart and Winston, 1965), pp. 48–50.
10. Ibid., pp. 48–50. An analysis of direction and intensity that emphasizes social rather than psychological factors may be found in Robert E.

Lane and David O. Sears, *Public Opinion* (Englewood Cliffs, N.J.: Prentice-Hall, 1964), pp. 6–9. ‾

11. From here on we shall refer to such an object or situation as an *attitude object*, a term that means anything about which an individual has an attitude.

12. Insko and Schopler, "Triadic Consistency," pp. 362–64.

13. Lewis A. Froman, Jr., *People and Politics* (Englewood Cliffs, N.J.: Prentice-Hall, 1962), p. 19.

14. One of the most interesting debates in the political science literature in recent years has been over the nature and importance of belief systems as they relate to both ideological and issue voting in elections. See Norman H. Nie and Kristi Anderson, "Mass Belief Systems Revisited: Political Change and Attitude Structure," *Journal of Politics* 36 (1974): 540–87; Norman H. Nie, Sidney Verba, and John R. Petrocik, *The Changing American Voter* (Cambridge, Mass.: Harvard University Press, 1976), passim; Hugh LeBlanc and Mary Beth Merrin, "Mass Belief Systems Revisited," *Journal of Politics* 39 (1977): 1082–187; and George F. Bishop, Robert W. Oldendick, Alfred J. Tuchfarber, and Stephen E. Bennett, "The Changing Structure of Mass Belief Systems: Fact or Artifact?" *Journal of Politics* 40 (1978): 781–87. The issues in this debate were first broached and the central definitions put forward by Philip E. Converse in "The Nature of Belief Systems in Mass Publics," in *Ideology and Discontent*, ed. David E. Apter (Glencoe, Ill.: Free Press, 1964), pp. 206–31.

15. A more sophisticated application of this heuristic device may be found in William A. Scott, "Structure of National Cognitions," *Journal of Personality and Social Psychology* 12 (1969): 261–78. For an argument that geometric shapes themselves may play a role in cognition, see J. A. Laponce, "Spatial Archetypes and Political Perceptions," *American Political Science Review* 64 (1975): 11–20.

16. This notion of organization closely parallels Philip Converse's definition of a belief system as "a configuration of ideas and attitudes in which the elements are bound together by some form of constraint or functional interdependence." "The Nature of Belief Systems in Mass Publics," p. 207.

17. Note the distinction between an attitude cluster and a belief system. An attitude cluster consists of an aggregate of affects and beliefs that need have in common no more than the fact that they refer to the same object. The direction of the affect in question or the logical compatibility of the beliefs is immaterial. A belief system, on the other hand, draws together preferences regarding multiple objects and imposes upon them a consistency of perception and direction.

18. Some theoretical support for this sort of mathematical treatment may be found in Milton J. Rosenberg, "Cognitive Structure and Attitudinal Affect," *Journal of Abnormal and Social Psychology* 53 (1956): 367–72; and in Martin Fishbein, "The Relationships Between Beliefs, Attitudes, and Behavior," in *Cognitive Consistency: Motivational Antecedents and Be-*

havioral Consequences, ed. Shel Feldman (New York: Academic Press, 1966), pp. 200–223.

19. For a debate over the nature of this linkage, see Martin Fishbein and I. Ajzen, *Belief, Attitude, Intention and Behavior: An Introduction to Theory and Research* (Reading, Mass.: Addison-Wesley, 1975); and P. M. Bentler and George Speckart, "Models of Attitude-Behavior Relations," *Psychological Review* 86 (1979): 452–64.

20. Insko and Schopler, "Triadic Consistency," p. 364. See also Alan J. Weinstein, "Predicting Behavior from Attitudes," *Public Opinion Quarterly* 36 (1972): 355–60.

21. Fishbein, "Beliefs, Attitudes, and Behavior," passim.

22. Lane and Sears, *Public Opinion*, p. 15.

23. Muzafer Sherif and Hadley Cantril, *The Psychology of Ego-Involvements: Social Attitudes and Identifications* (London: John Wiley, 1947), p. 132.

24. Milton Rokeach, "The Role of Values in Public Research," *Public Opinion Quarterly* 32 (1968–69): 550 f.

25. Converse, "Nature of Belief Systems," p. 208.

3

The Person Politic

Personality and Political Behavior

To this point we have been treating attitudes as if they were independent entities, psychological states that developed freely and randomly in whatever shape and direction they chose to take. That, of course, is clearly not the case. Rather, a person's attitudes are shaped and guided by two distinct sets of forces: those arising from the external social context in which the individual functions and his or her associated life experiences; and those arising from within the individual, from fundamental wants and needs and the individual's underlying character. The external or environmental factors influencing attitudes will be our focus in several subsequent chapters. In this chapter let us turn our attention to the set of forces that arises from what is generally termed the individual's *personality*.

Personality is a term that is bandied about rather freely in popular discourse, and most people have a sense that it refers to some very basic feelings that individuals have about themselves, about the world around them, and about the relationship between the two. Yet one of the most elusive goals in all of psychology is to arrive at a definition of personality on which most scholars can agree. It is not so much that personologists, as students of the subject refer to themselves, differ over what they are finding.[1] Rather, they differ even more fundamentally over how to conceptualize what it is they are studying. To get a grasp of the dimensions of disagreement here, reread the seemingly straightforward sentence with which this paragraph began. Upon inspection, that sentence can be seen as laden with ambiguity. How basic must feelings be in order to be regarded as part of one's personality? For that matter, what does "basic" mean in this context? Which are more important, feelings about oneself, about the world, or about the interaction of the two? Which sets of feelings should be considered? Where does one draw the line between an attitude and a personality characteristic? And we could go on. The point is that consensus exists at the general level: Personality is some fundamental component of the psychological makeup of each person and gives continuity to attitudes and behaviors alike. But that consensus dissipates rapidly as one begins to deal with specifics.

To some extent, this is probably unavoidable, for personality, whatever the fine points of its definition, is among the most difficult of phenomena to observe, even indirectly. Physiological activity (the mechanics of human life), which we shall consider later in this book, is not always well understood, but it is generally characterized by physical evidence (heart rates, blood pressure, and the like) that, if not already observed and comprehended, at least holds out the promise of discovery. The human body is a physical object, a machine, that we can observe directly; and it seems safe to assume that its operation is, to some extent, genuinely understood. Attitudes, in contrast, are not directly observable, but they do tend to be specifically oriented toward identifiable external objects or stimuli. So it is with reasonable confidence that we infer their existence and characteristics from a variety of observable behaviors not the least of which are direct answers to our questions about them. But personality is inherently latent, hidden from view. It may arise from human physiology (as we shall argue in Chapter 9), but it is not itself purely physiological. It may give rise to particular classes of attitudes, but it is not itself sufficiently stimulus-specific to be unmistakably revealed through them. It is, instead, something that ties the two together, something that links the biological being with its social environment, the political animal with the polity. Something—but what? Over that question there is much disagreement.[2]

Given the magnitude of discord among personologists themselves, we cannot hope to offer a definitive answer to the question here. To do so would be inherently misleading. What we can do is to suggest the outlines of some of the competing sets of definitions of personality, and to extract from those some sense of where the common ground may lie. It is to this task that we now turn.

THE PSYCHOANALYTIC APPROACH TO UNDERSTANDING PERSONALITY

The longest-standing, and to some readers perhaps the most familiar, conceptualization of the nature of personality comes from the tradition of psychoanalysis. According to what we shall call the *psychoanalytic approach* to defining and understanding personality, all human behavior is caused by some force acting within and upon the individual. For Sigmund Freud, to whose work the psychoanalytic approach traces, this force or drive could be self-preservative, dealing with such basic needs as thirst and hunger; it could be sexual in nature, where that term is defined broadly to include all forms of pleasure-seeking; or it could be aggressive, a term Freud associated with certain destructive tendencies. Proponents of this approach believe that these forces, or rather the tension among them and the psychological pressures that tension generates, are the key elements of personality, for it is these factors that give rise to behavior. Psychoanalytic theories of personality, then, are essentially theories of motivation. If we understand what makes a person act as he or she does, what interplay of forces lies behind any given action, we shall understand that person's personality.[3]

Nor is it necessary or even likely that the individual in question will be aware of what those forces are or how they interact with one another. Rather, psychoanalytic conceptions of personality distinguish among three levels of awareness: conscious, preconscious, and unconscious. The *conscious* part of the mind refers to cognitions of which we are fully aware at any particular time; it corresponds closely with the everyday use of the notion of consciousness as a sort of active thinking. The *preconscious* part of the mind stores cognitions that we are not using at the moment but upon which we could draw quite easily. Until you read the next words you are probably not thinking about them, but once you encounter them (affective component of an attitude), you will (I trust) recall them from the preceding chapter. They have just moved from your preconscious to your conscious mind. Finally, the *unconscious* part of the mind stores cognitions that are, at least as presented in Freud's early writings, beyond the individual's recognition. One becomes aware of them only in disguised or symbolic form. Yet it is these hidden forces that are most important in determining our behavior.[4]

Freudian psychoanalysts also distinguish among three key aspects or functions of personality that tie together the levels of awareness on the one hand with the important forces or drives that denote personality on the other. The first of these, the *id*, is the mechanism for psychological response to bodily needs. It is the part of the mind that senses and responds to a variety of internal and external irritants: hunger, thirst, temperature discomfort, and the like. According to this theory, the id causes us to release psychic tensions by engaging in some behavior that will gratify the need in question or, alternatively, reduce the irritation. Such behaviors are largely reflexive, and arise from the most basic of motivations. They do not, by themselves, differentiate among stimuli or situations and do not reflect conscious intellectual decision making. They are, in a sense, animal responses to animal needs.

But not every need can receive instant gratification. For we live in a real world, one that places social, economic, political, and physical constraints on our freedom of action. In other words, if people responded only to their respective ids, to basic reflexive drives, not only would society as we know it cease to exist because of constant interpersonal conflicts but each individual would become and remain extremely frustrated. Each would have gratification of his or her needs put off time and again, and each would be literally unable to tolerate the consequences. We would become a tribe of self-centered crybabies. Yet (most people believe) this is simply not the case. To the contrary, except for an occasional war or crime here and there, we get along together fairly well. We accept the constraints imposed by society. While we continue to feel and express our various needs, we are, in a word, realistic about the form and timing of their gratification. We adjust to our circumstances. This, the Freudians argue, is because there is operating a second function of personality, the *ego*. The ego is something of a safety valve; it modifies or postpones behavior to suit the circumstances. In a sense, the ego is for personality what conation is for attitudes: the mechanism by which specific behaviors are chosen from a menu of available options so as to maximize the attainment or expression of underlying preferences. The ego, then, is the force of reason, of compromise with reality, of intellect.

Finally, there is a third aspect of personality in this view, the *superego*. Where the ego adjusts to reality, the superego seeks the ideal. Where the ego is inherently empirical, taking things as they are, the superego is inherently normative, striving for things as they should be. The superego is a moral force; it imposes rectitude on behavior. In practice, this means that the superego inhibits behaviors arising from the id (where the ego merely channels those behaviors) and that it provides the motivation for self-sacrifice and altruism.[5]

What has all of this to do with political behavior per se? The answer may lie in the notion of a *hierarchy of needs*. It has been argued that an individual's behavior is governed by his or her attempts to gratify five different levels of need, and that in fact the gratification of one such level itself reveals or allows us to perceive the next. These levels of need include physiological, safety, love, self-esteem, and self-actualization, and the progression from one to the next roughly parallels the progression from the id to the superego.[6] Physiological needs refer to the body's demands for food, sleep, and the like. When these needs are not met, they become the motivating force for virtually all human action. All issues pale in comparison when one lacks fuel for the winter or the barest essentials of life. Once we attain these basic goods, however, we become concerned with preserving them and protecting ourselves. The person who has no food will risk danger to obtain it; the person who has food will avoid danger or devise institutions to defend against danger so as to protect what he or she has. Thus the second level of need is that for safety, safety from both bodily harm and psychological insecurity. Those among us who lived through the Great Depression and were without food or shelter are those who most jealously guard their food and shelter today; they understand deprivation in a way others do not. They value not just physical security but the sense of that security as well. Love needs, the third of our levels, refer to feelings of belonging and of affection such as nationalism, patriotism, or even ethnic identifications. At this level, the needs of the individual begin to be defined in more explicitly social terms. Acceptance and approval by one's peers, as we shall argue in Chapter 4, provide a psychological anchor for the individual within society and contribute to a still broader feeling of security, a kind of social security. That acceptance and approval, once accomplished, also makes possible the emergence of a fourth level of need, that for self-esteem. Here the individual goes beyond a mere sense of attachment to a group or society; that is no longer enough. Instead, the person seeks achievement, status, recognition, prestige, and, within the social context, perhaps even freedom and independence.[7] And finally, having achieved these, one turns outward. One gets involved in political activity for its own sake and seeks to define and pursue not just personal goals but collective ones.

These various needs, and the individual's attempts to satisfy them, give rise directly to sets of behaviors some of which may be political. But at each step along the way, these same needs help generate sets of beliefs about oneself, about others, and about the world generally, which in turn give rise to social and political values and preferences. It is from the combination of these beliefs and values that political attitudes emerge.[8] In this view, then, general needs arise from the very nature of personality, from the most basic of psychic drives. It is their application to specific stimuli or circumstances that gives them political significance.[9] In Chapter 6 we shall examine some ways in which this might take place.

THE TRAIT APPROACH TO UNDERSTANDING PERSONALITY

Where the psychoanalytic theorists see personality as a set of forces acting on the individual, other personologists see it rather as a set of traits or attributes describing propensities to behave in certain ways. These theorists define personality in terms of those enduring personal qualities that seem to offer the most consistent substantive description of the individual's actions. If the psychoanalytic notion of personality is one of verbs, or pressures rising to the surface, the trait theory of personality is one based on the adjectives, or more correctly the patterns of organization among the adjectives, that best characterize the individual.

This concept is probably best understood if we differentiate among three levels of analysis—the state, the trait, and the type— found in writings that define personality within this tradition. A *state* is simply an activity or condition that is taking place at any given time. Suppose, for example, you are taking a course from a very friendly and easygoing professor. And suppose further that your professor has just been denied tenure and is angry. That anger may be generalized well beyond the particular group of administrators or colleagues whose actions brought it on to include students, friends, or even family members. The professor may snap at students, or may even begin to impose harsher standards on examinations despite the fact that students were not involved in the tenure decision. But the professor's anger is, nevertheless, situation-specific. It arises not from some fundamental and enduring propensity toward such feelings but from a particular, and in the longer view rather limited, experience with a particular set of circumstances. It is, in short, a deeply felt response to a particular stimulus. It is different from an attitude because it lacks a distinctive affective-cognitive-conative structure, but it is stimulus-determined just the same. And precisely because it is generated in response to external forces rather than by the application of some long-running internal tendency in the professor's behavior, this state of anger is not regarded as a characteristic of the professor's personality.

But suppose, on the other hand, you are taking a course at the same time from another professor who is quite short-tempered. I am told such people exist in the teaching profession, though I have, of course, never encountered one. In any event, this undoubtedly mythical professor takes umbrage at student behavior that others simply take in stride, a case in point being that rare occasion when a student sleeps through an exam, turns in an assignment late, or, horror of horrors, shuffles some papers during a lecture. Vengeance, sayeth the professor, be upon ye. Such a person displays a longer-term kind of anger, a consistent behavioral tendency or inclination, which is regularly applied to a variety of stimulus situations. This superficial irritability, so easily aroused, is an enduring characteristic of the person in question that provides a relatively reliable description of the responses he or she is likely to offer to varied sets of stimuli. It is this type of internally generated continuity that distinguishes a *trait* from a state.[10]

If such traits are to offer a meaningful basis for defining personality, they must meet three criteria. First, they must be *comparable*. That is, attribution of a trait to one individual must be based on a comparison of that individual with others. Thus when we describe someone as cautious or independent, what we really mean is that such a person is *relatively* cautious or independent when measured against the range of caution or independence displayed by different people. Each such characteristic is part of a continuum, and its application to a particular individual serves to locate him or her on that continuum.

Second, traits must be *differentiable*. The qualities that enable or lead us to ascribe a given trait to a given individual must be sufficiently distinctive that we are able to discriminate between these particular qualities and any others the individual may possess. This requires in turn that underlying traits be defined as carefully and as precisely as possible and that a clear relationship be recognized between them and their more readily observable behavioral manifestations (their associated states).

Finally, traits must be *stable*. In describing a person's personality, we must recognize that the very notion of personality implies stability and that the attributes or traits of interest will be those that endure through time, those that recur in repeated observations, rather than those that are more transitory.[11]

A variety of underlying personality traits, or more correctly personality-trait continua, have been found to meet these criteria. Several of these are listed in Table 3.1, a review of which will give you a good sense of the sort of characteristics we are discussing.[12]

TABLE 3.1
Personality-Trait Continua

Adaptable	←——→	Rigid
Emotional	←——→	Calm
Conscientious	←——→	Unconscientious
Conventional	←——→	Unconventional
Considerate	←——→	Inconsiderate
Reserved	←——→	Outgoing
Sociable	←——→	Unsociable
Submissive	←——→	Dominant
Reserved	←——→	Venturesome
Tough-minded	←——→	Tender-minded
Trusting	←——→	Suspicious
Conservative	←——→	Experimenting
Group-tied	←——→	Self-sufficient
Relaxed	←——→	Tense
Cooperative	←——→	Obstructive

Sources: Adapted from Robert M. Liebert and Michael D. Spiegler, *Personality: Strategies and Issues* (3rd ed., Homewood, Ill.: Dorsey Press, 1978), pp. 226–29; and Raymond B. Cattell, *The Scientific Analysis of Personality* (Baltimore: Penguin, 1965), p. 365.

One of the difficulties with the trait approach to defining personality is its very richness. The fifteen sets of personality traits listed in Table 3.1, for example, are, to use a well-worn but telling cliché, no more than the tip of the iceberg. In some ways, our ability to identify relevant traits is limited more by our language skills and conceptual abilities than by the number of continua that may be argued to comprise one's personality. It is here that the inherent complexity of personality per se becomes wholly evident.

Personologists have responded to this problem by trying to identify unifying dimensions among the multitude of personality traits, or in other words, by seeking out particular sets or combinations of traits that almost always show up together. Their argument is that these clusters of related personality traits, which are termed personality *types*, are the real organizing bases of individual behavior. In effect, types of personality are the topmost component in a hierarchy of characteristics. At the base of this hierarchy are individual behaviors, particular and generally isolated responses to particular stimuli. These individual behaviors are, in turn, organized at the next level of the hierarchy into persistent patterns of behavior, or *habits*. On Tuesday, to oversimplify the point a bit, you talked about the recent election with a friend. On Wednesday, you discussed energy policy and prices with a service station attendant. On Friday, you got into an argument with a professor over the degree of honesty practiced by politicians. Each was an isolated act. But by Saturday, you were *in the habit* of discussing politics. That habit was a pattern of behavior developed over time and under differing circumstances. From the point of view of an outside observer, its effect was to impose a kind of unifying conceptual order on your more isolated behaviors. From your point of view, its effect was to accustom or predispose you to talk politics later in some other context. The repeated practice of a particular type of behavior in the past facilitates and makes more likely your engaging in that same type of behavior now or in the future.

In their turn, these habits are organized into traits. Talking politics, for example, may be a manifestation of an underlying trait of sociability. Seeking power may be an act of domination, running for office an act of venturesomeness, espousing a particular point of view an act of conscientiousness, and so forth. So it is that leaders may differ systematically from followers, participants in the political process from nonparticipants, or even ideological liberals from conservatives in terms of very basic personality characteristics that lead to different styles of political behavior.[13]

Finally, personality traits are themselves organized into a smaller number of types. One scholar, using a statistical technique called factor analysis, has identified three major types or dimensions including sociability, intelligence, and emotional stability. Another has reduced personality traits to four types based on two underlying dimensions: introversion-extroversion and stability-instability. In this latter view, the four types include (1) introverted-unstable, characterized by such traits as moodiness, anxiety, rigidity, pessimism, and unsociability; (2) introverted-stable, characterized by passivity, caution, thoughtfulness, self-control, reliability, calm, and even temper; (3) extroverted-unstable, with such traits as restlessness, touchiness, aggressiveness, excitability, changeability, impulsiveness, and optimism; and (4) extroverted-stable, including sociability, gregariousness, responsiveness, liveliness, an easygoing nature, and leadership.[14] Such analyses typify the trait approach to personality.

THE COGNITIVE APPROACH TO UNDERSTANDING PERSONALITY

We began our discussion of personality by examining the so-called psychoanalytic approach, which emphasizes the forces that drive the individual to behave, and have now considered as well the trait approach, which focuses instead on the identification of certain attributes of character. These two viewpoints have in common the idea that personality is inherently substantive, that it is to be defined by what people feel about themselves and others. There is, however, an alternative and rather more mechanistic way of defining personality, one that is concerned less with what people think or feel than with how they do it. Here differences in personality are conceptualized in terms of certain psychological processes, including learning, perception, and cognition, which are common to all people. The similarities in these processes from one person to the next are seen as a source of the broad continuities in human personality, while their differences are seen as helping to generate the more subtle differences among us. A brief review of these phenomena will help to make the point.

In its simplest sense, learning is the creation of memories, where memory refers not only to the recall of names, telephone numbers, and the answers to exam questions but also to the retention of patterns of behavioral responses to different classes of stimuli. Learning, then, refers to the development of these patterns. Drawing an association among the stimuli we encounter, the actions we take, and the consequences of those actions constitutes a primary mechanism by which we learn.[15] Such a process is termed *associative learning* and can be of least two types. *Classical conditioning* involves what we might term visceral learning, quite literally the learning of "gut reactions" to stimuli. It operates through the *autonomic nervous system*, a set of nerves that connect with muscles in such organs as the heart, stomach, and liver and with the sweat glands and adrenal glands.[16] Studies of physiological responses tell us that such organs and glands are very much involved in the emotional life of the individual. Classical conditioning refers to the process by which we learn to associate various outside stimuli with the internal experiencing of emotion or other forms of physiological change (such as the reduction of hunger) that are monitored by the autonomic nervous system. It is accomplished by the co-occurrence, and often by the *repeated* co-occurrence, within a relatively brief time span, of the external event that arouses the response in question and the internal feeling (tension, relaxation, nervousness, and the like) itself. Studies of classical conditioning have shown that responses learned in this way may be generalized to similar stimuli (i.e., what we learn about one situation or experience we are able to apply to other similar ones) and that we are able to identify characteristics of a learning situation that allow us to distinguish between one type of emotion-evoking stimulus and another. The significance of this is that we need not go through a whole new learning process for each new situation we encounter. Instead, we are able in many instances to anticipate what we would learn, which is to say, to use what we have already learned in new ways. Adolf Hitler viewed the concessions he was granted at Munich as a sign of the weakness of his adversaries and pressed his advantage. "No more Munichs" became the rallying cry of the West and a fundamental concern of its citizens during the cold war. The Vietnam war produced a decade of agony for Americans (not to mention its immeasurably greater impact on the Vietnamese). "No more Vietnams" became the touchstone of United States foreign policy in the 1970s. In just this way, classical conditioning contributes to both the emotional development of the individual and the commonality of feeling across whole societies.

A second type of associative learning, *instrumental conditioning*, refers to the development of behavior patterns in response to external, as opposed to internal, rewards and sanctions. We learn to avoid those situations that are socially unpleasant or to extricate ourselves from them once they have occurred, to pursue behaviors for which we have been rewarded and terminate those that have caused rewards to be withheld or taken away. In the context of personality development, these rewards are generally social in nature, and include such things as attention, approval, and praise from other people. The selective granting of such rewards by—and learning how to stay out of trouble with—parents, teachers, and peers helps an individual develop a sense of which behaviors are best to engage in. Thus instrumental conditioning is most important in the learning of actions and skills, and in helping the individual develop a sense of the norms for using these actions and skills that are most widely accepted by society.[17] We shall see the political importance of this learning at a systemic level when we discuss political culture in Chapter 4.

Before an individual can learn to respond "appropriately" to various stimuli, he or she must first be able both to recognize and to categorize those stimuli for what they are. This is where the closely related processes of perception and cognition come into play. Perception involves the psychological awareness (in a sense,

FIGURE 3.1   The Stimulus-Response Cycle.

STIMULUS → SENSATION → PERCEPTION → COGNITION → LEARNING → MEMORY → RESPONSE

consciousness) of the presence of stimuli, while cognition involves the organization of such stimuli into meaningful patterns.

Perception is, in effect, a threshold at which a physiological sensation such as sight or touch becomes a psychological one. It is the point at which we become conscious of something that is happening to or around us.[18] Cognition is the imposition by our minds of patterns and meanings upon whatever it is we perceive. It is both the product and the instrument of a continuing search for order, regularity, and correlation in the world around us based on visual and other forms with which we are already familiar. That is, in cognition we take what might otherwise be a set of random images or impulses and impose upon it some meaning or interpretation that both draws upon our existing storehouse of remembered sets of stimuli and may itself be added to that storehouse.[19]

The nature of this process is illustrated in Figure 3.1. In the figure, an outside stimulus, a news account, political speech, billboard, or any such item of information, is sensed by an individual and transmitted to his or her brain. (We shall explore the physiological process involved here in Chapter 9.) There it trips that amounts to an alarm that alerts the individual to its arrival. In less than a microsecond, the individual recognizes the presence of the information, compares it against past experience, draws upon some existing memories, and categorizes the new data (assigns them a meaning). Why, my goodness. . . . It's a billboard! This cognition, which will include both the content and the self-defined meaning of the information, is then channeled to memory (in which case it is "learned"), to an appropriate (previously learned) behavioral response, or perhaps to both.

Proponents of this cognitive view of personality argue that personality differences may arise from different learning experiences and, importantly, from differences in the ways that learning, perception, and cognition operate from one individual to the next. In other words, personality is to be defined not in terms of drives or traits but in terms of the way each person thinks, the way his or her mind works at a more mechanical level. In the view of these personologists, it is the distinctive operation of these fundamental psychological processes that best characterizes personality.

IN SUMMARY

For all their differences, these three views of personality have three critical points in common, and it is in those points that our own most important lesson lies. First, personality provides a fundamental organizing basis (whatever that might be) for behavior, one that imparts a degree of psychological momentum to our selection of preferences and behaviors, but one that is, at the same time, more a general tendency than a specific direction. Second, personality is not stimulus-specific in the same way that attitudes are; it is a propensity of behavior per se rather than of behavior vis-à-vis any given object or class of objects. But at the same time, and third, the manifestation of personality is to some extent a function of circumstances, of the opportunities that are available (or are denied) to the individual for self-expression. Thus, as we shall see in the next chapters, the character of the individual is interdependent with the character of his or her social and political milieu.

SUGGESTIONS FOR FURTHER READING

Several approaches to the study of personality are examined in detail in Jerry S. Wiggins, K. Edward Renner, Gerald L. Clore, and Richard J. Rose, *Principles of Personality* (Reading, Mass.: Addison-Wesley, 1976); and in Robert M. Liebert and Michael D. Spiegler, *Personality: Strategies and Issues* (3rd ed.; Homewood, Ill.: Dorsey Press, 1978). An alternative overview of personality research focusing more directly on the development of the literature and providing useful background for topics we shall take up in later chapters is Salvatore R. Maddi, *Personality Theories: A Comparative Analysis* (4th ed.; Homewood, Ill.: Dorsey Press, 1980). Harvey London and John E. Exner, Jr., offer reviews of a wide variety of politically relevant research in the trait tradition in their edited volume *Dimensions of Personality* (New York: John Wiley, 1978).

The best starting point for an examination of the application of these concepts to political analysis is Alan C. Elms, *Personality in Politics* (New York: Harcourt Brace Jovanovich, 1976), an overview of both theory and research written at an introductory level. Fred I. Greenstein's *Personality and Politics* (Chicago: Markham, 1969) provides a more sophisticated point of entry and includes an extensive review of the literature up to the date of publication. Gordon J. DiRenzo's edited volume of the same title (New York: Anchor Press, 1974) offers a selection of some of the more typical and better-known work in the field, as does Fred I. Greenstein and Michael Lerner's more extensive work, *A Source Book for the Study of Personality and Politics* (Chicago: Markham, 1971). Paul M. Sniderman's *Personality and Democratic Politics* (Berkeley: University of California Press, 1975) illustrates the application of personality concepts to problems of interest to political scientists.

NOTES

1. The nature of personology, as distinct from personality, is examined in Salvatore R. Maddi, *Personality Theories: A Comparative Analysis* (4th ed.; Homewood, Ill.: Dorsey Press, 1980), pp. 4–13.
2. For a discussion of this definitional difficulty, see Ervin Staub, "The Nature and Study of Human Personality," in *Personality: Basic Aspects and Current Research*, ed. Ervin Staub (Englewood Cliffs, N.J.: Prentice-Hall, 1980), pp. 2–7; and Robert M. Liebert and Michael D. Spiegler, *Personality: Strategies and Issues* (Homewood, Ill.: Dorsey Press, 1978), pp. 8–12.
3. Liebert and Spiegler, *Personality*, pp. 71–75.
4. Ibid., p. 93.
5. Ibid., pp. 97–100.
6. This notion of hierarchies traces to Abraham Maslow's *Motivation and Personality* (New York: Harper, 1954) and has received more recent treatment by Stanley A. Renshon in *Psychological Needs and Political Behavior: A Theory of Personality and Political Efficacy* (New York: Free Press, 1974).
7. For an interesting application of this notion, see James L. Gibson, "Personality and Elite Political Behavior: The Influence of Self-Esteem on Judicial Decision Making," *Journal of Politics* 43 (1981): 104–25.
8. Renshon, *Psychological Needs*, pp. 64–74.
9. For an application of this idea to identifying personality correlates of political ideologies, see Glenn D. Wilson, ed., *The Psychology of Conservatism* (London: Academic Press, 1973).
10. Richard S. Lazarus and Alan Monat, *Personality* (3rd ed.; Englewood Cliffs, N.J.: Prentice-Hall, 1979), pp. 97 f.
11. Wiggins et al., *Principles of Personality*, p. 70.
12. A number of specific traits including, but not limited to, authoritarianism, introversion, dogmatism, trust, and sensation-seeking are discussed at length in Harvey London and John E. Exner, Jr., eds., *Dimensions of Personality* (New York: John Wiley, 1978).
13. See, for example, the arguments developed in Paul M. Sniderman, *Personality and Democratic Politics* (Berkeley: University of California Press, 1975).
14. The personologists referred to here are Raymond B. Cattell and Hans J. Eysenck respectively. For a discussion of the connections between their theories, see Liebert and Spiegler, *Personality*, pp. 230–33. Political scientists have attempted to extend similar notions of personality typing to the assessment of leadership. See, for example, James David Barber, *The Presidential Character: Predicting Performance in the White House* (Englewood Cliffs, N.J.: Prentice-Hall, 1972); and James MacGregor Burns, *Leadership* (New York: Harper & Row, 1978). Lloyd S. Etheredge offers an interesting application of the trait approach to politics in "Personality Effects on American Foreign Policy 1898–1968: A Test of Interpersonal Generalization Theory," *American Political Science*

Review 72 (1978): 434–51. And Edmond Constantini and Kenneth H. Kraik report differences in self-confidence, achievement, dominance (all higher), abasement and deference (both lower) between party leaders and the general population, and additional differences between Republicans and Democrats in "Personality and Politicians: California Party Leaders, 1960–1976," *Journal of Abnormal and Social Psychology* 38 (1980): 641–61.

15. Wiggins et al., *Principles of Personality*, pp. 36–39.
16. Thomas S. Brown and Patricia M. Wallace, *Physiological Psychology* (New York: Academic Press, 1980), pp. 68–9.
17. Wiggins et al., *Principles of Personality*, pp. 36–44.
18. Russell Brain, "Some Reflections on Brain and Mind," *Brain* 86 (1963): 381–402.
19. James Deese, *Principles of Psychology* (Boston: Allyn and Bacon, 1964), pp. 195–205.

4

Political Culture

Individual Attitudes and the Political Matrix

Before we fully understand the sources and content of individual political attitudes, we must engage in one additional bit of preliminary analysis. For we must bring ourselves to the realization that those internal psychological processes described in Chapters 2 and 3 do not function in isolation. People do not simply go off into a corner and have political attitudes as the main purpose of their lives. Much to the contrary, we hold political attitudes precisely so that we may use them for guidance in our interactions with other people or groups in the political system. In fact, it is through the very process of such interaction that we come to acquire and to hold political predispositions in the first place, for that is the essence of politics. Thus we live not in isolation but in a dynamic social and political context that gives meaning to, and in a collective sense derives its own meaning from, our individual political attitudes. We are part of a "political culture," we are part of a shared sociopolitical environment that contributes a certain degree of consistency to our own attitudes and to those of others within our society. And as a result, our own individual attitudes can best be understood in terms of the larger social context within which they operate. Our purpose in the present chapter, then, must be to investigate the relationship between individual political attitudes and the political culture. For only in the context of societal pressures toward attitudinal compliance can we fully grasp the dynamics of individual attitudinal diversity.

POLITICAL CULTURE: THE MELTING POT

The term *political culture* refers to a set of common attitudes and beliefs about common objects, where the primary belief is that these objects bear a relationship to the political system.[1] In other words, if a society's members, or at least large numbers of them, accept certain objects (e.g., power, leadership, government, the state of the economy) as being inherently political, *and* if these individuals hold in common certain fundamental attitudes and beliefs regarding the objects in question, then we may refer to the intangible body of agreement that results as the political culture of the society. A political culture is a fundamental consensus of interest and evaluation with regard to a given set of attitude objects.[2]

This phenomenon of fundamental consensus may arise from common historical experience, from the necessity to deal with common problems, from exposure to common information (such as that from the mass media), as a result of collective geographic isolation, or from a wide variety of other sources.[3] And the objects of the consensus may be many or few (and the political culture correspondingly broad or narrow). But as long as such a fundamental consensus exists, as long as a society is built upon layer after layer of common experience and shared outlook, the political attitudes of individuals within that society cannot help but be influenced by the force of that consensus.

Not all of the component attitudes and beliefs of any given political culture, of course, are necessarily coequal in importance. Rather, some elements of the underlying consensus are more vital than others. In the American political culture, for example, attitudes about the freedom of speech are more widely shared than are attitudes about decentralized political parties, although both are present in the political culture.[4] Thus we might say that free speech as a cultural object displays a greater *extensive* importance than does the party structure. Similarly, the norm of governmental pragmatism, of solving problems in the most efficient possible manner, though it is seldom expressed in pure form, appears to be more fundamental among Americans than does a preference for restricting government actions according to the tenets of ideological liberalism or conservatism, although both a preference for pragmatism and a preference for ideology are present in the political culture.[5] Thus pragmatism as a cultural object displays a greater *intensive* importance than does ideology. And again, the distribution of party identifications among Americans is longer-lasting than is the distribution of views on any particular issue, regardless of its apparent import.[6] Thus party preference as a cultural object displays a greater *temporal* importance than do issues.

Certain attitudes and objects, then, are more critical than others to the basic nature of any particular political culture. Yet these differences of importance notwithstanding, it is the fact that all these objects—free speech, party structure, pragmatism, ideological preferences, party identification, and issue orientations, as well as many others—qualify as foci of the political culture as long as large numbers of people within that culture share politically relevant beliefs or attitudes about them. And the political culture is itself nothing more than a somewhat distilled collection of the variety of these widely shared political predispositions, a sort of attitudinal melting pot.

Two important characteristics derive from this view of the political culture as a melting pot. To begin with, the existence of objects and attitudes that are of greater or lesser importance within the political culture suggests that certain elements of that culture will be more susceptible to pressure for change than will others. Clearly, those components that are least fundamental, least widely shared, or least enduring in time will as a consequence be least stable, while those more basic elements, those constituting more intense and longer-term pressures on the society, will prove far more resistant to change. Thus the values that the Founding Fathers incorporated into the United States Constitution and governmental system have persevered, while their manner of speech and dress have been altered significantly. Yet at the time, both their values and their manners were part of the political culture.[7] And similarly, today's public opinion will be tomorrow's history, but today's basic values may serve as tomorrow's precedents. Yet both public opinion and basic values are part of the contemporary political culture. A political culture consists of peripheral and central components all of which constitute the foundation of political activity at a given point in time, but many of which will, by virtue of their less exalted position, decay in importance as new pressures come to bear.

The second point that follows from the melting-pot notion is that not everyone in a given society will share all or even most of the values characteristic of the dominant political culture of that society. Some people may share a greater or lesser proportion of cultural values in differing combinations; some people may indeed *share* all the dominant values of the society, but may interpret them in unique manners; and some people may reject the dominant values of the society altogether and seek to replace them with values of their own.[8] In this respect, the United States has been especially fortunate to enjoy a rather extended period of fundamental consensus among politically active groups and individuals, although the recent entry of newly active groups into the political arena and the accompanying rise in the salience of ethnic identifications seem to suggest at least a period of redefinition.[9] Such cultural unity, however, is not always the case. Indeed, where major groups with conflicting values closely rival each other in size and strength—as, for example, in the case of the Protestants and Catholics of Northern Ireland or the Christians and Moslems of Lebanon—the absence of a common political culture (augmented, of course, by other differences) and the unwillingness of important subgroups to arrive at a fundamental consensus can lead to the disruption, if not the outright destruction, of the established political order.

PSYCHOLOGICAL MOORING: WHAT CAN YOUR POLITICAL CULTURE DO FOR YOU?

Every political system, regardless of its size or its shape, is built upon an underlying structure of political beliefs, values, and expectations of the sort we have labeled political culture. Every political system rests upon a foundation of shared ideology and outlook that binds its citizens not only to the system itself but also to one another. For without such a linkage mechanism, without the umbilical cord of common perception, the citizen and the system would fail to reinforce one another in ways necessary to their mutual survival. Let us therefore investigate this relationship of mutual dependency, focusing first upon the benefits to the individual, later upon those to the system itself.

Put most simply, the political culture serves to identify and to make safe and/or desirable for the individual a wide range of "socially acceptable" political viewpoints. By nature, human beings value group reinforcements for their attitudes and actions. We like to know that others agree with our ideas, that we are part of a group of like-minded individuals. And since the adherents of the dominant political culture constitute by definition the biggest and most like-minded group of all, our own acceptance of that culture gives to each of us a set of norms with which we can safely identify, which we can take as our own, and which we can then employ in the process of interpreting and understanding what might otherwise seem to be the frenetic political activity that is taking place around us. In this way, the political culture provides us as individuals with a point at which we can psychologically anchor ourselves to the political system and its accompanying social matrix. It gives us a handle on political reality. And just as the political culture gains strength from the adherence of more and more individuals, each individual takes strength and direction from his or her adherence to the political culture.

But while it is encouraging for individuals to know that many people share certain of their beliefs and values, this may not be sufficient to give the sense of group identity which they desire. Such knowledge is, after all, quite intangible, and its validity must be inferred at a most abstract level. What is needed, therefore, is some form of concrete reassurance, some visible evidence that these beliefs and values are in fact widely shared. What is needed, in other words, is some sort of rallying point at which underlying attitudes may be converted to opinions and behaviors and their meanings shared in an overt display of communal attachment. Political symbols provide just such a rallying point.[10]

A *political symbol* is any object that takes on some political meaning exceeding its intrinsic qualities.[11] Thus the American flag, which is in essence merely a rectangular, tricolored piece of cloth, *comes to stand for* liberty, justice, capitalism, imperialism, or other values (depending upon one's point of view) not because any of these qualities is inherent in the flag itself, but rather because people have come to make the psychological association between the physical object and the values in question. Similarly, the White House, which is little more than a nice white building with a large lawn and an important occupant, *comes to stand for* all the prestige and authority of the executive branch of government. We hear phrases such as "The White House announced today..." or "The senators sought confirmation from the White House...." Who ever heard of a building making an announcement or confirming a rumor? Such statements would be pure nonsense except for one thing: *Everyone* understands that the "White House" is simply a shorthand reference to the President or some part of his administrative machinery; *everyone* makes the association between the term and its meaning; *everyone* shares the symbol, and through it a part of the political culture. For symbols are the common shorthand by means of which a political culture expresses itself. Indeed, symbols constitute a political language that is more or less peculiar to the culture in which they operate, a language that draws in large measure upon historical experience and contemporary psychological states unique to that culture. And by structuring the language and thought patterns of the individual according to the dictates of the

political culture, symbols serve to impose cultural patterns upon individual perceptions and preferences. They guide individual attitudes into culturally acceptable forms.[12] Or, to put that another
way, on the issues of greatest importance, those that bind the
citizens of a polity to one another, symbols provide a substantial
amount of continuity among the political attitudes of diverse individuals.

The list of political symbols for any single political culture or
subculture would be lengthy indeed. Every political system has its
symbol of power and authority, be it the White House, the Krem-
lin, or 10 Downing Street. Every political system has its symbol of
representation, be it Congress, Parliament, or an election. Every
political system has its symbol of autonomy, be it the Stars and
Stripes, the Union Jack, or the Hammer and Sickle. And every political system has its symbols of public concern, be they international
terrorism and Soviet expansionism, yellow ribbons, gangs of four,
running dogs of capitalism, antisocialist elements, or enemies of
the revolution.

Symbols can be used by political groups or leaders to obtain
tangible goals or to cover up, explain away, or rationalize inequities
within a society. Thus we are told to "buy American" even though
prices for imports may be lower or quality higher. We trade butter
for guns, collectively accepting somewhat higher levels of poverty
in exchange for an enhanced sense of national security. Similarly,
symbols can provide standards of judgment: They help us judge
what is right or wrong, what is good or bad, to whom we feel su-
perior or inferior. Being on "social security" is good; it is an extension of the work ethic. Being on "welfare" is bad because it is not.
Yet both programs have a similar purpose. Both redistribute a portion of the nation's wealth from one group, those who are employed (for the most part), to another, those who are not, so as to
provide subsistence income for the latter. But whatever the symbol,
and whatever its function, its importance lies not in its physical
properties but in the values with which it is associated in the
minds of acculturated individuals. Politics, like the proverbial filth,
is in the mind of the beholder.

Democracy, communism, valor, retreat, peace, war, love, hate,
humanity, destruction. Each culture has its values, each value has
its symbols, each symbol has its adherents. And each adherent, not
only by virtue of the acceptance of the dominant political symbols
and their attendant meanings, but also by the recognition that
others share this acceptance, anchors himself or herself to the political system and receives social reinforcement.[13] The political cul-

ture, by giving meaning and support to a particular view of political life that is (as we shall see) consonant with the needs and activities of the political system, serves to link the individual with that system and provides the substance necessary to make the relationship a meaningful one.

RULE SETTING: WHAT CAN YOU DO THROUGH YOUR POLITICAL CULTURE?

If the political culture gives to the individual an all-important basis for identification with the political system, it performs an equally vital function for the system itself, a function we may term *rule setting*, the delineation of a framework for political action. For the success of the linkage we have been discussing is as critical to the well-being of the political system as it is to the individual citizens of that system. No political system can endure without the support (in terms of physical goods as well as psychological states) of its populace, support that is the logical extension of the binding of individuals to the system through their acceptance of the political culture. Yet because the political culture is in fact dependent upon acceptance, because it can link citizens to the system only to the extent that large numbers of individuals within the society are *willing* to share in its values, the upper limits of this willingness come to be imposed upon the culture, and through it upon the political system, as a sort of de facto social contract. Through this chain of dependency, the popular will, insofar as it is reflected in the political culture, in effect establishes the rules of the political game, the guidelines within which political activity can and must take place.[14] Let us consider this proposition at some length.

When a political system is operating normally, the results that emerge from its complex processes of decision making generally take the form of public policy. The passing of a law, the adoption of a regulation, the establishment of a precedent, or even the mere expression of an intention are but a few examples of such policy. Each represents a response of the political system to some impetus, to some demand that has been placed upon it. Yet in order successfully to meet (or deflect) such demands, in order effectively to make policy, the political system must be able to call upon a supply of resources. It must possess the ways and means of political action. And while it is true that many of these resources are physical goods such as tax monies, the lives of soldiers, and the existence of a punitive system of justice, it is also true that many are psychological goods as well—goods such as loyalty, faith, acquiescence, fear, and credibility. Only when both the physical necessities and the psychological requisites are available to it in sufficient quantity can a political system create and enforce public policy.[15] And since through its linkage function the political culture is the principal source of large-scale psychological support for the system, the political system must draw upon and *be responsive to* the values reflected in that culture.

What this means in practical terms is that the actions of the political system must be—or at least must appear to be—consonant with the needs, the desires, and, perhaps most important, the expectations of the citizenry. In order to maintain the support of its citizens, without which it may well be unable to function effectively, the political system must appear similar enough to what those citizens want and expect for it to be able to retain its legitimacy, the popular acceptance of its right to function. It must reflect or appear to reflect the dominant values and interests of the society— or in other words, the political culture. For only so long as it remains within the bounds of propriety will the system retain its ability to draw upon citizen support in making and carrying out political decisions.[16] In this sense, then, not only individuals but political systems as well benefit from adherence to the political culture.

The importance of this set of cultural restraints on political decision makers is illustrated quite clearly by the so-called Watergate affair of the early 1970s. In that instance, officials of the executive branch of government, in whom rested all the symbolic legitimacy of that branch, committed a series of acts that lay outside the public expectations of what their proper roles should be. It was not that these acts were unique in the history of American political practice, though some may have been. And it was not that these acts were illegal, though indeed many were. Rather, it was because high officials in visible positions broke the unwritten rules of the game, because in effect they shocked the public by overstepping the loosely defined yet generally accepted bounds of their authority, that a crisis ensued. Because these individuals had committed *and been caught committing* actions considered taboo in the American political culture, the bonds between the people and the system were weakened, and a serious crisis of confidence followed, a crisis that reduced the level of public trust in all political leaders regardless of party identification and which threatened to paralyze the policy-making ability of the federal government.[17] The rules established by the political culture may be vague and unwritten, but their clear and purposeful violation can have the most serious of consequences.

THE CULTURAL INTERFACE: POLITICAL
CULTURE AND POLITICAL LIFE

Obviously, the rule-setting function of which we have been speaking is not a service formally performed at some fixed time and fixed point by the political culture. In most modern societies there exists no cultural tribunal that oversees the workings of the political system. Rather, this function is accomplished informally over an extended period of time at a variety of points in the political life of the society. Thus only when we assume a relatively broad perspective upon political life can we understand the real impact of a political culture. Perhaps we can clarify this by considering some examples of the political culture at work.

One outward manifestation of the political culture of a society is something we might term the *political style* of the society, the most general characteristics of political activity.[18] For example, we might be able to describe American politics as relatively open to a variety of participants, dependent upon interpersonal associations, and tolerant of voluntary participation, all characteristics reflective of the history and common experience of the American people.[19] Some other political culture might be more restrictive, more impersonal, and more compulsory, dependent upon an alternative history and an alternative common experience. Each of these traits represents a very general orientation toward acceptable political behavior, a sense of how individuals go about relating to one another and to their government. Each represents a manner or style of thought and behavior that helps structure political situations as they arise within the society. And as a result, each imposes a cultural imprint upon political activity at the most general of levels. All political systems have such stylistic traits, which are based in the common political culture and guide the patterns of political behavior.

A second outward manifestation of the underlying political culture, one that is perhaps more subject to the pressures of current history, is the so-called *political mood* of a society, something equivalent to the "temper of the times." The dominant mood of politics in any particular society might be, for example, revolutionary, imperialistic, chauvinistic, nationalistic, isolationist, or puritanical. Again, each alternative suggests the acceptability or unacceptability of various patterns of behavior based upon the willingness of the populace to concur in those actions. Thus acts of foreign entanglement might be applauded by a society whose mood is internationalistic or imperialistic, but those same acts might be wholly unacceptable to a society in which isolationist sentiment is in the ascendancy. Similarly, sex scandals of the sort that seem to plague various Western governments every decade or so would be accepted if not encouraged by a society whose mood was tolerant, but might bring down a whole government in more puritanical times. Like the customary style of politics, then, the mood of the moment also sets limits on political activity.[20]

There are other manifestations as well. The *tone* of political exchange in a society might be one of compromise, one of threat, one of hope, or one of trust, each reflective of broader social and political values and each giving unique direction to activity within the political system. The political *goals* of a society might be primarily substantive (the distribution of wealth or power within the society according to a certain formula, for example) or primarily ideological (the defense or proselytization of democracy, the fomenting of revolutions), again suggesting certain unique boundaries for political action. Indeed, even the more general sense that individuals have of what constitutes appropriate political behavior within their system represents an outward manifestation of the political culture.

Each of these illustrations denotes a point or a set of points at which the underlying beliefs and values of a society have a direct bearing on the political activity which takes place within that society. Each represents one means by which the political culture operates to establish the bounds of acceptable political behavior. And taken together, these elements of style, mood, and the like work to control the quality of political life in the society.

At the same time, it should be clear that public policy and other, less formalized forms of system behavior are frequently determined not by large and amorphous cultural groupings but by a more limited and easily identifiable group of political leaders.[21] And since these leaders may differ from the mass of citizens in terms of their personal resources (leaders control more physical and symbolic assets), of their social location (leadership positions entail considerable influence), and perhaps even of their personality traits (achievement of leadership may require disproportionate amounts of such attributes as confidence, aggressiveness, or opportunism), their presence introduces some margin for error in the translation of cultural mandates into public policy.[22] But we must keep in mind that to the extent that the political structure of a society is indigenous rather than imposed from the outside, the leaders themselves are likely to be *of* the political culture in question, or at least of some significant component subculture. That is, if the leaders of a society come from within that society, we can expect that they have been subjected to many or most of the same pressures and experiences that have helped shape the combination of contemporary attitudes and orientations that constitute the political culture. Thus not only will leaders *respond* to the pressures of the political culture, but to the extent that they share in that culture they will *reflect* those pressures as well. The bounds on the political activity of leaders, in other words, will be generated internally as well as externally.[23] And as a result, the judgments of these decision makers should not be grossly atypical of the collective judgments of their fellow citizens, and their actions should correspond more or less closely with the direction provided by the underlying political culture.

THE POLITICAL CULTURE OF THE UNITED STATES

Unfortunately, it is easier to formulate the abstract concept of political culture than it is to describe any particular political culture in detail. For while the public opinion on contemporary issues that lies at the periphery of such a culture is often easily measured, the more fundamental values that lie at the heart of the culture have proven more resistant to empirical discovery. This is the case in part because these values are so much more diffuse in nature than the opinions they foster, and in part because those who would observe these values are themselves often products of the very culture they would understand and hence (to use a hackneyed expression) may be unable to see the forest for the trees. Nevertheless, let us try briefly to suggest some outlines of the American political culture so that we may acquire some sense of the ways in which a particular political culture can work to structure political activity.

The *style* of politics in the United States emphasizes equality of roles and situations (as opposed to equality of individuals), individualism and personal freedom within a framework of majoritarianism and associated group superiority themes (including racism), and conformity with the external norms of the society.[24] We see these themes represented in such potent symbols and phrases as "equal opportunity" (in the pursuit as opposed to the attainment of happiness), "freedom of choice" (associated in the 1950s and '60s with the freedom of the [white] majority to avoid sending its children to schools attended by children of the [black] minority), and "the silent majority" (a Nixon-era catchphrase that excluded vocal nonconformists from the so-called mainstream of American politics). Indeed, the emphasis on majorities, group support, and equality of situations seems to have brought about not a democracy of individuals but a democracy of groups, a "pluralist" democracy where one's status and influence are often measured, not by who one is, but by the ethnic, social, political, or other groups with which one associates.[25] For all their tradition of rugged individualism and frontier independence, Americans seem to rely on group politics far more heavily than do adherents of other political cultures, and this reliance produces a certain pattern or continuity in the political outlooks of large numbers of individuals.[26]

The *mood* of American politics seems best to be described by four major "isms": humanitarianism, moralism, nationalism, and patriotism.[27] While it would perhaps be rather self-serving to attribute many acts of national policy primarily to humanitarianism on the part of the political leaders of the United States, it does seem fair to argue that much of the popular support for such policies as United Nations membership and financial support, the Marshall Plan for the reconstruction of Europe following World War II, and even the continuation of the Vietnam war after its futility had become apparent to many (not to mention the rationale put forward by the peace activists to end it) derived from an underlying humanitarian instinct. Certainly the leaders of the nation and many citizens recognized a certain national interest in the successful implementation of each of these politics, but equally certainly the general public accepted these policies at least in part for more altruistic reasons. The fact that some of these bases of support may have derived from myths or misperceptions, and the fact that other motives were involved as well, should not obscure the fact that such humanitarian ideals were at work. Indeed, that the political leadership could mobilize national resources in each instance by drawing upon this collective humanitarian instinct bears testimony to the importance of this inclination in the American political culture.

Often, however, the humanitarianism we have described is tempered by the remaining three elements of the American political mood: moralism, nationalism, and patriotism.[28] The Stars and Stripes, *The Star Spangled Banner*, the Pledge of Allegiance, Uncle Sam, the heroes of American history—each symbolizes an underlying theme of pride in the American heritage, but a pride that takes on near-religious proportions. We provide, as noted, for the social welfare of our less fortunate citizens, but we provide them, too, with a constant stream of contemptuous rhetoric about self-made men and women and the work ethic. We propagate Western-style democracy in the agrarian cultures of lesser developed nations, but where the lessons do not take (as in Vietnam), or where democracy takes what we regard as a false turn (as in Chile in the 1970s), we often reach an accommodation with proponents of other views who offer their support and proceed to delude ourselves into perceiving them as democrats. We assume from time to time that God is in fact on our side, and, secure in that knowledge, we incorporate His word into our public policy. In this, we have been aided and abetted throughout our history by such political leaders as William Jennings Bryan and Woodrow Wilson, and by such conceptions of purpose as "manifest destiny."[29] In more recent times, the application of these traits of national character to our dealings with other nations has led at least one observer to ascribe to us a certain arrogance in the exercise of our national powers and prerogatives.[30]

The *tone* of American politics is generally an admixture of pragmatism and optimism, laced with a belief in progress that can probably be traced both to the frontier imperatives of an earlier day and to the absence of any extended period of national adversity in United States history.[31] This tendency has been reinforced by the fact that the dominant political parties in the United States have generally engaged in evenhanded competition with one another while together working to coopt the support of those noncentrist third parties that have cropped up from time to time.[32] Thus in comparison with European democracies, the spectrum of American politics has been a relatively narrow one, and the polarization of factions along ideological lines has been avoided.[33] The muting of conflict and the historical success of various American enterprises have combined to set a generally progressive tone for politics in the United States.

The *goals* of the American political culture are rather more difficult to present in general terms, since one must differentiate among individual, group, and national levels. There do, however, appear to be at least two consistent themes, one substantive and one ideological, that are worthy of note. Substantively, Americans appear to value achievement, success, and material comfort, goals reinforced by the traditional capitalistic economic system as well as by the profound wealth of the nation. Ideologically, Americans pursue and proselytize in behalf of what they perceive to be democratic forms.[34] Both the achievement orientation and the preference for democratic politics contribute to an undertone of populism, of concern for abuse of the ordinary citizen by leaders who have lost touch with "the people," which has surfaced in domestic politics with some regularity ever since the election of Andrew Jackson, and most recently in international politics with the heavy emphasis placed by Jimmy Carter on attaining worldwide advances in human rights.[35]

Finally, we can describe the norms that govern personal participation in American politics. Compared with citizens of other democracies, Americans as individuals tend to have more frequent involvement in politics, to feel more of an obligation to play an active part in their community, and to possess greater feelings of political efficacy, of an ability to deal with and influence political affairs. They relate actively, openly, and often with considerable pride to their political system, and frequently view their involvement as an intensely personal experience, as a matter of considerable emotional concern.[36] Thus the American political culture is a highly participatory one.[37]

All these factors and others that we have undoubtedly overlooked contribute at a fundamental level to the manner and quality of political life in the United States. No single element and no static combination of elements allow us to predict the political behavior of Americans as a group, for, like individual attitudes, these traits interact with one another in continually shifting and realigning alliances. But if we view these cultural characteristics as collective predispositions, as consistent *tendencies* of behavior within American society, they do provide a context for understanding the day-to-day political activity that takes place in the United States. In this way, the political culture serves to summarize the dynamics of the interactions between individual citizens and their political system.

POLITICAL CULTURE AND POLITICAL STABILITY

But if, as we have suggested, the political culture reflects the dynamics of political activity at any particular *point* in time, that culture also operates through a complex teaching and learning process—generally termed *political socialization*—to maintain the continuity of political activity *through* time. As we shall see in the next chapter, the mechanisms of this process are many and varied, but all contribute to one ultimate result: the transmission, albeit at times in somewhat distorted form, of the principal values and orientations of a society from one generation to the next. The very preservation of the political system itself depends heavily upon the continuity of the political culture and, as a consequence, upon the successful transmission of the constituent attitudes, beliefs, and patterns of behavior of that culture to the heirs of the political order.[38]

Considered within this framework, the process of system-supportive political socialization has about it a certain quiet inevitability. We, as members of a particular society, may continue to do things in a particular manner, may continue to respond to political stimuli according to a consistent pattern, simply because that is the manner—quite possibly the only manner—in which we have seen them done before. Because our collective experience is limited, we are unaware of alternatives. Like a needle on a phonograph record, we follow the prescribed groove because it is there. Similarly, we may go along with, and in fact adopt as our own, certain cultural norms because everyone else seems to accept them and because as a consequence such acceptance entails social support. (Here the group dynamic that we detected in the American political culture becomes especially important.) We hold sets of attitudes that we perceive as consonant with the dominant values of the political culture because it is more rewarding, both socially and psychologically, to hold those attitudes than it is to question them. Indeed, perhaps we have never learned how to question them; perhaps we are to some extent unable to question them. And as a result, to the benefit of the established political order and by no means necessarily to the detriment of its citizens, the values of the system tend to be preserved and the way of life which it represents maintained.

This tendency toward stability is reinforced by a second and rather more overt psychological dynamic that has its basis in the functions performed for the individual by culture-related attitudes. As we have suggested, these attitudes help the individual to locate herself socially with respect to an infinitely large range of events and other individuals in the political system. In a very real sense, they tell her who she is; they help her to define her existence in political terms.[39] These attitudes, then, play a very important role in the political life of the individual—the role of anchoring her to a political world which she experiences with some frequency. And the more fundamental any particular attitude is in its contribution to the individual's sense of accommodation with political reality, the greater the level of personal significance that attitude will assume.

As a consequence, we can expect that those particular shared attitudes and orientations that are most used by individuals to identify with politics at the societal level—those attitudes and orientations that, in other words, constitute the heart of the political culture—will be extremely resistant to pressures for change. In fact, these most highly valued political attitudes, *precisely because they are so highly valued*, will be the most likely of all political attitudes to be passed along purposefully to succeeding generations. And thus, despite the short-term vicissitudes of history and the revolutionary prophecies of occasional visionaries, most political cultures will retain their distinctive characteristics through time. Those elements of belief and value, those critical determinants of the nature and quality of political life, that the most people feel are the most important will generally persevere.

This is not by any means intended to suggest that no individuals in a given society can or do ever question the cultural norms and political orientations that dominate that society. Clearly, such an assertion could not be supported. But the inherent stability of culture-based attitudes does serve to point up two considerations relative to the likelihood of fundamental change arising from within a given political culture. First, those individuals who *meaningfully* question dominant norms are likely to be relatively few in number except in the most unusual of circumstances. Only an act of uncommon personal assertion combined with a high degree of perspicacity is likely to provide the vantage point necessary for effective criticism of so fundamental a feature of political life as the political culture. Second, and perhaps more important, there is operating within any given polity at any given moment a widespread state of psychological inertia, either an unwillingness or even a basic inability to question cultural norms and the status quo. This inertia is the source of considerable stability in the political culture and, as a result, in the political system.[40]

And on those rare occasions when internally generated change does occur in the political culture, it is likely to occur not so much despite but in a sense because of the same kinds of psychological processes that lead to maintenance of the political culture. Individuals, as we have pointed out in the preceding chapter, interpret their encounters with politics in terms of their previous perceptions of political reality, perceptions that are generally governed by the cultural status quo. Thus new information and experience tend to be understood in terms of established concepts. If in a given society, however, we have a new generation that had a significantly different collective experience from that of the parent generation, something equivalent to a devastating economic collapse or an extended national tragedy, we might then expect this difference of baseline experience to influence the way in which the later generation would interpret both the norms expressed in the political culture and the events and personalities of the contemporary political scene. This differential experience could then serve as a basis either for challenging the cultural norms themselves, which would amount to a "cultural revolution" of the sort attempted some years ago in the People's Republic of China, or, as seems more likely, for challenging the ways in which those norms were being interpreted and applied by those in power, which would amount to cultural evolution.[41] In either event, the same functions of attitudes that generally work to maintain the political culture would in effect be working to change it.

IN SUMMARY

The political culture, then, works to the advantage of both individuals and the political system. At the same time that it provides individuals with a cognitive link to the polity around them, the political culture draws upon the collective beliefs, wants, and expectations of the individuals so linked to provide both direction and continuity to the larger political system. Thus each party to the political process—people and their institutions—has a stake in the maintenance of the political culture, and we can understand the functioning of one only in the context provided by the other.

SUGGESTIONS FOR FURTHER READING

Must reading for anyone interested in the study of political culture is a book by Gabriel A. Almond and Sidney Verba entitled *The Civic Culture* (Princeton: Princeton University Press, 1963). This seminal work provides a theoretical framework for the analysis of political culture and reports the results of a survey research project designed to compare the political cultures of five nations (the United States, Great Britain, Germany, Italy, and Mexico). A more contemporary treatment of the topic, and probably a better initial point of entry to the literature, is Walter A. Rosenbaum's *Political Culture* (New York: Praeger, 1975), which sets forth a broadly based framework for understanding many of the issues raised in this chapter.

Several books are of interest for the study of the political culture of the United States in particular. *The First New Nation* (New York: Basic Books, 1963) by Seymour Martin Lipset takes a developmental and comparative approach to American history and outlines over time the interaction between the political culture and the social environment. The nature of the American national character—if such a thing can in fact be divined—is suggested by Robin M. Williams, Jr., in *American Society: A Sociological Interpretation* (3rd rev. ed.; New York: Alfred A. Knopf, 1970); and by Donald J. Devine in *The Political Culture of the United States* (Boston: Little, Brown, 1972). The latter volume is both more limited in scope and more empirically sophisticated in presentation. The linkage between the political culture and the political structure of the United States is treated in Daniel J. Elazar, *American Federalism: A View from the States* (New York: Thomas Y. Crowell, 1972), while that between political culture and public policy is explored in Jarol B. Manheim, *Déjà Vu: American Political Problems in Historical Perspective* (New York: St. Martin's, 1976). Finally, relevant aspects of public opinion, some of which lie closer to the periphery of the American political culture than to its core, are examined by Richard E. Dawson in *Public Opinion and Contemporary Disarray* (New York: Harper & Row, 1973); and by Dan Nimmo in *Political Communication and Public Opinion in America* (Santa Monica, Calif.: Goodyear, 1978).

NOTES

1. This definition is based on the treatment of political culture by Samuel C. Patterson in "The Political Cultures of the American States," *Journal of Politics* 30 (1968): 187–209, as well as that by Gabriel A. Almond and G. Bingham Powell in *Comparative Politics: A Developmental Approach* (Boston: Little, Brown, 1966), pp. 50–64.
2. David Easton suggests that the objects of political orientations may be classified into three categories: government, regime, and political community. *A Systems Analysis of Political Life* (New York: John Wiley, 1965), pp. 171–219.
3. See Lucian W. Pye, *Aspects of Political Development* (Boston: Little, Brown, 1966), pp. 104f., and Daniel J. Elazar, *American Federalism: A View from the States* (2nd ed.; New York: Thomas Y. Crowell, 1972), pp. 89 f. The specific application of this notion to the American case is illustrated by Elazar, pp. 90–126, and by Seymour Martin Lipset in *The First New Nation* (New York: Basic Books, 1963).
4. Donald J. Devine, *The Political Culture of the United States* (Boston: Little, Brown, 1972), p. 362.
5. Elazar, *American Federalism*, pp. 90–93.
6. Philip E. Converse, Warren E. Miller, Jerrold G. Rusk, and Arthur C. Wolfe offer an interesting analysis of the relationship between party and issue preferences in "Continuity and Change in American Politics: Parties and Issues in the 1968 Election," *American Political Science Review* 63 (1969): 1083–1105.
7. Lipset, *First New Nation*, passim.
8. Almond and Powell, *Comparative Politics*, pp. 63 f.
9. Some examples of the rise in ethnicity are documented by Roger Ricklefs in "Small Ethnic Groups Enjoy Revived Interest in Cultural Heritages," *Wall Street Journal*, July 11, 1973, pp. 1, 21.
10. Roger W. Cobb and Charles D. Elder, "The Political Uses of Symbolism," *American Political Quarterly* 1 (1973): 307 ff.

11. L. White, *The Science of Culture* (New York: Grove Press, 1949), p. 25, cited in Cobb and Elder, "Political Uses of Symbolism," p. 307.
12. Murray Edelman, *The Symbolic Uses of Politics* (Urbana: University of Illinois Press, 1964), chapter 6. See also Murray Edelman, *Politics as Symbolic Action* (Chicago: Markham, 1971), chap. 5.
13. Edelman, *Symbolic Uses*, passim.
14. Patterson, "Political Cultures of the American States," p. 190.
15. David Easton, "An Approach to the Analysis of Political Systems," *World Politics* 9 (1957): 383–408, and Almond and Powell, *Comparative Politics*, pp. 25 ff.
16. Cobb and Elder, "Political Uses of Symbolism," pp. 329 ff. See also Walter Dean Burnham. "Crisis of American Political Legitimacy," *Society* 10 (1972): 24–31.
17. This assessment tends to be supported by the results of the Harris polls of 18–22 July 1973 and 6 August 1973, as reported in *Watergate: Chronology of a Crisis*, 2 (Washington, D.C.: Congressional Quarterly, 1973), 1:240, 262, and in the more extensive results reported by Everett Carll Ladd, Jr. in "The Polls: The Question of Confidence," *Public Opinion Quarterly* 40(1976–77): 545.
18. This and other components of a political culture discussed below are treated briefly in Richard E. Dawson and Kenneth Prewitt, *Political Socialization* (Boston: Little, Brown, 1969), p. 26. The concept of political style is developed by Sidney Verba, who deals with these same themes in a rather less differentiated manner, in "Comparative Political Culture," in *Political Culture and Political Development*, ed. Lucian W. Pye and Sidney Verba (Princeton: Princeton University Press, 1965), pp. 544–50.
19. Gabriel A. Almond and Sidney Verba, *The Civic Culture* (Princeton: Princeton University Press, 1963), pp. 440 f.
20. For an interesting analysis of this point with respect to American foreign policy, see William R. Caspary, "The 'Mood Theory': A Study of Public Opinion and Foreign Policy," *American Political Science Review* 64 (1970): 536–47.
21. Indeed, it may be precisely because the political culture is quite vague and quite general in its operation that political leaders are literally forced to emerge as a mechanism for the application of ill-defined cultural norms to specific situations. See G. Lowell Field and John Higley, *Elites and Non-Elites: The Possibilities and Their Side Effects*, Module no. 13 (Andover, Mass.: Warner Modular Publications, 1973), pp. 1–38.
22. For a related discussion see Stephen V. Monsma, "Potential Leaders and Democratic Values," *Public Opinion Quarterly* 35 (1971): 350–57.
23. In this regard, Elihu Katz and Paul F. Lazarsfeld suggest that participation in the shared values and interests of their followers may actually be a prerequisite for leaders in a group setting. *Personal Influence* (Glencoe, Ill.: Free Press, 1955), pp. 101 f.

24. Robin M. Williams, Jr., *American Society: A Sociological Interpretation* (3rd rev. ed., New York: Alfred A. Knopf, 1970), pp. 472–87, 495–500.

25. Robert A. Dahl, *A Preface to Democratic Theory* (Chicago: University of Chicago Press, 1956), pp. 145–48. For contrary evidence on this point, see Thomas R. Dye, *Who's Running America?* (2nd ed.; Englewood Cliffs, N.J.: Prentice-Hall, 1979).

26. Almond and Verba, *The Civic Culture*, p. 191.

27. Williams, *American Society*, pp. 461–64, 489–92.

28. Ibid., pp. 462–64; and Elazar, *American Federalism*, pp. 96–99.

29. Louis W. Koenig, *Bryan: A Political Biography of William Jennings Bryan* (New York: C. P. Putnam's, 1971), passim; Arthur S. Link, *Wilson the Diplomatist* (Baltimore: Johns Hopkins Press, 1957), pp. 11–16; and Julius W. Pratt, *Expansionists of 1898* (Baltimore: Johns Hopkins Press, 1936), pp. 1–33.

30. J. William Fulbright, *The Arrogance of Power* (New York: Vintage Books, 1966).

31. Daniel J. Elazar argues the frontier hypothesis in *American Federalism*, pp. 104–14, and in *The Metropolitan Frontier: A Perspective on Change in American Society* (Morristown, N.J.: General Learning Press, 1973). The point regarding national adversity is an extension of Louis Hartz's familiar arguments in *The Liberal Tradition in America* (New York: Harcourt, Brace and World, 1955). See also Devine, *Political Culture of the United States*, pp. 54–60.

32. See Frank J. Sorauf, *Party Politics in America* (2nd ed.; Boston: Little, Brown, 1972), pp. 28–58.

33. Indeed, Maurice Duverger in *Party Politics and Pressure Groups* (New York: Thomas Y. Crowell, 1972), p. 23, describes the American party structure as a "pseudo" rather than a genuine two-party system. For an alternative and especially interesting perspective on this argument see David R. Segal, "Classes, Strata, and Parties in West Germany and the United States," *Comparative Studies of Society and History* 10 (1967): 66–84.

34. Williams, *American Society*, pp. 454–61, 469–72, 492–95.

35. The most recent manifestations of this phenomenon in domestic politics have been the Wallace movement of the late 1960s and early '70s and the Carter campaign of 1976. See Converse et al., "Continuity and Change in American Politics," pp. 1101–5.

36. Almond and Verba, *The Civic Culture*, pp. 440 f. This argument notwithstanding, the consensus that permits for continuity in the political process may be more shallow than generally believed, and may in fact depend for its acceptance on its absence of clear definition. See Herbert McClosky, "Consensus and Ideology in American Politics," *American Political Science Review* 58 (1964): 361–82.

37. Practice may be an imperfect reflection of these cultural characteristics. According to a study of voting rates in the period between World War II and 1980, the United States ranks last among 20 nations in the propor-

tion of its population that actually votes in elections. See Ivor Crewe, "As the World Turns Out," *Public Opinion* 4 (1981): 52–53.

38. Dawson and Prewitt, *Political Socialization*, p. 27.
39. Roberta S. Sigel, "Learning and Development," in *Learning About Politics*, ed. Roberta S. Sigel (New York: Random House, 1970), pp. 9 f.; and Dawson and Prewitt, *Political Socialization*, p. 203.
40. For an alternative view, see Louis M. Seagull, *Youth and Change in American Politics* (New York: New Viewpoints, 1977).
41. Almond and Powell, *Comparative Politics*, p. 65. For an example of this phenomenon, see Alex Inkeles, "Social Change and Social Character: The Role of Parental Mediation," *Journal of Social Issues* 11 (1955): 12–23.

5

Political Socialization

A Continuing Apprenticeship

In the final pages of Chapter 4 we suggested that political socialization plays a vital role in maintaining the continuity of political life in a society. By providing for the transmission of acceptable patterns of perception, expectation, and behavior from one generation to the next, from the institutions of a society to its citizens, or from one group of citizens to another, the socialization process in effect lubricates the gears and wheels of the political machine. By assuring that the values and orientations that give meaning to political reality will be passed along to those who need them, socialization preserves the essential character of the political process. Only when its requisite psychological supports are successfully conveyed to newly arrived participants can the political order endure.

But if the process of political socialization plays such a critical role in the life of whole societies, it is certainly no less vital to the individuals who make up those societies, for political socialization helps each such individual understand and adjust to the political realities of the social environment. Indeed, by the very acts of preserving the political order and communicating the existing body of political wisdom, political socialization works to integrate each new generation of novices into the political mainstream. Thus what society considers the transmission of established values and orientations comes to the individual as a revelation of the mysteries of political life.

THE LEARNING OF POLITICS

Putting all of this a different way, political socialization, the process of teaching and learning about politics, gives rise to individual political attitudes of the sort we described earlier. It is through the process of political socialization that an individual acquires the values and beliefs of the political culture (as well as other politically relevant values and beliefs), that he continually learns to interpret or to reinterpret his personal encounters with political reality, and, in fact, that he even learns to define what constitutes political reality to begin with. Indeed, not only the values passed along to or gathered in by the individual subjects of the socialization process but the very act of observation—the identification and understanding of relevant political "facts"—is structured by the particular characteristics of each individual's own socialization experience. The capabilities and limitations of each individual to understand political reality are a function of his own personal political history.[1]

The linkage between this individual perspective on political socialization and the societal perspective we developed earlier may be made clear if we consider the nature of the relationship between a person and his political system. As we have suggested previously, a political system is composed in large measure of the politically oriented attitudes and behaviors of the people who live within. The most basic elements of a political system, then, are the actions and attitudes of individual citizens and the particular contributions each makes to political life. Each person has a certain set of functions that he is able and/or expected to fulfill if the system itself is to perform as required. These tasks may range from simply believing in the system to the act of voting, to working for a favored candidate for office, or even, perhaps, to actually holding office. But whatever his task, whatever his "role" in the political system, each individual must somehow learn what is expected of him and how he is to respond to particular political stimuli. Each individual must somehow acquire the information and orientations upon which to base his interpretation and his conduct of his own role in the political life of his society. That "somehow," that binding tie between the individual and the system, is political socialization.[2]

Individuals learn to make demands upon political leaders, or perhaps they learn not to make such demands. They learn to offer support to the political system, or perhaps to withhold that support; to expect certain concessions from the political system, or perhaps to expect nothing. Those who will ultimately become political leaders learn first how to become leaders, later how to perform as leaders.[3] In other words, the beliefs and expectations that govern every encounter with politics must be acquired; the attitudes and perceptions that guide every political action must be learned. And the position in political life that each individual defines for himself derives from his own personal learning experience, from his own personalized version of the socialization process. We saw in Chapter 3 the potential importance of learning in the development of one's personality, one's fundamental psychological predispositions for perceiving and dealing with the surrounding world. Here I am suggesting that a part of that same learning process provides the cues necessary to cope with and use politics per se.

Political socialization is an interactive process that continues from early childhood until the individual loses touch with political life through death, senility, social or informational isolation, or other similarly complete forms of withdrawal from society. As long as one continues in some way to relate to politics, even if that relationship involves a rejection of overt political participation, the process of political socialization remains incomplete. There exists no universally identifiable endpoint, no state of being "completely socialized."[4] Truly, political socialization represents for the individual a continuing apprenticeship in political life.

That is not to suggest that an individual's early experience is not highly significant in structuring the relationship between person and politics. To the contrary, most evidence indicates that most people acquire the bulk of their political orientations and learning at a relatively early stage of life, and certainly before reaching adulthood. But it should help us to perceive these early experiences in their proper context, which is, in its simplest terms, that of preparing the individual to understand and to deal with later experiences which he may encounter. In general, by giving him a relatively broad base of political orientations, early experience prepares the individual more or less adequately for the assumption of adult political roles. His later experience in those roles then further influences his attitudes and expectations as they apply to subsequent political events. Thus political learning is cumulative, and the lessons learned are subject to both preexisting expectation and subsequent modification.[5]

We have already examined the psychological mechanisms of learning, and in Chapter 9 we shall consider the physiological events that are associated with it as well. Here our emphasis is on the social context in which learning occurs. Students of the process have suggested at least four different models or theories that describe the ways in which political and other learning comes about. These include the "accumulation" theory, the "interpersonal transfer" theory, the "identification" theory, and the "cognitive developmental" theory. As we look briefly at each of these models, the most important point to keep in mind is that, while each represents a distinctly different characterization of the learning process, none is intended to explain all instances of learning. Rather, each seeks to identify and to explain a different aspect of the acquisition of information. Thus socialization in one attitude area at one point in time may best be understood in terms of one particular theory, and socialization in another attitude area or at another point in time may best be understood in terms of another. The overall corpus of political learning will result from an admixture of all four.

The first of these explanations, the so-called *accumulation theory*, begins from the premise that political learning is an incremental process that proceeds by the addition of discrete units of knowledge, information, and belief. Thus an individual's attitudes are seen as the sum at a given point in time of the inputs she has received up to that time. In this view, there is not necessarily any logical sequence by which learning takes place; rather, information is acquired when and as it becomes available. In other words, there is implicit in the accumulation theory no consistent pattern to the learning of politics, and there need be no systematic connection among the various elements of new information that an individual acquires.[6] As a consequence, the accumulation theory is useful primarily for explaining the acquisition of bits of factual knowledge which contribute principally to the cognitive component of political attitudes.

The second theory of political learning, that of *interpersonal transfer*, is rather more useful for explaining affective judgments and relationships with political figures. Here the individual is presumed to possess a storehouse of experience in interpersonal relations that can be transferred over to expressly political situations. This amounts to a sort of guilt by association. For example, when a child comes to identify the President as an authority figure, she is likely to make the association between her father's role of authority in the family, with which she has considerable direct experience, and the President's role of authority in the nation, with which she has none. Thus she develops an image of the President as quite literally the father of her country. Her understanding of the concept of "President" is less a product of newly acquired information which relates directly to the object in question than it is simply an extension of earlier, possibly nonpolitical forms of understanding.[7]

The *identification model* is similar in that it too derives from interpersonal relations, but here the learning process is rather more direct. Identification operates when an individual identifies herself with some other person whom she holds in high esteem and proceeds to imitate the attitudes or behaviors of that person. In this view, then, learning proceeds without teaching, and the transmission of values from source to recipient may be inadvertent. The individual herself chooses the lessons she will learn and the conditions under which she will learn them.[8] Furthermore, just as the accumulation model allows for the learning of unconnected facts, the identification model permits the adoption of preferences or behaviors without understanding. It is the ritual of imitation, and not the force of reason, that results in learning of this type. It is the personal stature of the individual's role model and not necessarily the substantive sources of the role model's attitudes and behaviors that motivates learning by identification. The student who adopts the political outlooks of a professor she admires might well provide an example of such learning.

Our final conceptualization of political learning, termed *cognitive developmental*, derives from the cognitive conceptualization of personality we examined in Chapter 3 and is rather more demanding in its structuring of the learning situation. According to this theory, an individual is limited in her ability to understand political phenomena by the amount of relevant information she already possesses and by the level of conceptual ability she has achieved. The more developed her general mental capabilities in dealing with abstractions, for example, the better able she is to grasp the subtleties of fairly abstract political ideas such as ideologies. Similarly, the more information she possesses about candidates and political competition, the better able she is to perceive and respond to the complexities of an electoral situation. The cognitive developmental model, in other words, argues that learning is heavily dependent upon the inherent capabilities of the individual to think, and suggests that learning of increasingly complex political information can take place only as the individual acquires increasing critical skills. Accordingly, the level of sophistication of the information one is *able* to learn, and, therefore, the limits on the potential sophistication of one's understanding of politics, is at least in part a function of age.[9]

Each of these theories of political learning is of differing importance at different stages of the socialization process, in interaction with different socializing agents, in different situations, or at different times. Each has its greatest impact on the learning of

different kinds of political lessons. And each makes different demands upon the mental state and capabilities of the individual in
question. But taken together, the four models provide us with a
satisfying intuitive sense of just how it is that political learning
takes place, and of just where it is that individual political attitudes
come from.

To this point, then, we have some understanding, first, of
how important political learning is, and second, of the ways in
which one might go about acquiring it. Yet an all-important question remains: From whom or from what do we in fact learn about
politics? Who or what constitutes the source of our political information? Or, in the jargon of the political scientist: Who or what
are the "agents of political socialization"?

An *agent of political socialization* may be defined as any person,
institution, event, or other source from which we take cues as to
how we should think or behave with regard to politics. Thus such
things as one's parents and family, the schools, peer groups, and
the mass media would, in performing certain of their functions that
we shall investigate shortly, be considered agents of political
socialization. Indeed, any source to which we can trace the acquisition of information relevant to or directly bearing upon our perceptions of political reality constitutes an agent of political socialization. And while we shall, in the remainder of the present chapter,
focus our attention somewhat narrowly on political socialization as
performed by those few agents found to have an especially profound impact on the political development of the individual, we
must keep in mind the fact that no single one of these sources of
political learning can remain uniformly effective in perpetuity. It is
instead the unique combination and the ongoing interaction of various of these and other socializing agents that help define any particular political individual at any particular moment in time. With
this in mind, let us turn our attention to several of the more important contributors to the political maturation of the individual.

INTERPERSONAL SOURCES OF POLITICAL LEARNING

In childhood, the first experiences that are or may become politically relevant remain largely undifferentiated from other aspects of social learning. If a child encounters authority, for example, it is
usually a very direct and highly personalized kind of authority,
often familial, and the abstraction of such experiences to less direct,
less personalized political relationships will develop only later and

more gradually. Similarly, if a child acquires a sense of the restraints that operate on his personal behavior, those restraints are
perceived as being situation-specific, and their relevance to more
generalized forms of political behavior will be perceived only later
and more gradually.[10] In other words, the individual must first define to his own satisfaction his immediate sphere of personal and
social existence, and only then, within the constraints thus
obtained, may he proceed to expand his consciousness to encom-
pass political reality.

Within this context, the earliest and perhaps the most significant influence on the nascent individual comes from his family. It
is, after all, the family which commands virtually the full attention
of the child during his earliest formative years. Almost all of the
social experience which an individual acquires at this stage of life
he acquires through interaction with his parents and siblings. The
family is thus not only the gatekeeper of such social experience,
but is in most instances the ultimate source of that experience as
well. Drawing upon our earlier analysis, then, we can think of the
family as effectively controlling the stimuli which reach the child
during this period. Moreover, unlike any other agent of socialization, the family starts with a clean slate. The family has the earliest
access to the virgin mind of the young child. Thus while other
would-be sources of political influence must in large measure either
counter, reinforce, or work around existing attitudes, the family is
in a position to create basic orientations, an advantage which is limited only by the family's willingness and ability to do so and by
the willingness and capabilities of the child to learn.[11]

The prime importance of the family as an agent of socialization
comes about for a number of reasons. To begin with, as we have
suggested already, the family is simply there first, and for a significant period possesses a virtual monopoly on the child's time and
attention. During the first critical months and years the child has
no friends with whom he can communicate effectively, no meaningful interactions with mass media or other outside sources of
stimuli to provide him with substantive ideas. His only link with the
outside world is through non-verbal—and later limited verbal—
communication with those who look after him—generally, the
members of his family. His only sources of social support and interpersonal communication, of warmth and affection, are those
same family members. As a consequence, the members of his family provide the only models of thought and action available to the
individual at this earliest stage of development.

It is, in fact, this same dependence of the child upon the family for support that provides parents and perhaps siblings with yet a second potential source of influence. For precisely because the family is his only point of contact not only with his social environment but with the very means of physical sustenance, the young child necessarily holds the members of his family in high esteem and will behave according to patterns of conduct which they set forth for him. That is, precisely because he senses that his very survival rests upon the whim of those who provide for him, the child will begin to behave in manners dictated by or exemplified by his presumed benefactors. The child will imitate or emulate because he regards such behavior as essential to his personal well-being.[12]

A third source of parental influence arises as well from the special nature of the parent-child relationship, and most especially from the development of trust. Put most simply, parents generally constitute a "high-credibility source" of information, one whose positive affective relationship with the child transfers over to any information that might be communicated. At this point in the life cycle, the lessons learned from one's parents are not generally questioned, but are instead accepted as inherently believable. Indeed, the learning of these lessons itself becomes a goal that is positively valued. And as a consequence, the potential impact of parental instruction is likely to be substantial.[13]

Finally, during his early developmental stages the child is dependent upon his family not only for sustenance, but for identity as well. As he begins to perceive of himself as an individual, as he begins to sense that he possesses a separate and independent place in the world, the child seeks to define for himself an appropriate set of social roles. Yet given the unavailability of alternative judgmental criteria, the only basis he has for defining his own role is his perception of how others whom he considers relevant see him. Indeed, because those "relevant others" are at this point likely to be precisely those people upon whom he has been so dependent for his well-being all along, it is once again the family that serves as the principal source of cues even for independent social behavior. The individual learns to see himself and his place in society as he and that place are seen by the members of his family.[14]

Psychologists tell us that the most important lesson a child learns during his earliest months and years is that of coexistence with his environment. Discussions of child development often center on the importance of toilet-training and early feeding patterns, arguing that styles of behavior that a child acquires in the process of learning to perform these most basic activities will influence (among other things) his general feelings of efficacy later in life.[15] But other, more complex interactive situations arise as the child gets older which have the potential of providing him with similar feelings of self-satisfaction and/or potency. Examples include helping at home (cooking, dishwashing, babysitting for younger children), venturing out from home on his own and later crossing streets or using public transportation, going shopping alone or with his peers, or even getting a part-time job. Generally speaking, the earliest experiences of a child in testing the basic aspects of his existence and in expanding the boundaries of that existence help greatly to determine the kind of personal identity he defines for himself. This emergent self-definition may later be transferred to the areas of political perception and political activity as required by circumstance.

As a child emerges from infancy and acquires increasing physical mobility and communicative skills, his relationship with his parents becomes, from a socialization standpoint, rather more complicated. Verbal communication and formal instruction take on increasing importance, and the child gradually acquires the ability to conceptualize. He learns to think, to deal with ideas. And it is the development of this ability to perceive the world in some organized fashion, and with it the ability to hold attitudes, which brings the child to the threshold of social and political reality.[16]

From this point on, and most particularly as he continues through school, the individual starts to acquire a more analytical view of his family, its social role, and his role in it—all largely because of his interactions with other, outside socializing agents that constitute more or less competing models of reality. But even then, throughout his early years, the lessons and outlooks that he learns in the family offer something of a fallback position, a referent against which other stimuli may be compared.

More than that, his family experience provides the individual with what amounts to a social version of a stacked deck. For just as the family creates in large measure the basic orientations that an individual will bring to a given social situation, the family further exercises a significant degree of control over the kinds of situations in which that individual is in fact likely to find himself. That is to say, each family possesses certain group identifications and social locations—be they economic, linguistic, ethnic, religious, or political— which it may be expected to pass along to its offspring as a matter of course.[17] Thus the child who grows up in a middle-class family is likely to live in a middle-class neighborhood, to attend a middle-class school, and to have middle-class friends. He simply will not experience either ghetto life or that of the jet set. The child in the United States who is raised in a setting in which Spanish or German is the primary language may relate most easily to those who share his language and may not feel pressured to adjust to the larger, English-speaking society. In this way, the family may cushion the child's exposure to the larger social environment and may act, even if unintentionally, to preserve its own value preferences. In such instances, only later experience derived from other sources can suggest to the individual either the existence or character of alternative modes of political perception and behavior.[18]

Potentially one of the most important of these external influences that may challenge the basic attitudes and patterns of thought established by the family is that exercised on the individual by his peers. The term *peers* here refers to one's friends, associates at work, childhood playmates, or more generally to any small, unstructured or at least informally structured group with whose members one has close personal contact. From the very moment he begins to acquire acquaintances of his own age outside his family, from the very moment he establishes what we may term peer-group relationships, the individual opens himself to alternative points of view which may have a considerable impact upon his attitudes, his expectations, and his behavior.

Remember that until he ventures on his own out into the real world—that which exists beyond the door of his home—the child has existed in a social vacuum of sorts. All ideas and concepts which his parents have rejected, deemed irrelevant, consciously guarded him against, or themselves been unaware of have been effectively purged from the realm of his perception. They have, for all practical purposes, simply not existed. Suddenly he finds himself confronted with other individuals, some of whom he values as friends, who have had more or less different experiences and who may espouse more or less different points of view. The growing realization that there exist these alternative experiences and value structures may gradually lead the individual to reexamine his own outlooks in a new light as well as to accept an expanding variety of new attitudes, interests, and understandings.[19]

Peer groups play differing roles as agents of socialization at different stages of life. At the outset, when as a young child the individual first crosses the social threshold, peer relationships supplement familial relationships by broadening the scope of his awareness and by helping him to identify his family as part of an emerging social matrix. It is through the development of peer-group interactions that the individual first begins to lose his "pre-Copernican" notions about the central dependence of all life upon his family and to sense the full breadth of his social environment.

During the years of formal education, peer groups become increasingly important in a different way by furnishing alternative value structures and alternative emotional foci which, in concert with the school experience, begin to provide the individual with the motives and the skills requisite for developing his own sense of social independence.[20] In fact, by the time a child reaches high school age—a period when he is beginning to sense his own maturity—peer-group relations in combination with other socializing factors may largely supplant the family as a reference point for personal norms, at least to the extent that the individual in question is conscious of making choices.[21] Thus young people tend to prefer the company of their contemporaries to that of their "old-fashioned" parents, and in the extreme case, adolescent rebellion assumes the character of a group as opposed to an individual phenomenon.[22]

And finally, by the time an individual reaches adulthood, peer groups may have become the dominant socializing force in his life, once again, as was the case with the family, due largely to proximity. Once an individual is out of school and on his own, he is most open to influence by those persons he most values: his spouse, his friends, his fellow workers. At this point in life, peer groups provide the most salient social referent; they constitute the principal locus of social support for his attitudes and behavior.[23] We shall in fact see that even the potential influence of the mass media on the individual seems to be affected by the nature of his peer-group relationships.

Peer-group socialization is politically significant in at least three ways. To begin with, by increasing his awareness of alternatives to the kinds of value formulations promulgated by his parents and later by the school, peer groups give to the individual a degree of social leverage with which he may challenge those formulations. By expanding the consciousness of the individual, by giving him a broader perspective upon his own beliefs and values, they can prove a potentially significant instrument of social change. Second, peer groups often develop and offer support for their own alternative value structures. That is, not only may they motivate the individual to rethink his learning from other sources but they may also provide him with competing models of reality. Thus peer groups may be not only destructive of established social outlooks but constructive of new ones as well. And finally, peer groups may offer directly political kinds of cues. They may support (in the psychological sense) particular party identifications, ideological orientations, or even issue and candidate preferences. Indeed, if only by making the individual cognizant of the broader social system itself, peer groups help make meaningful the whole concept of "politics."[24]

It goes without saying that peer groups can reinforce those values that an individual acquires from parents, school, or other sources as well as call them into question. We have in fact suggested earlier that families tend to place their children into social situations that make this outcome reasonably likely. But the real political significance of peer-group relationships lies in the fact that they help broaden the individual's perceptions of social and political reality and provide the individual with alternative points of anchorage to the social system. Precisely because they bring together— under conditions of positive affect and intense contact—individuals of differing background and experience, precisely because they serve as the interface of two or more products of different social and psychological circumstance, peer-group relationships are considerably more likely than are familial relationships to facilitate changes in political orientation.

INSTITUTIONAL SOURCES OF POLITICAL LEARNING

While interpersonal factors such as family and peer associations have a significant influence on the political development of the individual, we must realize that these relationships operate within a larger, institutional framework. For not only do small and more or less closed groups of individuals have a stake in and an impact upon political learning, but the society itself, working through a variety of larger and more formal organizations, also defines for itself a significant role in the socialization process. Indeed, political learning from family and peers is often implicit and incidental, developing largely as a by-product of social activities that are at best only marginally political, while the transmission of political knowledge or skills to an individual from institutional sources may be a good deal more explicit, more purposeful, and more structured.

Perhaps the most important institutional agent of political socialization with which almost every individual in a modern society must come into contact is the school. Without question, schools teach lessons with clear and intended political content in ways that are designed to take advantage of the student's skills in and orientations toward interpersonal relations. And while the general thrust of formal education in a given society may or may not be predominantly political in nature (depending, in part, upon whether one learns to count apples and oranges or capitalists and imperialists), students will, in the process of being schooled, acquire values, beliefs, and patterns of behavior which are clearly relevant to political life.

The socializing aspects of the school experience are numerous, and it goes without saying that not all of them have a direct bearing upon political learning. It should be apparent, however, that within the classroom the child learns to relate to authority figures from outside the family, is imbued with the norms and symbols of the state, acquires skills that have direct applications to political life, and is formally instructed in the goals, mechanisms, and functions of his government. It is during his years in school that a child learns to deal in more abstract terms with such concepts as power, government, and authority.

Besides perhaps the policeman, the teacher is usually the first extrafamilial authority figure with whom most children come into contact. In the child's eyes the teacher is a spokesman for all of society, a symbol of linkage with what is at first a vaguely understood "they." And just as the child has learned to identify himself by observing the behavior of others as they relate to him, he now learns to relate to a more remote power structure through his interactions with and observations of the teacher.[25] Although the child does learn to abstract his notions of power and the like, the fact that the teacher personalizes those concepts much as his parents had before helps to expand his understanding of those concepts and to integrate them into his own life experience. The teacher thus becomes a new standard of judgment in the process of learning by identification.[26] The teacher becomes an affective symbol, either positive or negative, and a more or less credible source of political information.

In essence, the teacher creates in the classroom a *learning culture*, a system of rules and values to which the child is expected to aspire. For his part, the child uses these rules and values to help define and interpret for himself the larger political culture.[27] Elements of this learning culture might include competition, cooperation, self-help, self-sacrifice, discipline, freedom of expression, participation, obedience, fairness, independence, loyalty, truthfulness, or the converse of any of these or a lengthy list of other characteristics. The point is that those norms that are emphasized in the classroom are likely to be learned effectively. And because they are learned from the teacher, a symbol and agent of some greater authority, their learning (or the absence of their learning) has some very direct political consequences.

The teacher, and through her the state, uses a variety of instruments to transmit values to students. Principal among these are classroom ritual and, of course, the curriculum itself. Classroom rituals are numerous and generally overt in their attempts at political indoctrination. Saluting the flag, reciting a pledge of allegiance, singing the national anthem and other patriotic songs, honoring national heroes and events with special activities or (even more significantly) with special school holidays, and exposure to pictures of and quotations from great national figures are all common fare in the classrooms of every nation. A sense of the nation and of one's identity with it is created and reinforced, at least during the early school years, by participation in rituals of this kind.[28]

Yet there is a latent and equally significant second dynamic at work here as well: Classroom rituals are generally collective rituals. Everyone takes part; everyone shares in a common experience. Thus classroom rituals provide social support for the acceptance of those norms to which the various rituals attach. In this manner, dominant social values come to be accepted as peer-group norms, a situation that reinforces them. In loyalty, patriotism, or nationalism there is brotherhood, friendship, and the security of identification with one's peers.[29]

The formal curriculum, too, has its overt political manifestations and its subtleties. The former are best typified, of course, by formal instruction in good citizenship, government, and political affairs. Such courses are often highly normative in that they present an idealized picture of the political system as it is designed to operate, rather than an objective appraisal of its strengths and weaknesses, the things that one quite literally "does not read in the textbooks." Here, perhaps more than elsewhere, community norms may be introduced in a controlled and effective manner through the exercise of the prerogatives of the school board or the school principal in the selection of course materials. At least one study has found that there are systematic differences in the basic themes presented in civics textbooks and that different communities tend to select texts that reflect their particular value preferences. Indeed, educators and community leaders freely admit that they see the curriculum as a proper instrument for training the student in political roles and civic responsibilities.[30]

This willingness to manipulate the curriculum to the advantage of the political system is somewhat less apparent but equally pronounced in other areas of study as well. Courses in history tend to be highly selective and to reflect limited viewpoints, a fact that has been highlighted in recent years by our growing awareness of the role of blacks in American history. In music courses emphasis is placed on patriotic songs, songs that glorify events or actors in the nation's history, and songs, including hymns and other essentially religious songs, that reflect dominant social values. And similarly, selections of readings in literature courses often emphasize the same kinds of themes.[31] The school curriculum is literally saturated with political content and social comment and provides an extensive, intensive, and highly effective agency for political socialization.

The school, then, can prove a potent force in the political development of the individual, one that is often more direct in its political teaching than both family and peer groups, but that nevertheless acts in conjunction with the latter in guiding the maturing individual into assuming his proper role in political life. Furthermore, the socialization process that takes place in the school is much more carefully structured and much more purposive than comparable political learning from family or peers. As a consequence, the substance of political learning that derives from the school is relatively more likely to conform to the content that the political leadership of the society considers appropriate. With regard to their political function, the schools are designed to build good citizens—citizens who both accept and by their own lives reflect the self-defined virtues of the society in which they live. In other words, the schools are expected to conserve the social and political status quo.

We should emphasize, however, that our discussion of the school experience should not necessarily be taken to include college education. Very often there are elements in the college education that lead one to question the dominant values of one's society rather than accept them unthinkingly, elements that are missing from the elementary and secondary school experiences. Indeed, in a society that enjoys a relatively high degree of intellectual freedom, college teachers tend more than primary or secondary teachers to be in a sense subversive, to force their students to question, *though not necessarily to reject*, dominant (political) values. Similarly, colleges tend less effectively to indoctrinate students in societal orthodoxies than to provide an atmosphere in which examination and inquiry into those orthodoxies may be both guided and facilitated. Thus higher education may differ fundamentally in purpose from both primary and secondary schooling. And as a consequence, while the mechanisms of socialization may remain more or less unchanged from elementary and secondary schools to colleges, the substantive content of political learning may change significantly. More specifically, one could safely argue that the impact of higher education upon a society may be traced to the fact that colleges not only communicate additional facts but also provide individuals with a diversity of outlooks and experiences that helps them develop their critical capabilities.[32]

The college experience is also different from earlier formal education simply because it follows that education. That is, while elementary and secondary schools must do their share to create knowledgeable, functioning social entities, the college is able in some degree to assume their existence.[33] Students attend college at a later and presumably more mature stage of life having successfully overcome a variety of obstacles. By the time they reach college, students are beginning to perceive that they have a vested interest in increasing their understanding of the social and political independence that is soon to be thrust upon them. Attending college may in fact represent the first exercise of that very independence. And the combination of these factors may make college students acutely susceptible to persuasive communication.[34] The potential thus exists in the college experience for the introduction and development of a more or less radical divergence from the norms with which individuals may previously have identified. The college experience, therefore, is potentially a locus for the emergence of insurgent value structures and, in the extreme case, for the introduction of instability into a political system. At the least, the social and intellectual environment to which college students are exposed is likely to give them a broadened outlook on society in general and on politics in particular.

Everyone, of course, does not attend college. In fact, if college education has the potential to induce widespread questioning of the political system and its established norms, there exists a second institution with which individuals of roughly the same age, maturity, and persuasibility as most college students may come into contact and which seeks instead to emphasize the alternative value of strict obedience. I refer here to the military services. By definition, military life involves an intensive program of mental and physical discipline, adherence to established standards of order, and loyalty both to one's comrades and to one's country. The much-publicized rigor of military training and the particular (and militarily functional) values that it instills brings a very different kind of pressure to bear on the individual than does college life. Here the individual is trained not to inquire but to conform, not to reason but to react. Discipline, honor, and integrity are presented in a unique context.[35] Indeed, an individual's military training may lead him (or her) to define responsible social behavior in altogether different terms than might be suggested by the college—or, for that matter, by almost any other agency in the whole of social experience.[36] Nevertheless, we see the same socializing mechanisms at work here that we have seen elsewhere. Just as elsewhere, a particular set of norms is presented and then continually reinforced. Just as elsewhere, both direct and indirect cues are provided regarding the limits of acceptable thought and behavior. It is the substance of socialization and not the process that varies.[37]

Virtually all individuals in the United States today have been exposed to a significant amount of primary and secondary schooling, some in combination with college, some in combination with military service, and many in combination with both. Yet, regardless of their individual differences, and regardless of the extent and order in which they are combined, these three institutions taken together share one important characteristic. As agents of political socialization, the school, the college, and the military all make extensive demands on the time and the emotions of those who participate in them, and collectively they constitute the last intensive institutional pressures that will be brought to bear upon most citizens during their political lives.[38] For once an individual receives his (or her) last formal certification—be it a high school diploma, a college degree, or a military discharge—he is in a very real sense on his own. He must at last support himself, raise a family, and in general meet all the demands, including political ones, entailed in the assumption of adult roles. He has, in short, come of age.

From this point on, the political socialization of the individual becomes rather haphazard. Certainly much of his learning will come in the context of peer-group relationships, most especially those with his spouse and his fellow workers. In addition—though by no means independent of the peer-group dynamic—he may come to rely rather heavily on one or another of the mass media to provide him with political stimuli, a phenomenon we shall investigate momentarily. And he may join one or more of what sociologists refer to as secondary groups—organizations such as labor unions, church groups, political associations, and the like—that provide a source of limited but continuing social and political education. In any event, the individual continues to acquire new politically relevant stimuli long after he departs the ivy-covered walls or the mess hall, but he usually does so under more relaxed and less structured circumstances. Politics, or the exclusion of politics, becomes to a much greater extent a matter of leisure and of choice.

MASS MEDIA AS SOURCES OF POLITICAL LEARNING

There remains one additional and temporally pervasive set of socializing agents, the mass media of communication, to which we must devote our attention. Mass media provide various forms of politically relevant information to the individual at virtually every stage of the life cycle, and there can be little question that encounters with mass communication have significant impact upon the perceptions of political reality held by the citizens of technologically advanced societies. Because they facilitate vital forms of social and political exchange in such societies, but most especially because individuals in such societies rely upon them as sources of information, social contact, entertainment, release, and fulfillment, mass media provide an effective and significant agent of political and other learning. Indeed, in the development and dissemination of a widely shared set of cultural values, it is unlikely that any other socializing agent exceeds the scope of the mass media.

While the mass media are potentially powerful socializing agents, one difference nevertheless exists between mass media and other agents of socialization which may serve to limit the ultimate effectiveness of the former. That difference lies in the quality of the interaction between the individual and the socializing agent. On the one hand, socialization by family, school, peer group or other similar experiences is in almost every instance a matter of direct, small-scale, interpersonal communication. An individual acquires his role orientations by observation, by acquiescence, and perhaps by imitation of others whom he esteems. There is, in effect, a face-to-face confrontation between the "socializer" and the "socializee." In contrast, socialization through the mass media introduces an intermediary into the process, a technological middleman. Considered narrowly, the media themselves possess no capability to create information of their own, but only to process and distribute information provided by the people who control them.[39] At the same time, individuals who receive and interpret politically relevant information from the media, as we shall see shortly, often rely upon interactions with other media users in the process. As a result, political socialization through the mass media is in every case less direct than that conducted through other agents, and the effectiveness with which these media function is subject to restraints that would be extraneous to simple interpersonal communication.

The particular political content transmitted by the various media that thereby becomes grist for the mills of political socialization is determined by the confluence of three distinct social forces.

Most simply, media operators make production decisions within financial constraints dictated by their sponsors and within political constraints dictated by various public and/or governmental figures. So in effect, the information that reaches us through the mass media represents the resolution of conflicts among numerous technological, economic, and political pressures, and the content of the media is the operational compromise that emerges from the interaction of these three spheres of influence.[40] Because of one interest common to *all* the sources of such pressure, however, one consistent pattern of media content frequently emerges, at least in the United States. For those who hold informational, economic, or political power have in common the desire to preserve their respective positions, and to this end must act to maintain the established system of values from which they so clearly benefit. In the United States, that system of values is, as we have seen, primarily majoritarian, and the majority is middle class. As a consequence, and almost without exception, the language patterns, life styles, and thought processes reflected in the nation's media, and most especially on television, continually reinforce the dominant norms of the American culture to the virtual exclusion of alternative or minority orientations. This results in the broad dissemination and continual reinforcement of these values—and perhaps consequently in the stability of the political structure.[41]

In addition to the pressures of vested interests, two other factors contribute to insuring the consistency of this life-style bias in American mass media content. To begin with, middle-class orientations accurately reflect the life styles of precisely those media managers who make content decisions. Life can be reflected in the mass media only as it is perceived by the mediators themselves. And because these mediators are for the most part members of the middle or upper middle class, because they are constituents of the cultural majority, whose social vision is restricted by the blinders of their own experience, it is only reasonable to expect that the values and orientations of that majority will be predominant in their decisions.[42]

In the case of commercial media such as network television, this predominance of middle-class values is further reinforced by yet a second consideration. Most simply, dominant values are safe values, both socially and economically. Because of the structure of American mass media and their dependence on selling information to the public, the selection of content must involve a consideration of what information that public is willing to buy.[43] And we may surmise from our earlier discussion that there is always an easier and more extensive market for information that is supportive of the most widely held attitudes and outlooks in the society than for that which is disruptive. Hence the commercial media are likely to provide pablum rather than problems, reinforcement rather than reevaluation. The profitability of majority rather than minority viewpoints, of dominant rather than secondary values, thus works through the institutional structure of the media to support the preservation of those viewpoints and values. And insofar as dominant political, social, and economic values are incorporated into media content, the media as socializing agents tend to be conservative of the cultural status quo.[44]

To the extent that the mass media are effective socializing agents, the impact of this consistent media world view upon political life in the United States is fairly predictable. Children grow up with middle-class outlooks that reflect life as they see it on television or in the movies, as they read of it in their school texts, and perhaps as they are exposed to it by other agents of socialization. They acquire an orientation toward property and security, the focal points of middle-class culture.[45] People in decaying urban centers are exposed to repeated media images of what must seem to them to be the entire remainder of their society in a state of affluence. They become restive, and perhaps at times even turn to violence, a form of behavior that is also in effect condoned by the disproportionate frequency with which it occurs as a theme in the mass media.[46] In each instance, the mass media point up with phenomenal frequency and consistency the dominant values of the society. *Where these media images are supportive of and supported by other cues about political reality that the individual might receive, they help create and reinforce a system-supportive political orientation. But where media images are in sharp contrast with other cues received by an individual, the likelihood of the development of system-disruptive political orientations may be generally increased.*

This is *not* to suggest that the mass media are omnipotent, that they are able to exercise total control over our minds and our deeds. To the contrary, it should be clear for a number of reasons, not the least of which are the contextual pressures exerted by other agents of socialization, that this is not the case. But the mass media do exercise substantial influence as agents of political socialization, and the direction which that influence takes is in large measure reflective of the pressures acting upon media decision making.

THE INTERACTION OF SOCIALIZING AGENTS

The ways in which individuals receive this information from the mass media provide one of the best examples of interaction among socializing agents, for more than any other source of political learning, the mass media are themselves literally dependent upon a combination of agents for their effectiveness. According to one of the most widely accepted theories of mass communication, messages from the mass media influence most people *indirectly* through a relatively small group of intermediaries whom we may term *opinion leaders* (and who should not be confused with public figures, who might be considered *opinion makers*). These opinion leaders are more active in receiving messages from the media than are most other people and possess other characteristics that allow them to elicit a certain deference from their acquaintances. They purposefully seek information from the mass media, they process this information according to their own cognitive requirements, and, finally, they pass along the processed information through interpersonal communication to a larger number of people who respect their opinions.

This larger group, the so-called *opinion followers*, consists of individuals who are for the most part less avid users of the mass media. The messages in the media serve less to influence members of this group directly than simply to arouse their interest or curiosity. When the opinion followers become interested or when the opinion leaders become active advocates, each seeks out his opposite number. The opinion leaders then interpret the information from the media and guide those who respect their opinions to an understanding of the implications of the new information within the context of their own social or political situations. Information moving from the medium to the audience, in other words, is digested by the audience through a process of social interaction among opinion leaders and their followers. In this way, information from the media provides an impetus to peer-group activity, while the ultimate meaning which attaches to that information is determined by the peer-group dynamic.[47] And just as the form and content of messages carried by the media are the result of an interplay among several competing or reinforcing demands, the ultimate (political) lessons derived from those messages can be directly traced neither to the medium nor to the peer group, but rather to the interaction of the two. Here, as elsewhere, one agent draws strength from another, and the result reflects the characters of both.

PRIMACY AND RECENCY: THE TIMING
OF POLITICAL LEARNING

Before we conclude our discussion of political socialization, we should touch more directly on one point that has been implicit in much that we have already said. That point relates to the timing of political learning, to the stage of life at which the more important aspects of socialization occur.

One argument on this point, called the *primacy model*, holds that fundamental attitudes and values are formed early in life (say by age ten), that these attitudes and values endure, and that they provide the basic developmental framework within which adults later perceive and respond to their environment. A second argument, termed the *recency model*, holds that because people do not develop the cognitive skills required for political activity at least until their adolescence, and because, in any event, few experience many overtly political stimuli until well beyond childhood, it is the most recent learning rather than the earliest that is most politically relevant.

Each model seems to provide the best explanation for certain kinds of political learning. The primacy notion seems best to explain basic political attachments, identifications, and loyalties vis-à-vis political institutions and customs, to account for general ideological tendencies, and to describe the learning of the generally accepted beliefs and values that bind together members of a given political culture. These lessons, once learned, provide the standards of comparison against which subsequent learning will be evaluated. The recency notion, in contrast, seems best to explain the learning of explicitly political information, that relating to particular issues and actions, to candidate images, policy preferences, and most especially to being "political," to identifying and developing patterns of action that will be instrumental to achieving sets of political goals. The "student" at this point is more sophisticated and his or her political needs more complex, both criteria that are reflected in the type of learning that occurs.

In general, then, the political learning that occurs early is relatively more general in nature and in some ways more affective. That which occurs later in life is more specific in nature, more cognitive and instrumental. The former is most important for coping with politics as a fact of life, the latter for dealing with politics as a part of life.[48]

IN SUMMARY

In concluding our discussion of the agents of political socialization, let us reemphasize four points that have emerged. First, it should be apparent from our analysis that *political* socialization is basically a subset of a more general teaching/learning process, and as such abstracts from that process only those elements which have relevance to political objects, values, or activities. Thus toilet-training can be as significant a factor in political socialization as indoctrination in the tenets of Marxism or Jeffersonian democracy, but it is only of interest in this context insofar as it has discernible applications to expressly political behavior.

Second—and this is of critical importance—the fruits of political socialization are aggregative and interactive. As we suggested at the outset, no one is ever completely socialized until his or her involvement in political life ceases entirely. Rather, people are continually subjected over time to a variety of new and changing pressures, not the least of which may be their own life situations and states of mind. These new experiences and changing circumstances are incorporated into an ever-expanding body of information that provides individuals with a constantly updated standard they may employ to evaluate and understand encounters with political reality. Political socialization, in short, is an ongoing process.

Third, the process of political socialization is comprehensive. That is, political socialization encompasses all phenomena that are even remotely associated with political learning. Any contact, experience, or circumstance from which a person derives any information whatsoever about politics constitutes a bona fide agent of political socialization. And while we have discussed several of the more obvious and quantitatively more significant agents here, a complete catalog of sources of political stimuli would be considerably longer and would reflect a veritable maze of complex personal associations.

Next, and closely related to the preceding point, we must keep in mind the fact that every individual represents a more or less unique combination of socializing experiences. The varieties of family life, peer-group associations, educational experiences, and life styles are virtually infinite, and since political socialization involves the interaction of these and other forces, the potential products of such socialization must be more numerous and more diverse still. To be sure, similarities in the experiences of many individuals permit us to study the process of political socialization by making generalized observations; but we should not allow these general theoretical statements to obscure the proliferation of highly individualized adult political roles.

Finally, it is worth noting that most individuals operate on both sides of the political socialization process. Everyone learns, but by the same token, virtually everyone teaches. Whether as a parent or a childhood peer, a teacher or a member of a secondary association, a letter writer, a co-worker or a poker buddy, we provide for others the same kinds of socializing cues many of them provide for us, and we are as much a part of their socialization experience as they are of ours. That we seldom think of ourselves in this role says much about the spontaneous character of political socialization. That the process nevertheless continues with undiminished effect says still more about its inexorable contribution to the flow of political life.

As we pointed out in the preceding chapter, political socialization plays an important role in the political life of a society as the communication process by which political systems and their value structures endure over time. At the same time, this same socialization process provides a vital linkage between the society and its constituent members by helping the individual citizen acquire the attitudes and expectations that will be useful in grasping and fulfilling his or her requisite political roles. Thus the process of political socialization at once constitutes both a training ground for the political culture and a continuing political apprenticeship for the individual.

SUGGESTIONS FOR FURTHER READING

Perhaps the most complete overview of political socialization is provided in Richard E. Dawson and Kenneth Prewitt, *Political Socialization* (Boston: Little, Brown, 1969). These authors deal at some length with the conditions under which socialization takes place and with the processes and agencies by which it is brought about. Robert Weissberg presents a slightly narrower but rigorous and highly stimulating analysis of the topic in *Political Learning, Political Choice, and Democratic Citizenship* (Englewood Cliffs, N.J.: Prentice-Hall, 1974). Roberta S. Sigel, in her edited volume *Learning About Politics* (New York: Random House, 1970), provides an extensive and most interesting collection of research in all areas of political socialization, while several of the same articles as well as others appear in the much shorter *The Learning of Political Behavior* (Glenview, Ill.: Scott, Foresman, 1970), edited by Norman Adler and Charles Harrington.

Three books that focus upon particular areas of political socialization are worthy of note. *The Development of Political Attitudes in Children* (Chicago: Aldine, 1967) by Robert D. Hess and Judith V. Torney reports the results of a nationwide study of the role of the elementary school in the political socialization process. *Television in the Lives of Our Children* (Stanford, Calif.: Stanford University Press, 1961) by Wilbur Schramm, Jack Lyle, and Edwin B. Parker focuses on the role of the mass media and most especially television in the educational development of schoolchildren. And *Personal Influence* (Glencoe, Ill.: Free Press, 1955) by Elihu Katz and Paul F. Lazarsfeld provides a somewhat dated but important discussion, in the context of an analysis of peer-group relationships, of the social mechanisms by which individuals interact with mass media.

Jack Dennis offers an extensive bibliography of the literature of political socialization in *Political Socialization Research: A Bibliography*, Sage Professional Papers in American Politics no. 04-002 (Beverly Hills, Calif.: Sage Publications, 1973).

NOTES

1. Nor, of course, are these abilities and inclinations independent of individual personality characteristics. See Giuseppe Di Palma and Herbert McClosky, "Personality and Conformity: The Learning of Political Attitudes," *American Political Science Review* 64 (1970): 1054–73.
2. Kenneth P. Langton, *Political Socialization* (New York: Oxford University Press, 1969), pp. 14 ff. For a related discussion, see Eduard A. Ziegenhagen, "Political Socialization and Role Conflict: Some Theoretical Implications," in *Learning About Politics*, ed. Roberta S. Sigel (New York: Random House, 1970), pp. 466–75.
3. William C. Mitchell, *The American Polity* (Glencoe, Ill.: Free Press, 1962), chap. 7.
4. Richard E. Dawson and Kenneth Prewitt, *Political Socialization* (Boston: Little, Brown, 1969), pp. 42 f.
5. Ibid., chap. 4.
6. Robert D. Hess and Judith V. Torney, *The Development of Political Attitudes in Children* (Chicago: Aldine, 1967), pp. 19 f.
7. Ibid., pp. 20 f.
8. Ibid., p. 21.
9. Ibid. See also Joseph Adelson and Robert P. O'Neil, "Growth of Political Ideas in Adolescence: The Sense of Community," *Journal of Personality and Social Psychology* 4 (1966): 295–306; and Richard M. Merelman, "The Development of Political Ideology: A Framework for the Analysis of Political Socialization," *American Political Science Review* 63 (1969): 750–67.
10. David Easton and Jack Dennis, "The Child's Image of Government,"

Annals of the American Academy of Political and Social Science 361 (1965): 40–57.

11. Dawson and Prewitt, *Political Socialization*, pp. 107 f.

12. James C. Davies, "The Family's Role in Political Socialization," *Annals of the American Academy of Political and Social Science* 361 (1965): 11 f.

13. David Easton and Robert D. Hess, "The Child's Political World," *Midwest Journal of Political Science* 6 (1962): 229–46.

14. Davies, "The Family's Role," pp. 10–19 et passim.

15. James Deese, *Principles of Psychology* (Boston: Allyn and Bacon, 1964), pp. 240 ff.

16. Easton and Hess, "The Child's Political World," passim.

17. Dawson and Prewitt, *Political Socialization*, pp. 109 f.

18. Russell J. Dalton describes the family as a formative agent of broad import in "Reassessing Parental Socialization: Indicator Unreliability Versus Generational Transfer," *American Political Science Review* 74 (1980): 421–31; Richard M. Merelman offers a contrasting assessment in "The Family and Political Socialization: Toward a Theory of Exchange," *Journal of Politics* 42 (1980): 461–86.

19. James J. Best, *Public Opinion: Micro and Macro* (Homewood, Ill.: Dorsey Press, 1973), p. 111.

20. Hess and Torney, *Development of Political Attitudes*, pp. 120–25.

21. The developing sense of maturity is treated in Joseph Adelson and Robert P. O'Neil, "Growth of Political Ideas in Adolescence," pp. 295–306.

22. Urie Bronfenbrenner cautions that this may be a culture-specific phenomenon dependent upon the autonomy of the peer groups themselves. "Response to Pressure from Peers versus Adults among Soviet and American School Children," *International Journal of Psychology* 2 (1967): 199–207.

23. Best, *Public Opinion*, pp. 122–29.

24. Elihu Katz and Paul F. Lazarsfeld, *Personal Influence* (Glencoe, Ill.: Free Press, 1955), pp. 48–65; and Dawson and Prewitt, *Political Socialization*, pp. 134 f.

25. Dawson and Prewitt, *Political Socialization*, pp. 158 f. M. Kent Jennings and Harmon Ziegler suggest that there is broad diversity in the way teachers represent community norms. "Political Expressivism among High School Teachers: The Intersection of Community and Occupational Values," in Sigel, *Learning About Politics*, pp. 434–53.

26. Hess and Torney, *Development of Political Attitudes*, pp. 111–15.

27. Dawson and Prewitt, *Political Socialization*, pp. 162–67. Some long-term effects of this learning culture are discussed in Gabriel A. Almond and Sidney Verba, *The Civic Culture* (Princeton: Princeton University Press, 1963), pp. 332–34, 352–63.

28. Hess and Torney, *Development of Political Attitudes*, pp. 105–8.

29. Dawson and Prewitt, *Political Socialization*, pp. 157 f.

30. Edgar Litt, "Civic Education, Community Norms, and Political Indoctrination," *American Sociological Review* 28 (1963): 69–75.

31. Dawson and Prewitt, *Political Socialization*, p. 147.
32. Philip E. Jacob, *Changing Values in College* (New York: Harper, 1957), pp. 38–57. These changes may in fact occur despite rather than because of the college curriculum, as suggested by Albert Somit, Joseph Tanenhaus, Walter H. Wilke, and Rita W. Cooley in "The Effect of the Introductory Political Science Course on Student Attitudes Toward Personal Political Participation," *American Political Science Review* 52 (1958): 1129–32. Alternatively, the selection of particular college curricula may reflect other preexisting attitudes on the part of the student, attitudes that are also reflected in his political life. See David D. Dabelko and Craig P. Caywood, "Higher Education as a Political Socializing Agent: Some Effects of Various Curricula," *Experimental Study of Politics* 2 (1973): 1–24.
33. Joseph Adelson, "The Political Imagination of the Young Adolescent," *Daedalus* 100 (1971): 1013–50.
34. Roberta S. Sigel, "College and University," in Sigel, *Learning About Politics*, p. 376.
35. Social control as an element in military training is discussed by Samuel A. Stouffer, Edward A. Suchman, Leland C. DeVinney, Shirley A. Star, and Robin M. Williams, Jr., in *Studies in Social Psychology in World War II*, vol. 1, *The American Soldier: Adjustment During Army Life* (Princeton: Princeton University Press, 1949), pp. 410–29.
36. The extreme case of this unique definition, that of the combat situation, is discussed by Charles C. Moskos, Jr., in "Why Men Fight," *Trans-Action* 7 (1969): 13–23.
37. Richard J. Tobin, "The Impact of Military Service Upon Political Attitudes" (Northwestern University, April 1970), passim.
38. See E. Goffman, "The Characteristics of Total Institutions," in *Complex Organizations: A Sociological Reader*, ed. Amitai Etzioni (New York: Holt, Rinehart and Winston, 1961), pp. 312–40, but especially pp. 313 f., for an analysis of the importance of pervasiveness in institutional experience. These notions are applied to a combination military-college experience by Tod A. Baker, Robert P. Steed, and Paul R. Benson, Jr., in "A Note on the Impact of the College Experience on Changing the Political Attitudes of Students," *Experimental Study of Politics* 2 (1972): 76–88.
39. For a comprehensive survey of research on this process of intermediation, see George A. Donohue, Phillip J. Tichenor, and Clarice N. Olien, "Gatekeeping: Mass Media Systems and Information Control," in *Current Perspectives in Mass Communication Research*, Vol. I, ed. F. Gerald Kline and Phillip J. Tichenor (Beverley Hills, Calif.: Sage Publications, 1972), pp. 41–70. The practical implications of the process are illustrated by Bernard Roshco in *Newsmaking* (Chicago: University of Chicago Press, 1975) and by Herbert J. Gans in *Deciding What's News: A Study of CBS Evening News, NBC Nightly News, Newsweek and Time* (New York: Pantheon Books, 1979).
40. Melvin L. DeFleur and Sandra Ball-Rokeach, *Theories of Mass Communication* (3rd ed.; New York: Longman, 1975), chap. 7.

41. Paul F. Lazarsfeld and Robert K. Merton, "Mass Communication, Popular Taste, and Organized Social Action," in *The Process and Effects of Mass Communication*, ed. Wilbur Schramm and Donald F. Robert (rev. ed.; Urbana: University of Illinois Press, 1971), pp. 554–78. For supportive evidence, see Frank Gentile and S. M. Miller, "Television and Social Class," *Sociology and Social Research* 45 (1961): 259–64; Melvin L. DeFleur, "Occupational Roles as Portrayed on Television," *Public Opinion Quarterly* 28 (1964): 57–74; and Nathan Katzman, "Television Soap Operas: What's Been Going On Anyway?" *Public Opinion Quarterly* 36 (1972): 200–212.

42. Harry J. Skornia, *Television and Society* (New York: McGraw-Hill, 1965), chap. 3.

43. DeFleur and Ball-Rokeach, *Theories of Mass Communication*, chap. 7.

44. See, for example, J. David Colfax and Susan Frankel Sternberg, "The Perpetuation of Racial Stereotypes: Blacks in Mass Circulation Magazine Advertisements," *Public Opinion Quarterly* 36 (1972): 8–18.

45. Russell H. Weigel and Richard Jessor, "Television and Adolescent Conventionality: An Exploratory Study," *Public Opinion Quarterly* 37 (1973): 76–90.

46. David O. Sears and John B. McConahay, "Racial Socialization, Comparison Levels, and the Watts Riot," *Journal of Social Issues* 26 (1970): 121–40, and William L. Rivers and Wilbur Schramm, *Responsibility in Mass Communication* (New York: Harper & Row, 1969), pp. 175–89. For useful insights concerning the theme of violence in the mass media see Douglas A. Fuchs and Jack Lyle, "Mass Media Portrayal: Sex and Violence," in Kline and Tichenor, *Current Perspectives*, 1:235–64; and F. Scott Andison, "TV Violence and Viewer Aggression: A Cumulation of Study Results 1956–1976," *Public Opinion Quarterly* 41 (1977): 314–31. The interaction of race, media use habits, and violent content is treated in a most interesting manner by Bradley S. Greenberg, "Mass Media Behavior and Attitudes of the Urban Poor," testimony before the President's Commission on the Causes and Prevention of Violence, Washington, D.C., 15 October 1968.

47. This communication process, generally termed the *two-step flow*, was first noted in early election studies and received its most extensive investigation from Elihu Katz and Paul F. Lazarsfeld as reported in *Personal Influence*. The development of the two-step flow hypothesis has been summarized and subjected to a critique by Elihu Katz in "The Two-Step Flow of Communication," *Public Opinion Quarterly* 21 (1957): 61–78. Modification of this theory has been proposed by several subsequent studies, notable among which is Verling C. Troldahl's "A Field Test of a Modified Two-Step Flow of Communication Model," *Public Opinion Quarterly* 30 (1966–67): 609–23, in which the author attributes a more active role to opinion followers in the initiation of peer group interaction.

48. Robert Weissberg, *Political Learning, Political Choice and Democratic Citizenship* (Englewood Cliffs, N.J.: Prentice-Hall, 1974), pp. 23–31.

6

Political Persuasion

Information Processing and the Dynamics of Influence

In its simplest terms political socialization is a social process that involves the issuance and reception of persuasive and/or instructive information. Individuals and institutions interact with one another in a more or less structured set of teacher-learner relationships in which the individual acquires a role orientation toward political life and by virtue of which, as a consequence, the substance and distribution of cultural values are retained. And as we have seen, the effectiveness of the socialization process is largely dependent upon the nature of the social relationships among the various parties to it.

But if, as we have suggested, political socialization is the process by which individual political attitudes are acquired or altered —or, alternatively, if political socialization is the source of variations in individual political perception—there must exist yet a second dimension to the socialization process: There must exist not only an external or social dynamic according to which attitudes and perceptions are developed but an internal dynamic as well. For in the final analysis, attitudes and perceptions are primarily psychological phenomena, and while the social situation in which an individual finds herself may facilitate, impede, or otherwise influence the flow of new information she takes in, the ultimate impact of that information on her mental state will of necessity be determined by the structure and status of her existing attitudes, beliefs, and expectations.

In the present chapter, then, we shall turn our attention to the internal dynamics of attitude maintenance and attitude change. We shall investigate the various processes by which attitude change is believed to come about, the susceptibility or resistance of individuals to efforts at persuasion (where the term is used broadly to include attempts to create new attitudes as well as those to alter existing ones), and some potentially effective means of inducing attitude change in a given individual. Before we may proceed, however, we must discuss in somewhat greater detail a concept introduced in an earlier chapter.

THE STAGES OF PERCEPTUAL SCREENING

In Chapter 2 we suggested that information which is to interact with an individual's existing storehouse of attitudes and knowledge must first pass through a filter of sorts, which we termed a *perceptual screen*. We pointed out that this screen, which consists of the psychological wants, needs, and expectations of the individual, serves both to protect the individual against unwanted information and to give personalized meaning to the information that finally does penetrate. Since we shall be concerned in the remainder of the present chapter with the form and substance of precisely the latter category of information—that which *does* get through—it is imperative that we understand in somewhat greater detail the forces that govern its reception. Let us therefore focus our attention more closely on the process of perceptual screening.

Students of the process have identified four distinct yet highly interdependent stages in the perceptual screening of information, each of which is worthy of some consideration. The first of these stages, which is generally termed *selective exposure*, means precisely that. An individual who does not accept or have interest in New Left ideas simply does not read New Left publications. An individual who is not concerned with a particular public issue either avoids or at the very least does not seek out information on that issue. An individual who prefers one television newscaster over another adjusts her viewing habits accordingly. In other words, the first thing one does in coping with the numerous messages issued in her direction every day is simply to make a series of choices, some conscious and others not, as to which if any of these messages she will allow to reach her for consideration. Based upon personal interests, needs, beliefs, predispositions, and the like, each of us acts to determine which of the universe of available messages we will come into contact with at any particular time.

Sometimes the act of making such a choice is purposeful, as in the instances noted above, while at other times it follows as the inevitable consequence of other, possibly unrelated, social decisions. For example, carrying out a decision to attend a football game at once entails exposure to the advertising billboards at the stadium and precludes viewing a news documentary that happens to compete for the same time period on television. Similarly, a decision to drive to work down Main Street rather than Central Avenue increases, wholly as a by-product, the likelihood of exposure to some items of information (particular advertising or traffic signs), while reducing the likelihood of exposure to others. In either event, whether purposefully or inadvertently, and with varying degrees of efficiency, individuals nonetheless expose themselves to information in a selective manner according to whatever criteria they consider appropriate. And as a result, only some of the many messages that might reach any particular individual actually arrive on target.[1]

The screening process does not stop there. Suppose, for example, that we have in fact chosen to watch a particular news program in its entirety. We may then safely say that we have been exposed to all the news content of that program. But on any particular newscast there might appear one item about the state of the nation's economy, in which we are in this hypothetical instance quite interested, and another about a part-time peapicker from Punxsutawney, Pennsylvania (or some similarly innocuous human interest item), in which we are not. Because of our interest, we *pay closer attention* to the economic news and more or less tune out whatever it is they are saying about the peapicker. That is to say, once we have allowed ourselves to come into contact with a particular collection of messages, we still retain the option of distributing our full or partial attention in a selective manner among the messages to which we are exposed. We may refer to this second stage of the screening process, then, as *selective attention.*[2]

This same mechanism can operate on a more localized level as well. Suppose for the sake of argument that we are watching the aforementioned report on the state of the economy and that we have a preexisting feeling that the economy is in poor condition. The visual portion of the report shows a series of graphs of leading economic indicators, all of which are plummeting, while the audio portion carries an interview with a government economist who claims that conditions have bottomed out and the future is indeed bright. Because of our attitudes at the outset, because of our sense of impending economic doom, we may very well attend closely to the video portion of the telecast, which tends to support those views, and at the same time ignore the commentary. Thus only a part of a message to which we have in fact been exposed and given attention claims our full notice. Again we have a process of selective attention, but one that operates *within* rather than *among* messages.[3]

But is this picture that attracts our attention one of continuing decline or one of turnaround? Is it cause for continued pessimism or rather for renewed optimism? Is the spokesman a prophet or a charlatan? Even if we were to see the picture *and* hear the words, would we give equal weight to each in our personal interpretation of the report? Indeed, what do we consider to be the real meaning of this message? In formulating our individualized subjective response to these and other, related questions, we must rely to some extent on how we are *predisposed* toward this information in the first place. In interpreting and understanding what we see and hear and feel, we must fall back on our own personal "encyclopedia" and "dictionary" of beliefs, interests, goals, and so forth. In other words, we must fall back on our existing attitudes. In this sense, what we *want* to perceive (namely, information that supports our initial point of view) and what we *expect* to perceive both go a long way toward determining what in fact we *do* perceive.[4] Where the pessimist sees recession, the optimist sees turnaround. Where the pessimist sees decay, the optimist sees rebirth. Where the pessimist finds chicanery, the optimist finds truth. The same message is there for all to see, but the interpretation of its content by each of us is unique and highly personalized. We see things as we want and expect them to be, even where such perception may distort "objective" reality. We perceive reality in a selective manner, and such *selective perception* constitutes the third stage of the screening process.

The final stage in the screening process is *selective retention*, which refers essentially to the memory function. Given all the new perceptions and appraisals that arrive in our cognitive system daily, which do we remember? And perhaps more important, with which of our earlier attitudes and beliefs do we associate this new information as we file it away? How readily accessible is this new item in our memory? Based upon the particular preexisting attitudes and beliefs that we call upon to help us interpret new information, we tend to place that information in a recall context or filing system such that certain future cues will call to mind both it and the earlier information with which we have associated it. (In

Chapter 9 we shall examine the mechanism by which such creation and access to memory are believed to occur.)

If, for example, we receive information that Candidate Smith is an honest man, we could, for future reference, file that information away in the portions of cognitive space (see Chapter 2) reserved for items about Smith, about political candidates, about politicians in general, about some upcoming election, and/or about some intention to buy a used car from Smith's company. And our future recall of that information will depend upon the particular categories to which we assign it. In this way, we label data for future access, and the labels we assign exercise control over all of our subsequent uses of those data.[5] Indeed, it is in this process of making what we judge to be appropriate associations between new and existing information that the new information itself becomes fully integrated with our original attitudes and beliefs and becomes part of the basis upon which subsequent new information will be interpreted. It is in this process of integration that the potential for influence and attitude change exists.

Thus the perceptual screening process sets up a series of increasingly restrictive barriers, some, like selective exposure, primarily quantitative in character and others, like selective perception, predominantly qualitative, which must be penetrated by incoming informational stimuli. In this way, the screen acts to eliminate information that fails to meet various criteria of interest, importance, and acceptability. At the same time, the state of the perceptual screen at any particular moment represents the status quo ante of the attitude structure itself. After all, those criteria of interest, importance, and acceptability must come from somewhere, and that somewhere is the existing attitude and belief pattern of the individual in question. The structure of the perceptual screen reflects the structure of existing attitudes, and the dynamics of the perceptual screen are inextricably bound to the dynamics of attitude change—or, in other words, to the process of political persuasion.[6]

ATTITUDE STABILITY AND CHANGE

Theories regarding attitude change abound in social psychology, and we could never hope to do any of them full justice in the present forum. We can, however, indicate some of the principal areas of concern in these theories by outlining some general categories of inquiry and then suggest some of the common lessons to be derived from the various approaches. To that end, let us consider four different perspectives on attitude change.

The first such perspective, which is in a way the most straight-forward, is generally referred to as the *functional approach*. We have already suggested in Chapter 2 that attitudes perform a variety of functions for an individual, ranging from the expression of one's value preferences to the protection of one's self-concept. Adherents of the functional approach suggest that attitudes develop and change as required to serve a variety of such needs in a given indi-vidual. As the social environment of the individual changes, her psychological needs change; as the psychological needs of the indi-vidual change, her attitudes must change. Effective persuasion, then, may be accomplished by altering the actual social situation of the individual, or at least her understanding of that situation.[7]

In this view, for example, attitudes held by the individual to maximize rewards (positive evaluations of objects or ideas that are potentially rewarding) or minimize sanctions (negative evaluations of objects or ideas that might lead to punishment) may be changed by altering the perceived structure of rewards or sanctions. Thus the "halo effect" that is believed to operate when the electoral sup-port for a winning candidate reported in postelection surveys exceeds his proportion of the actual vote may be understood as a response to an altered structure of social rewards: Most simply, peo-ple tend to find that identifying with the winning side—regardless of which it might be—is both easier and often more socially re-warding than identifying with the losers. The change or clarifica-tion of party fortunes, then, facilitates a change in party or candi-date preferences.[8]

Similarly, one can help to induce change in attitudes whose function is defensive either by removing perceived threats from the presence of the individual in question or, conversely, by increasing the salience of those threats. Thus an individual who masks his (or her) own insecurity with prejudice against minorities may have his prejudice amplified or reduced respectively by increasing or de-creasing his proximity, his perceived social distance, to those groups. As the apparent threat to his self-concept becomes more remote, the cost of a liberalized attitude is lessened and the chances of inducing change in this direction improve. As the threat becomes more immediate, the reverse is true. In either event, a ·change in the perceived social situation brings with it pressure for a change in attitude. And more generally, the functional approach holds that where the particular function performed by an attitude can be identified, that attitude may be modified by altering the individual's perception of those aspects of the social environment that are most relevant to the function of the attitude.[9]

The second perspective on attitude change derives from learning theories such as those we outlined in the preceding chapter. Here the emphasis is on four elements of the learning situation: the source of new information; the nature of that information; the predispositions of the recipients of the information, including their relevant group identifications and personality factors; and the responses of those recipients in terms of acceptance and retention of the material communicated.[10] The *learning approach* thus draws very heavily on the communication model we presented earlier. Proponents of this approach contend that systematic manipulation of the contextual elements of the learning situation can serve to facilitate or to impede attitude change. Since much of our analysis of political socialization was essentially reflective of the learning theory perspective on attitude development and change, however, we mention it here only in passing.

The third approach to attitude change is reflected in a set of propositions of a rather different nature, which are generally referred to as *balance theories* or *consistency theories*. The main argument of these theories is really quite simple. In essence, they maintain that each of us has various attitudes and beliefs rolling around in our heads and that we feel somehow compelled to keep these attitudes and beliefs more or less compatible with one another so that they will remain, in a special sense, logically consistent. That is, we feel ourselves under some sort of psychological pressure to preserve a "balanced" or "consistent" state of mind. Dissonance (or imbalance), then, is the condition in which two or more of our attitudes, beliefs, or perceptions come into basic disagreement with one another, often as a result of our having received some new information. This condition of imbalance is believed to bring on a state of discomfort which in turn compels us to take some kind of action to restore consistency. The extent of this compulsion to change is a function of the degree of imbalance. More particularly, the greater the perceived disagreement among our cognitive elements, the greater the need we will feel to resolve that disagreement.[11]

Once we find ourselves in this condition of cognitive imbalance, there are several ways, these theories suggest, in which we can respond to restore ourselves to a state of consistency. For instance, we can change our behavior patterns to conform with our new perceptions. We can look for new supporting evidence that could restore the original balance. We can delude ourselves into perceiving reality incorrectly or incompletely so that our beliefs are allowed to stand. We can try to influence those people who have expressed opinions contrary to our own. We can try to gain (or to regain) social support for our views. We can try to discount the credibility of individuals or groups who have expressed contrary opinions. Or, *as only one option among many*, we can change our own attitude. In each case the problem for the individual is either to find an excuse for discounting the information which threw him out of balance or to accept the veracity of that information and then find some way of adjusting to it.[12] In many cases, the path followed may simply be that of least resistance.[13]

Concomitantly, say adherents of the balance approach, the problem for the would-be persuader is not to identify and take advantage of the purposes to which the attitude in question is put, as would be argued by proponents of the functional approach; nor is the problem one of controlling the learning situation as an end in itself, as might be suggested by proponents of the learning approach. Rather, the problem is to restrict the alternatives to attitude change that are available to the subject of the persuasive attempt. An example or two may make this clear.

Senator Smith said that Senator Jones, my favorite senator, is just a troublemaker and can't get along with his colleagues, *but we all know how backward Senator Smith is*. The newspaper said this country is in danger of collapse, *but they have been printing that same line for seventy-five years*. In each instance, we defend our original position with ease by denigrating the source of contradiction. By deflecting the thrust of the new information, we are able to cope with the message and at the same time preserve the attitude in question.[14] If, however, one's goal is to change such an attitude, one may attempt to close off this avenue of escape by issuing a persuasive message from such a highly credible source that it cannot be easily discounted. My professor, whose political judgment is invariably correct, says Senator Jones is not competent. The President, *whom I greatly esteem*, says the country is in danger of collapse. If the source cannot be discounted but some response is still required, it becomes increasingly likely that this response will take the form of attitude change.[15]

Similarly, we might appeal to the group identifications of the individual whose attitudes we hope to change. For instance, we could suggest to the individual that some group with which she identifies no longer shares the opinion she holds and then we could provide irrefutable evidence to that effect. In this way, we first introduce imbalance and then reinforce our attack with evidence that makes attitude change a more likely outcome. Alternatively, we might use the positive aspect of the same appeal, suggesting that those groups with which the individual identifies now favor some new position that she should consider accepting as well.[16] The much-heralded "bandwagon effect" is an example of this technique as applied to a very loosely defined reference group. *Nobody* believes that anymore. *Everyone* is doing it.[17] Again, we force change by creating an awareness of inconsistency; we direct it by reducing the options. By taking advantage of the strain toward consistency and by channeling the response to imbalance in the direction of attitude change, we increase our ability to persuade.

The final perspective on attitude change is that provided by the so-called *social judgment–involvement approach*. This theory starts from the premise that an individual feels some variable degree of personal emotional commitment to each attitude that he holds. This commitment to an attitude is termed "involvement," and a person is said to be highly involved in an attitude when he associates the holding and maintaining of that attitude very closely with his own personal and/or psychological well-being. According to the theory, because an individual is emotionally involved in his attitudes, he becomes rather protective of those attitudes. (This, incidentally, is quite the reverse of the functionalists' argument that attitudes protect the individual, though the two positions are not necessarily incompatible.) Indeed, the greater his feeling of involvement, the more protective he becomes; and the more protective he becomes, the less open he is to persuasive communication. Thus information that is widely discrepant with his existing attitudes and beliefs will be rejected, and only that which at least moderately resembles his existing mental state will have a chance at interaction.[18] As a result, potential influence is seen as restricted to a rather narrow spectrum of acceptable inputs.

In essence, then, advocates of the social judgment–involvement approach argue that the more involved in a given attitude an individual is, the less likely it is that he or she may be successfully influenced in the opposite direction. We can best clarify the implications of such an argument using the illustration in Figure 6.1. Let the figure in the mortarboard and gown represent any attitude that you hold. For the sake of argument, let us say that this attitude (or, more correctly in this case, attitude cluster) is a feeling you have that the United States is a glorious nation and should be proud of its accomplishments in the world. The second figure represents some item of slightly different information, suggested perhaps by your professor, who is no doubt an aging Ivy

FIGURE 6.1   The Social Judgment–Involvement Approach.

League type. Suppose, for example, he suggests to you that the
United States is indeed great and should be justly proud, but that
it is precisely because of that greatness and pride that the nation
should face and resolve certain pressing social problems. This
might well strike you as a reasonable variation of your earlier notions, and you might be willing to change your mind in the direction of closer agreement with this new position. But then along
comes another piece of new information, represented by the final
figure in the illustration, which is radically different from your own
ideas. In this case, perhaps it is an argument that the United States
has always had a sordid record of lacking social concern and must
now pay a price in social disorder which is richly deserved. Let us
suppose that this argument is so diametrically opposed to your original view that you reject it out of hand. This rejection of information
that is "too" discrepant would be in line with the predictions of the
social judgment–involvement approach.

    And just how discrepant is too discrepant? The answer to that
question varies from one individual to the next, from one attitude
to the next, and possibly even from one situation to the next. But
involvement theory does tell us that to the extent that an individual becomes more and more emotionally involved in holding a
given attitude, he or she will find fewer and fewer bits of contrary
information to be acceptable. Thus attitude change can be effected

only incrementally by the provision of moderately discrepant information, and as the level of involvement of the individual increases, the opportunities for influence decline.[19]

We can illustrate this point in Figure 6.1 as well. Drawing upon our earlier notions of cognitive space, let us draw around the original attitude a circle representing a boundary called the "threshold of rejection." Any new information that is similar enough to the original attitude to fall within this boundary is accepted, while less similar information falling beyond the boundary is rejected. Involvement theory would hold that as the emotional attachment of the individual to the original attitude increases, the threshold of rejection is drawn closer and closer about the center so that less and less new information has a chance of being "acceptable," a chance of bringing about some change in attitude. This is just another way of saying that those individuals who are most zealously committed to a particular point of view are least likely to be open to having that point of view challenged, let alone changed. In the more specific terms of our illustration, if you were at the outset rather intensely committed to your views on the greatness of the United States, you might actually draw in your threshold of rejection to a point at which you would reject even the more moderate variation. Were you less intensely committed, your threshold might expand to the point of approaching or even embracing the more extreme view. In either event, according to proponents of the social judgment–involvement approach, the degree of involvement acts to restrict the kinds of persuasive messages which may be most effective.

THE ATTITUDE DYNAMIC AND
THE PERCEPTUAL SCREEN

It is difficult to reconcile the various points of view outlined in the preceding section, and indeed that is not our purpose here. Suffice it to suggest that, much as the various theories of political learning discussed in Chapter 5 have situation-specific applications to the political socialization process, each view of attitude change may have explanatory power under certain circumstances or for certain kinds of attitudes. To be sure, nothing in our discussion suggests that these four perspectives on attitude change are mutually exclusive. To the contrary, all four seem to have considerable intuitive appeal, and it seems reasonable to expect that more than one might be operative at the same instant. The threshold of rejection from involvement theory, for example, might simply denote a point at which attitude change becomes more or less desirable than other alternatives in reducing the imbalance suggested by the consistency theories. Similarly, the role of the high-credibility source or of group identification in the consistency formulation may have its parallels in the role assigned to these same agents in the learning theory approach. Thus the most valid theory may yet prove to be a synthesis of all four of the perspectives mentioned.

Be that as it may, all these theories of attitude change do suggest one common conclusion: Attitudes do not change of their own volition. Furthermore, when attitudes do change, they change only to a limited extent and only in response to certain kinds of stimuli. Only when appropriate pressures are applied under conducive circumstances can the structure of attitudes be altered. Another way to state this is to say that attitudes are not changed, but only modified. Attitudes are modified in the sense that they become more or less firmly held, more extreme or more moderate in direction, more or less reorganized in substance—in each case depending upon the strength, content, and direction of the new information with which they interact. But the only time that a change in the *direction* of an attitude is likely is where the attitude itself is held rather tentatively and/or where the original intensity of the attitude approaches neutrality.

And just how do attitudes act to restrict or facilitate the flow of new information into the cognitive structure? How is it, in other words, that attitudes influence their own susceptibility to persuasion? The answer is readily apparent: By defining the wants, needs, beliefs, and expectations of individuals at a particular point in time, by guiding their understanding of their encounters with reality, attitudes provide the substantive basis for the operation of the filtering process. Because they constitute the standards of judgment that individuals value, attitudes set the terms of recognition and understanding that give meaning to the perceptual screen. The perceptual screen, then, constitutes a behavioral manifestation of the underlying attitude structure. This point is illustrated in Figure 6.2.

In essence, the existing attitudes of the individual operate to preserve themselves in two ways, both of which become operational in the form of the perceptual screen. First, information that is wildly discrepant from that which is expected and/or acceptable has an exceptionally difficult time passing through the filtering process and is relatively less likely than more "orthodox" forms of information eventually to interact with the attitudes themselves. The gateway to our cognitive structure is guarded, and only those messengers with proper credentials may enter. Moreover, in the later

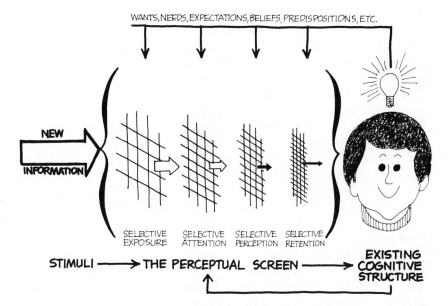

FIGURE 6.2 Perceptual Screening and the Resistance to Change.

stages of the screening process, information that does persevere will be interpreted in terms of existing concepts and orientations so that even new information assumes old and previously understood meanings. Information is continually recycled, with the effect that much of the original essence of the attitude structure is retained. And as a result, contrary information is unlikely to penetrate the screening process to the degree necessary, or in the form necessary, to work fundamental change on the attitudes of the individuals.

AVOIDING THE PERCEPTUAL SCREEN

Over the course of this chapter, we have suggested a variety of ways of inducing attitude change. These have ranged from altering the functional attributes of the attitude in question or the contextual attributes of the persuasive situation to restricting either the options available to the individual or the actual content of the message itself. But while each of these techniques is derived from a different view of the attitude dynamic, all have one important characteristic in common. Either by bringing pressure on the individual in the hope that it will lead to cognitive change, or by trying to channel that change in the particular direction of an individual's attitudes, each of these approaches attempts to employ the very factors that operate to stabilize attitudes as a lever to facilitate attitude change. Much as a person might use the gravitational pull upon a boulder to roll it down a hill to a new position, each of these techniques tries to use the inertial properties of the cognitive structure to induce modification.

There is, however, a second general approach to attitude change that is at least potentially as effective, one that involves attempts either to avoid or to overload the perceptual screening process itself. One popular means of accomplishing this is by the use of *saturation*, or multiple exposure. The idea here is that some amount of information is probably going to pass through the screening process without resistance simply because the sheer volume of messages beamed at an individual is too great for screening to be totally effective. If this is in fact the case, it then stands to reason that those messages that are repeated more frequently will have a proportionately greater chance of penetrating this breach in the defenses. The advertisers of popular brand-name products are probably the most pervasive practitioners of this kind of persuasive attempt, but we see it in politics as well when every candidate tries to saturate every utility post and television screen with voter appeals.

It is probably true that if enough messages are issued toward individuals, some of them are indeed likely to penetrate their screening process unmolested. But the saturation technique has one disadvantage: Messages or bits of information passing into cognitive space in this way have no opportunity to interact with the individual's attitudes or perceptions on the way in; they have not been interpreted and properly catalogued. As a result, they tend not to be attached to or integrated with any particular attitude or belief, but rather to float around in a sort of limbo. Thus they are unlikely to influence attitudes very effectively until they become so numerous that they can no longer be ignored. Eventually, everyone has to have some thoughts about, say, Coca-Cola—but not necessarily about Candidate Jones, who is running for the city council and who is trying on a much smaller scale over a much shorter period of time to make use of the saturation technique.

One way to increase the probability that this unconsciously received information will have some impact is to give it thematic consistency. That is, even though such messages may travel at different times over different media, they should possess a certain identifiable similarity with respect to both their substantive content and their format. They should, in short, have a common theme:

the Pepsi Generation . . . the Greatest Show on Earth . . . the Candidate of the People. And this theme should always be present, no matter what else is in a particular message, to serve as a link calling to mind all of the earlier, related messages.

Other technical factors can be used to advantage as well. If the vehicle itself is attractive, for example, the message it conveys may penetrate more or less unnoticed. In the early 1970s Coca-Cola received several million requests for a recording of one of its commercials because the tune was so catchy. The lyric was ultimately purged of advertising and issued as a phonograph record, which immediately became a best seller. And every time it was heard, everyone naturally thought of Coca-Cola, even though the name of the product was no longer mentioned.[20]

Similarly, the timing of messages may be controlled to advantage. Analysis has shown that persuasive messages have their greatest impact immediately after they have been issued, and that this impact decays as time passes. Thus the longer one waits to reinforce a given message, the smaller will be the cumulative impact of that series of messages of which it is a part. If, on the other hand, persuasive messages are issued in rapid succession, their cumulative impact will be relatively greater.[21] Based upon these findings, techniques have been developed for increasing the impact of messages by adding one upon another until a peak of effectiveness is reached. Manipulations of this sort are particularly useful in election campaigns, in which most of the advertising is designed to maximize the impact of the message at one point in time—election day.

Certain of the mass media, and most especially television, are better equipped than others to take advantage of these and other perceptual screen-avoidance techniques. This variable capability arises from the fact that each medium offers somewhat different types of informational stimuli and demands somewhat different degrees of an audience member's time, effort, and attention if it is to be effective. In particular, a given medium provides to the audience member more or less complete information, and in inverse proportion requires that the individual fill in the details. The more complete the message provided by the medium, the more passive can be the recipient; the less complete the message, the more active must be the recipient in completing the image communicated. As a result, information communicated over *active* (high-audience-participation) media will inevitably interact with the perceptual screen of the individual audience member, since the very use of such media requires the conscious activation of his or her attitudes.

Information communicated over *passive* (low-audience-participation) media, on the other hand, might succeed in avoiding the screen to some extent, since media of this type make far fewer demands upon the recipient.[22]

A practical example may clarify this difference. Let us consider two different media representations of the same scene: a child sitting under a tree. Representation I is the printed statement you have just read: "a child sitting under a tree." Now consider the following questions regarding this statement. Is the child a little girl or a little boy? What is the child wearing? Is the child happy or sad? Aside from sitting, what sort of activity is he or she engaged in? What kind of a tree is it? Is the tree located on a hill? Is it surrounded by flowers or grass? Is the scene set in summer or winter? As you read the phrase "a child sitting under a tree," you probably conjured up in your mind some image of a child sitting under a tree. Perhaps, *depending upon your own experience*, your personal image offered responses to some or all of these questions, perhaps to others that could be asked as well. In any event, chances are that you created in your own mind some kind of mental image of a child sitting under a tree. Assuming you did, the details of that image were provided neither by the medium nor by the message, but by your personal *interpretation* of the simple six-word phrase. That is, in the act of reading the message, you used your own experience and expectations to give it meaning. You filled in the blanks, as it were, with your imagination. And as a consequence, the message was individualized and perhaps raised to the level of consciousness.[23] Thus we see that the medium of print is not conducive to the avoidance of the perceptual screen.

In contrast, let us suppose that representation II involves the same message—a child sitting under a tree—as presented on television. The television image fills in many of the details omitted in the print message: It shows and tells us what the child looks like, what he or she is doing, the nature and location of the tree, and so forth. Indeed, if the image is on color television, still more details are provided. The message is more nearly complete, and in fact uniformly complete, even in ways of which we may be unaware.

On which portion of his anatomy was newsman Les Nesmond wearing a bandage in that last episode of "WKRP in Cincinnati"? What kind of car do the officers on "Hill Street Blues" drive? What objects were beside the President on his desk the last time he gave a televised speech? Specific, detailed information of this type is invariably available from television broadcasts, but because the image presented is relatively complete, because we need not ask ourselves questions to understand it, we tend not to notice such details. Because we are not required to think, to imagine, to personalize the message, because its understanding has in effect been prefabricated by the medium itself, we can literally vegetate in front of the television set and still engage in meaningful communication. It is not that we communicate less with television than with print, but only that as individuals we are required to contribute less to the process and are permitted to take more for granted.[24]

Precisely because low-participation media such as television provide substantially more information than do high-participation media such as print, they require less effort on the part of the individual user to interact with the message, with the result that her (or his) perceptual screen may be lulled into inactivity. Where a person is actively working to receive a message, chances are that she will consciously try to integrate that message with her established attitudes and beliefs. But where she is the passive target of persuasive information, she is ripe for unconscious influence. And it follows that if in communicating a message we wish to avoid the perceptual screen, if we wish to minimize the degree of individual interpretation or conscious consideration of new information (and at the same time reduce the chances of outright rejection), we should present that information in a medium—such as television—which is less conducive to personalized message evaluation.

We can see, then, that there are ways not only to use the screening process to effect attitude change, but either to avoid it or to overwhelm it as well. At the same time, many of the messages that arrive in this manner, and particularly those designed to evade the perceptual screen, are less likely than those that interact with that screen to be effectively integrated into the attitude structure of the individual. In a qualitative sense, then, attempts at influence that take this form may be at a competitive disadvantage.

IN SUMMARY

Above all, this chapter should make it clear that the holding of political attitudes is not simply a passive exercise. Rather, it involves a continuous interposition of those attitudes between the environment and the individual—or, in terms which we have suggested earlier, between the stimulus and the response. For attitudes give meaning to every encounter with reality; attitudes help to explain every phenomenon of which one becomes aware. And because in so doing they inadvertently act to restrict the experiencing of alternatives, existing attitudes tend continually to reinforce themselves through the elimination of competition. This process is relative rather than absolute, and it is surely less than completely effective. But it nevertheless serves to introduce a significant degree of stability into the attitude structure of the individual and to establish a highly constrained setting for attempts at political influence, the practical implications of which we shall explore in the following chapter.

SUGGESTIONS FOR FURTHER READING

The dynamics of attitude change are discussed at a relatively elementary level in Philip Zimbardo and Ebbe B. Ebbesen, *Influencing Attitudes and Changing Behavior* (Reading, Mass.: Addison-Wesley, 1969). This book also includes several case studies showing the application of certain theories of attitude change to particular situations.

At a more advanced level, the tenets of several theories of attitude change are set forth in the selections in Richard V. Wagner and John J. Sherwood, eds., *The Study of Attitude Change* (Belmont, Calif.: Brooks/Cole, 1969). A more complete but rather less readable survey may be found in Charles A. Kiesler, Barry E. Collins, and Norman Miller, *Attitude Change: A Critical Analysis of Theoretical Approaches* (New York: John Wiley, 1969).

Dan Nimmo reviews the practical considerations associated with political persuasion per se in *Political Communication and Public Opinion in America* (Santa Monica, Calif.: Goodyear, 1978), especially chapter 4. Doris Graber examines some related themes as they apply to mediated persuasion in particular in chapter 5 of *Mass Media and American Politics* (Washington, D.C.: Congressional Quarterly Press, 1980).

In a book entitled *When Prophecy Fails* (Minneapolis: University of Minnesota Press, 1956), Leon Festinger, Henry W. Riecken, and Stanley Schachter apply the theories of attitude change to an analysis of the members of a group that unsuccessfully predicted the destruction of the world on a certain date. The book is both illustrative and highly entertaining. A similarly entertaining effort that bears on, among other points, the effectiveness of perceptual screening is Hadley Cantril's analysis of the panic following the famous "War of the Worlds" broadcast in 1938 in *The Invasion from Mars* (Princeton: Princeton University Press, 1940).

NOTES

1. David O. Sears and Jonathan L. Freedman consider both purposeful and de facto selectivity in "Selective Exposure to Information: A Critical Review," *Public Opinion Quarterly* 31 (1967): 194–213. For an example of selective exposure in action, see Fred W. Grupp, Jr., "Newscast Avoidance Among Political Activists," *Public Opinion Quarterly* 34 (1970): 262–66. Contrary evidence as to the effectiveness of the process is presented by Michael A. Milburn in "A Longitudinal Test of the Selective Exposure Hypothesis," *Public Opinion Quarterly* 43 (1979): 507–17.

2. Percy H. Tannenbaum, "The Indexing Process in Communication," *Public Opinion Quarterly* 19 (1955): 293 f. In Chapter 9 we shall develop a related argument on the physiological correlates of attention.

3. Ibid.

4. David Krech and Richard S. Crutchfield, "Perceiving the World," in *The Process and Effects of Mass Communication,* ed. Wilbur Schramm and Donald F. Roberts (rev. ed.; Urbana: University of Illinois Press, 1971), pp. 235–64. The applications of selective perception to the electoral process are suggested by Bernard R. Berelson, Paul F. Lazarsfeld, and William N. McPhee in *Voting: A Study of Opinion Formation in a Presidential Campaign* (Chicago: University of Chicago Press, 1954) chap. 10, and in a more formal balance theory framework by Drury R. Sherrod. "Selective Perception of Political Candidates," *Public Opinion Quarterly* 35 (1971–72): 554–62.

5. The importance of this indexing of new information is discussed in Tannenbaum, "The Indexing Process in Communication," pp. 292–302. See also Claire Zimmerman and Raymond A. Bauer, "The Effects of an Audience on What Is Remembered," *Public Opinion Quarterly* 20 (1956): 238–48.

6. In this context, it is of more than passing interest to note that perception may in fact be culturally defined, so that certain kinds of events or meanings might lie entirely beyond the grasp of an acculturated individual, while the frequency of perception of others would be multiplied by adherence. For some interesting arguments and research on this point see Marshall H. Segall, Donald T. Campbell, and Melville J. Herskovits, *The Influence of Culture on Visual Perception* (Indianapolis: Bobbs-Merrill, 1966).

7. Two principal attempts have been made to develop a functional approach to attitude change. The conceptualization by Daniel Katz reported in "The Functional Approach to the Study of Attitudes," *Public Opinion Quarterly* 24 (1960): 163–204, provides the basis for the present discussion. A second and somewhat different perspective may be found in two articles by Herbert C. Kelman: "Compliance, Identification, and Internalization: Three Processes of Attitude Change," *Journal of Conflict Resolution* 2 (1958): 51–60, and "Processes of Opinion Change," *Public Opinion Quarterly* 25 (1961): 57–78.

8. This might be an alternative source of error to those suggested by Angus Campbell, Philip E. Converse, Warren E. Miller, and Donald E. Stokes in *The American Voter* (New York: John Wiley, 1960), pp. 75 f.

9. Katz, "The Functional Approach," passim, but especially p. 192.

10. Richard V. Wagner, "The Study of Attitude Change: An Introduction," in *The Study of Attitude Change*, ed. Richard V. Wagner and John J. Sherwood (Belmont, Calif.: Brooks/Cole, 1969), pp. 7–11. For a broad overview of learning theory approaches to the development and modification of attitudes, see Winfred F. Hill, *Learning: A Survey of Psychological Interpretations* (San Francisco: Chandler, 1963). One of the earliest and most interesting studies representative of this approach is Carl I. Hovland, Arthur A. Lumsdaine, and Fred D. Sheffield, *Studies in Social Psychology in World War II*, vol. 3, *Experiments on Mass Communication* (Princeton: Princeton University Press, 1949).

11. Wagner, "The Study of Attitude Change," pp. 12–18, provides a brief overview of research on the balance theories, as do John J. Sherwood, James W. Barron, and H. Gordon Fitch in "Cognitive Dissonance: Theory and Research," in Wagner and Sherwood, *The Study of Attitude Change*, pp. 56–86, and Steven Jay Gross and C. Michael Niman in "Attitude-Behavior Consistency: A Review," *Public Opinion Quarterly* 39 (1975): 358–68. The topic is treated at greater length in Charles A. Kiesler, Barry E. Collins, and Norman Miller, *Attitude Change: A Critical Analysis of Theoretical Approaches* (New York: John Wiley, 1969), pp. 155–237. The emphasis in the present discussion is centered in particular on the theory of cognitive dissonance since it is at present the focus of the largest share of balance theory research. For a noteworthy critique of dissonance theory, see Russell H. Fazio, Mark P. Zanna, and Joel Cooper, "Dissonance and Self-Perception: An Integrative View of Each Theory's Proper Domain of Application," *Journal of Experimental Social Psychology* 13 (1977): 464–79.

12. Sherwood et al., "Cognitive Dissonance," pp. 70–74, and Kiesler et al., *Attitude Change*, pp. 197–200.

13. Leon Festinger, *A Theory of Cognitive Dissonance* (Evanston, Ill.: Row, Peterson, 1957), pp. 28 f. This point is actually in some dispute. See Sherwood et al., "Cognitive Dissonance," pp. 74 f.

14. Robert E. Lane and David O. Sears, *Public Opinion* (Englewood Cliffs, N.J.: Prentice-Hall, 1964), pp. 47–53, provide an extended discussion of such options.

15. The literature on source credibility is critically reviewed in Brian Sternthat, Lynn W. Phillips, and Ruby Dholakia, "The Persuasive Effect of Source Credibility: A Situational Analysis," *Public Opinion Quarterly* 42 (1978): 285–314. For an analysis of the attributes of a high-credibility source, see David K. Berlo, James B. Lemert, and Robert J. Mertz, "Dimensions for Evaluating the Acceptability of Message Sources," *Public Opinion Quarterly* 33 (1969–70): 563–76.

16. For some related experimental results, see Elaine Walster, "The Temporal Sequence of Post-Decision Processes," in *Conflict, Decision, and*

Dissonance, ed. Leon Festinger (London: Tavistock Publications, 1964), pp. 112–27.

17. For a related discussion, see Richard F. Carter, "Bandwagon and Sandbagging Effects: Some Measures of Dissonance Reduction," *Public Opinion Quarterly* 23 (1959): 279–87.

18. Carolyn W. Sherif and Muzafer Sherif, "The Social Judgment–Involvement Approach to Attitude and Attitude Change," in *Social Interaction*, ed. Muzafer Sherif (Chicago: Aldine, 1967), pp. 342–52. The reference to involvement here relates to what proponents of this approach term "ego-involvement," and as that term suggests, the approach itself derives rather straightforwardly from the psychoanalytical notions of personality we presented in Chapter 3.

19. Sherif and Sherif, "The Social Judgment–Involvement Approach." The discussion that follows represents a simplification of the Sherifs' notions of areas of acceptance, neutrality, and rejection. For some recent evidence supporting the theory, see Richard R. Halverson and Michael S. Pallak, "Commitment, Ego-Involvement, and Resistance to Attack," *Journal of Experimental Social Psychology* 14 (1978): 1–12. Physiological differences associated with varying levels of discrepancy are described in John T. Cacioppo and Richard E. Petty, "Attitudes and Cognitive Response: An Electrophysiological Approach," *Journal of Personality and Social Psychology* 37 (1979): 2181–99.

20. This, of course, is the well-known argument of Marshall McLuhan in *Understanding Media: The Extensions of Man* (New York: McGraw-Hill, 1964), but it may be seen to underlie more rigorous methodological inquiry as well. For some examples, see note 22, below.

21. Hubert A. Zielske, "The Remembering and Forgetting of Advertising," *Journal of Marketing* 23 (1959): 239–43. There is evidence, however, that excessive exposure can have a negative effect. See Richard L. Miller, "Mere Exposure, Psychological Reactance and Attitude Change," *Public Opinion Quarterly* 40 (1976): 229–33.

22. Herbert E. Krugman, "The Impact of Television Advertising: Learning Without Involvement," *Public Opinion Quarterly* 29 (1965): 349–56; idem, "The Measurement of Advertising Involvement," *Public Opinion Quarterly* 30 (1966): 583–96; idem, "Brain Wave Measures of Media Involvement," *Journal of Advertising Research* 11 (1971): 3–10; and Philip Anast, "Personality Determinants of Mass Media Preferences," *Journalism Quarterly* 43 (1966): 729–32. See also Ivan L. Preston, "A Reinterpretation of the Meaning of Involvement in Krugman's Models of Advertising Communication," *Journalism Quarterly* 47 (1970): 287–95, 323. For a critical analysis of the potential impact of society's increasing reliance on passive media, see Jarol B. Manheim, "Can Democracy Survive Television?" *Journal of Communication* 26 (1976): 84–90.

23. Anast, "Personality Determinants," p. 731.

24. Ibid.

7

Political Competition

Candidates, Voters, and Electoral Decisions

At least from a heuristic standpoint, no element of political life better illustrates the confluence of the various social, political, and psychological phenomena we have described in these pages than the period of machination and competitive image making that we commonly call the political campaign. Inherent in the campaign situation are both an overt attempt on the part of the campaigners to persuade large numbers of individuals to work or at least vote for them and a more or less clearly defined effort on the part of those individuals themselves to choose among the electoral alternatives offered. Inherent in the campaign is a natural interplay between the need of various candidates to find employment for the next few years and the needs of the voters to seek their own forms of electoral gratification. And because these pressures operate on all parties to the process, because they serve to constrain the behavior of vote seeker and voter alike, the campaign—and more particularly its focal point, the election itself—literally forces an interaction among persuasive stimuli (campaign propaganda), intervening attitude and belief structures (the wants and needs of the individual voter), and actual behavior (the reading and implementation of decisions relating to casting a vote). As a result, the campaign situation provides us with an excellent laboratory in which to investigate the practical manifestations of our analysis in the preceding chapters.

THE POLITICAL CAMPAIGN:
A MEETING OF THE MINDS

In the context provided by those chapters, we can view the political campaign as an exercise in mutual psychological mapping—the matching of cognitive needs with informational stimuli. On one side of this process we have a variously defined group of voters, each of whom possesses some more or less carefully constructed conceptualization of what constitutes the ideal political candidate and each of whom is faced with the task of selecting the one actual candidate who most closely approximates (or seems to approximate) that ideal. Each of these voters projects his or her electorally relevant wants, needs, and expectations into the campaign situation in an effort to identify the most viable of the available alternatives. In contraposition to this group of voters, we have a considerably smaller group of candidates, each of whom wishes to create a positive symbolic representation (image) based upon a controlled presentation of his or her various attributes and to convey the image in such a way that as many different kinds of voters as possible will be able to identify with it. Each candidate will try to project this desired image into the campaign situation in an effort to persuade prospective voters of his or her own merits. The political campaign, then, is that period of time during which a variety of manipulations, modifications, and compromises take place, both in the minds of the voters and in the activities of the campaigners, each of which is designed to maximize the chances that these two sets of images will resemble one another closely enough that a vote may be cast accordingly.[1]

Figure 7.1 may help us visualize this process. The figure shows two more or less similar images being projected upon a screen. The image projected from the left represents the electoral desires of any individual prospective voter based on his own wants, needs, and expectations. It consists of the traits that the individual considers to be most necessary in a "qualified" political hopeful. In the United States, for example, most voters seem to place considerable emphasis on the amount of experience a candidate brings to the campaign, with such traits as honesty, integrity, education, and intelligence also considered quite important. Other candidate characteristics that are frequently attributed by American voters to their ideal candidate include independence, the ability to make decisions, leadership and administrative skills, good health, a pleasant personality, sincerity, and a stable family life. Indeed, the list is longer still.[2] Clearly no single voter is likely to project all these desired

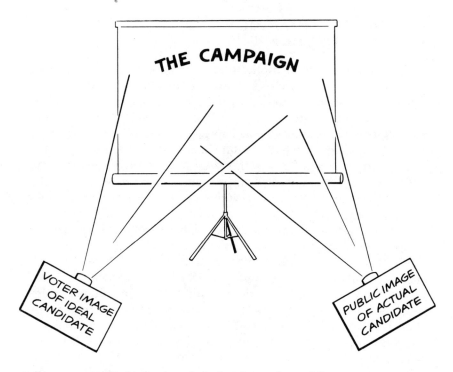

FIGURE 7.1   Mutual Mapping of Ideal and Actual Candidate Images.

characteristics into his or her electoral decision making. But equally clearly, each voter is likely to take into consideration at least several of these and other traits. As a result, the image of the ideal candidate which each voter brings to the campaign will be both highly individualized and highly complex. It is the task of the voter to compare this idealized candidate image with the available campaign stimuli and thereby to identify that candidate who best reflects his or her own interests.[3]

The image on the right in Figure 7.1 represents those characteristics projected by the actual candidate or attributed to the candidate by others who seek to create an image in his (or her) behalf. This image consists of the elements of his public personality, the sound and relative fury of his positions on the issues, his party identification, and such other factors as may become important to the voters during the period of decision-making. It is the task of the candidate to present a package of image characteristics that will prove appealing to the broadest possible group of voters without at the same time introducing so many inherent contradictions or limitations upon himself that his image collapses from its own weight.

Not all candidates, of course, are able to approach this task with equal resources. Some simply do not possess the personal characteristics, the political acumen, or the financial muscle to match themselves effectively against idealized voter expectations. Others choose not to do so. But regardless of the realities of the situation, the nature of the campaign is such that all must try at the very least to *appear* to assume godlike proportion, for it is the appearance and not the reality that is communicated to the voter. Thus each candidate must emphasize his assets and deemphasize his liabilities in what amounts to the "selective projection" of a campaign image.[4]

During the period of the campaign, an effort is made by both parties to the electoral process to blend these two images together. For his part, a candidate may, in a figurative sense, move his image to a different location on the screen (by altering some of his positional or other characteristics), or, as is more often the case, he may simply blur his image either by reducing the clarity of his attributes and positions or by avoiding public appearances. Each of these techniques may be illustrated with reference to the most recent presidential campaigns of Ronald Reagan, and more particularly to his perceived need to broaden the base of his appeal to voters. Running against the incumbent Gerald Ford in 1976, Reagan used the first of these strategies, albeit unsuccessfully, when, in an effort to reduce his extremist image in advance of the Republican convention, he named Richard Schweiker, a party liberal, to be his running mate should he receive the presidential nomination. The result, in large measure because of bad timing and inadequate preparation, was confusion and dismay among his staunchest supporters. Reagan was more successful in portraying himself as both moderate and responsible during the preliminaries of the 1980 race by adopting a sort of "cactus garden" strategy. This time he avoided conflict and confrontation with other Republican candidates through the simple expedient of staying home and staying quiet, while his opponents scrambled and scrapped. By this technique he succeeded in attaching to his person the aura of 'authority that most citizens associate with the presidential office. In both instances, it was the recognition that candidates must provide images of themselves that match the requirements of voters that prompted Reagan's actions. And more generally, by using strategies of this sort, any candidate may broaden his or her appeal *within the established context of voter wants, needs, and expectations.*

By the same token, in the absence of any candidate closely resembling his ideal image, the voter may decide that any particular positions or personality traits of a given candidate are not really as important as they seemed at the outset. After all, *compared to his opponent* the candidate may very well be perceived as the lesser of two evils—or to rephrase, as the closest available approximation to the ideal. Thus the voter may shift from a strategy of maximizing benefits from the election of one or another candidate to one of minimizing costs, or he may simply alter his judgment regarding the relative salience of candidate characteristics. In either event, and probably as a result of his interactions with various campaign stimuli, the voter adjusts the image which he projects onto our hypothetical screen to fit his perception of the available alternatives.[5] And based upon these mutual efforts to resolve the inconsistencies between the image of the candidate as selectively projected and that same image as selectively perceived, the campaign may be viewed not only as a period of persuasion but as one of accommodation as well.

THE INDIVIDUAL AS VOTER

Inasmuch as they provide both the social and the informational context within which electoral competition takes place, it seems appropriate that we begin our analysis of political campaigns with an investigation of the voters themselves. A voter is in every sense of the word an individual: she has her own attitudes, her own perceptions of reality, and her own beliefs about what is important and what is not. Indeed, as we have pointed out earlier, each individual is the product of the unique combination of her own personal socializing experiences, and there are potentially as many different kinds of individual voters as there are imaginable combinations of politically or socially relevant experience. We might even liken individuals in the political process to sets of fingerprints: Given the task of analyzing millions of them, we would still find no two exactly alike.

But, like fingerprints, groups of voters tend to display certain recurrent characteristics which allow us to make more general statements about them. That is, just as particular combinations of peaks and swirls make it possible for us to classify fingerprints systematically into one category or another, particular combinations of social and psychological characteristics arising from similarities of situation or socialization experience enable us to identify individual voters as members of groups with certain common voting habits.

Thus we may speak of the "farm vote," the "youth vote," or the "liberal vote" as a means of summarizing the voting patterns of many individuals. But only to the extent that these shorthand references reflect underlying individual voting propensities—only to the extent that they summarize consistent tendencies in the resolution of individual electoral dilemmas—do these concepts and others like them have real meaning.

A number of social characteristics have the potential to influence electoral decision making by helping the individual structure his perceptions of political reality. These might include such factors as the racial, religious, educational, occupational, economic, and party identifications of the individual in question, to list only a few.[6] For example, blacks, while giving consideration to other issues as well, might by virtue of their racial identification be strongly influenced in casting their votes by the belief that one or another of the candidates will be either a help or a hindrance to the cause of social equality. Similarly, Catholics might, because of their religious identification, be psychologically pressured to oppose a candidate who favors legalized abortion. Farmers might, by virtue of their occupation and life style, favor a candidate because he is associated with a more sympathetic approach to the problems of agriculture, while urban white-collar workers might oppose that same candidate because they fear that if he were elected the price of food might go up. In general, then, *to the extent that an individual identifies with a particular group in the society, and to the extent that the group's members see their group interests as relevant to the election itself, the psychological force of that social identification and of the common political perspective it entails will exercise pressure on the individual both to interpret the campaign in certain ways and to respond to the campaign accordingly.*[7]

The political significance of these social identifications is clearly reflected in voting patterns in the United States in that each of the two major political parties finds consistent support among certain groups in the society whose members perceive that party as best representing their common interests. Republican strength, for example, tends to center in towns and small cities, while the Democrats are strongest in urban centers and the rural South. Republicans draw support disproportionately from higher-income groups, while the Democrats draw from the less affluent; Republicans draw from the more extensively educated members of the society, while Democrats receive the support of those with less schooling. And similarly, Republicans traditionally do well among whites, Protestants, those engaged in professional or managerial occupations, farmers, nonmembers of unions, and older voters; Democrats traditionally do well among ethnic minorities, Catholics and Jews, and both skilled and unskilled laborers, especially union members. Republican strength tends to be centered in the Midwest and West and is growing in the South, while Democratic strength is greatest in the East.[8]

The individual who identifies with any of these groups acquires the perspectives that define the group's common cause and is likely to acquire those political orientations which receive group support as well. As a result, there develops within such groups a collective and relatively uniform preference that often serves over an extended period to benefit one or the other political party and most of the candidates associated with that party. In this way, group identifications contribute to the stability of the American two-party system.

In contrast, other kinds of individual psychological considerations tend to have a rather more temporary and more fragmented impact on electoral partisanship. In this category we may include such factors as the personality traits and the elements of the self-concept which underlie the structure of individual attitudes. For example, a person's degree of maturity might influence his political activity and preferences, both in terms of what he seeks from a candidate and in terms of the extremity of his own views. Similarly, a sense of personal insecurity might prompt one to support a candidate who presents an image of authority, while a sense of frustration might induce one to oppose any and all incumbents. In each instance, a set of personal psychological conditions becomes— or may at least be perceived by the individual to become— relevant to electoral politics. Unlike the enduring and pervasive social pressures mentioned above, these psychological considerations seldom accrue consistently to one political party or another. Rather, because they are so highly personalized and because they often arise in response to the particular options presented in a particular campaign, these factors are essentially short-lived assets that accrue to particular political personalities or to particular types of appeal. Nevertheless, these pressures may significantly influence the individual's definition and perception of the political process, and in the aggregate they may greatly affect the electoral outcome. This is most particularly the case, it would seem, when the appeal of one of the candidates involved is primarily charismatic in nature, or in other words, when the personality of the candidate is especially attractive and provides a locus of support. In such cases, the quasi-personal relationship between candidate and voter may provide the principal cue for the electoral decision.

In the light of our analysis of attitude dynamics, the impact of social identification and psychological need on voting behavior should come as no surprise. The social attachments of the individual and his psychological state provide the cues that help him understand his political situation and that lead him to establish certain expectations relative to the electoral process. These expectations then guide him in his encounters with campaign stimuli. In other words, the social and psychological pressures we have described help the individual to establish his perceptual screen in the area of electoral politics. And the derivative attitudes that give substance to the screening process thus play a critical role in voting determinations.

While these group identifications and psychological factors greatly assist us in our efforts to characterize voting behavior, it is nevertheless important to realize that no individual is so simple in nature that he may be understood in terms of one or another summary category. No one is simply a Catholic, simply a professional, simply more or less secure or mature. To the contrary, any given individual might display any particular combination of these and other characteristics. We might in fact find in the electorate mature Catholic managers, moderately educated Protestant laborers, urban Jewish professionals, and any of an almost infinite variety of other voter configurations. Indeed, the more categories we consider, the more room for variation we introduce; the more room for variation we introduce, the greater the likelihood that any particular individual will be found to possess conflicting loyalties or perspectives. And because the number of potential electorally relevant characteristics in the real world is quite great, it becomes rather likely that various of the identifications and needs which an individual voter manifests will in fact conflict with one another, each pressuring him to respond somewhat differently to political stimuli. Thus one set of identifications may suggest to the voter that his best interests lie with one party or candidate at the same time that other identifications suggest the desirability of supporting an opposing party or candidate. As might be expected, these competing pressures contribute to a sense of imbalance between two or more of the individual's political orientations, a perceived inconsistency that must be resolved before the actual vote may be cast.[9] The following description of Jewish voters during the 1972 presidential campaign illustrates the point quite nicely.

One gets a picture of a middle aged parent, a modestly successful businessman. His temple would be either Conservative or Orthodox. He is distressed over the crime seeping into his own neighborhood; he resents the "hippies" around McGovern, and he is worried about his college age daughter infected by this strange cult; he frets about the future of Israel, distrusts McGovern's "fuzzy" views on economics, and is critical of the job "quotas" demanded by militant blacks and Puerto Ricans that appear to threaten the aspirations of Jewish boys and girls from poorer families.

But he's still a Jew, still deeply committed to human dignity, to offering a helping hand to the less fortunate, still imbued with that special social consciousness, and not a little wary of all "those Germans" around Nixon in the White House and the way they play around with something as precious as personal liberties. He's appalled by the waste and bloodshed in Vietnam. *Politically, he's become two men*—one tugged to the right by the troubling aspects of a society in upheaval, the other imbued with the liberalism of the past.[10] [Emphasis added.]

To the extent that an individual is subjected to conflicting internal (i.e., private) forces of this sort, we speak of him as being *cross-pressured*—pushed in opposing directions by his various identifications and preferences.[11] And to the extent that the conflict among forces is external (i.e., social) in nature, where it is defined for the individual by his society in terms of competing sets of values or social positions, we speak of such a voter as displaying *status inconsistency*.[12] Where identifications of widely differing strengths are involved, it is relatively safe to predict resolution of the conflict in favor of the stronger identification. But where the forces involved are deployed more evenly, the simplest resolution may be indecision, a reduction in cognitive imbalance by withdrawal from the conflict situation.[13]

It is also important to note that precisely because he is searching for a resolution to the inconsistencies in his own original position, precisely because he is attempting to arrive at an electoral decision, the cross-pressured or status-inconsistent individual is among the most open of all potential voters to persuasion during the period of the campaign, particularly if he receives information that helps him reduce his apparent inconsistencies. To the extent that he wishes eventually to arrive at a partisan preference, such an individual actively seeks to reconcile conflicts among his attitudes and perceptions.[14] Consequently, in anticipation of the needs of such voters, a candidate may choose to blur his image, to move, as one political pundit has put it, to the "extreme center" on all issues.[15] By doing so, the candidate increases his chances of attracting support from undecided voters and at the same time reduces the likelihood that any of his positions will force a choice among his own supporters' underlying identifications, a forced selection that might, as often as not, work to the candidate's disadvantage.

ATTITUDE STRUCTURE AND ELECTORAL DECISIONS

From the standpoint of the would-be persuader, then, several characteristics of electorally relevant attitudes are of interest. The most obvious, of course, is the substantive content of the evaluative process as conducted by each individual—the questions of what knowledge, how much knowledge, and what affective associations the voter brings to decision making. We could expect, for example, that—other things being equal—a voter who has based his preliminary assessments upon a substantial amount of information about his own situation and about the available electoral alternatives might be less subject to persuasion than one who bases his preliminary judgments on somewhat less information. The sheer weight of established support for the chosen position or candidate, in other words, might limit the chances of successful influence in another direction. Similarly, the actual substance of the information that a voter has at the outset has certain clear implications for any subsequent attempts at persuasion. The nature of a person's beliefs sets limits on the ways in which he might be influenced. And of course the direction and momentum of the views of a particular individual may indicate that any persuasive attempts are either unnecessary (in the event that he is favorably inclined toward the candidate in question in the first place) or unlikely to produce any meaningful results (in the opposite circumstance).[16]

Even more basic than these considerations is the question of just what attitude objects the individual relates to the electoral process to begin with and what relative importance he attaches to each. Not everyone who votes in an election votes for the same reasons. To the contrary, each individual has his own set of criteria, which he applies to candidate selection, and these criteria may relate variously to some or all of the issue positions taken by the candidates, to some or all of the personality characteristics of the candidates (or even to those of some of their most easily identified supporters), or, as we have seen, to various aspects of the economic, social, and political well-being of the individual voter himself. Even though I disagree with many of his positions, for example, I still support Candidate Church because he opposes legalized abortion. I could never vote for Candidate Liberal because he is too young—and besides, all those longhairs and radicals support him. Even though I like Candidate Dove, I want to support Candidate Hawk because he will see that the company I work for will continue to get new contracts so that I may keep my job. In each case, the voter defines the attitude objects by which he will judge the electoral alternatives according to their relative salience as he himself assesses it and then applies the resultant evaluation to his voting decision.

These examples suggest—and, on the basis of our earlier analysis, we should indeed expect—that to a certain extent each voter will take from a political campaign only those kinds of electoral cues he seeks.[17] A voter who comes to the campaign with an eye on the issues will garner from that campaign some notion of each candidate's positions on those issues. A voter who comes to the campaign with the idea that all politicians or all members of one party or another are untrustworthy will no doubt come away with some evidence to support his beliefs. And a voter who comes to the campaign seeking reassurance that his original choice of candidate is a "proper" one will find that reassurance almost regardless of what takes place in the campaign. In each instance the political attitude–perceptual screen cycle is at work, and in each instance the voter perceives what he wants and expects to perceive.

Suppose, for example, that Candidate Sortof A. Radical is running for the Presidency, and suppose that Ms. Radical has taken a strong and forthright position in favor of busing to achieve racial integration of the public schools. During the campaign, the candidate comes to the realization that in order to broaden her electoral support, she will have to moderate her position on busing and be very careful to use phrases that will not inflame those potential supporters who happen to disagree with her on this particular issue. Recognizing that her policy preferences can be implemented only if she wins the election, she adjusts her public pronouncements accordingly. The voter who typically seeks information from the campaign regarding the substantive positions of the candidates will conclude from her change in behavior that Ms. Radical has moderated her position on the issue of busing. The voter who typically distrusts politicians will see her change in phraseology as yet one more indication that every politician will do or say whatever is necessary to get elected regardless of principle. And the voter who typically seeks reassurance might decide (depending on his original preference) either that Candidate Radical has displayed the willingness to compromise that is necessary in a President and that justifies his faith, or that Candidate Radical is indecisive and that he has been correct in opposing her. In each case we have the same stimulus—a modification in the position statements of the candidate; but in each case we have a different interpretation of the event depending upon the particular expectations that were initially brought to the campaign situation by the voter.

In addition to these expectations that a voter brings to the campaign, our analysis of attitude change suggests that at least one other voter attribute—the degree of personal emotional commitment that the individual attaches to his electorally relevant attitudes—can greatly influence his persuasibility as well. Most simply, we may expect that voters who are most highly involved in those of their attitudes that they most closely associate with the electoral situation will be the least open to persuasion during the period of the campaign. This is the case for two basic reasons. First, by virtue of the fact that these voters are emotionally involved in their attitudes, we may assume that they have formulated some more or less clearly defined preferences with regard to the campaign. In other words, these are by no means "undecided" voters, but rather individuals who have established for themselves a relatively unambiguous set of priorities. At the same time, precisely because these individuals are highly involved in their attitudes, they will raise their thresholds of rejection, they will stiffen their defenses against information which contradicts their original attitudes—in short, they will resist attempts at influence.[18]

To put all of this another way, those people who are the most emotionally involved in their election-related attitudes will be the most closed-minded during the period of the campaign. They will be the least open to persuasive communication, the least open to conversion regarding their candidate preferences. Yet precisely because these individuals are highly involved in campaign-related attitudes, they are also the ones most likely to be intensely interested in the campaign itself. Because the questions raised by the campaign are most salient to these attitude-involved voters, they tend to have a proportionately greater psychological stake in the outcome of the election and may be expected to display a proportionately greater interest in related events.

The implications of this analysis are indeed significant, for if the most interested and the most involved voters are the least open to persuasion during the period of the campaign, it must follow that those most open to persuasion are relatively lower-interest, lower-involvement voters, people who in fact may not have defined for themselves any stake in the outcome of the election whatsoever. It is these latter voters, constituting at least as many as one-third of the voting population in the United States in nationwide elections, who make up their minds during the period of the campaign; it is these voters who are most fluid in their intentions.[19] And as a consequence, it is at these uncommitted and more or less unconcerned individuals, in whose hands rests the balance of electoral power, that the political campaign must in large measure be directed. What is more, because these individuals are comparatively uninvolved and disinterested—because, in other words, they are potential *nonvoters*—they must not only be convinced of the merits of one candidate or another but must actually be motivated to take an interest and become involved in the whole process in the first place. Thus political campaigns must stimulate not only support but participation as well.

One additional comment is in order before we turn our attention from the voters to the vote seekers, for underlying much of our discussion of individual participation in the electoral process has been an assumption about the nature of the voting act itself which should be made clear. One basic question in the analysis of voting activity is whether electoral decisions are arrived at as a result of reasoned evaluations of the available alternatives or rather as a by-product of built-in and continually reinforced behavioral propensities (behavior-oriented attitudes) which arise from the self-perceived social location of the individual in question. In other words, does the voter somehow ascertain the presumed social and personal costs and benefits of his actions, consciously plug this information into a decision-making equation, and then behave (vote) in a way he believes will minimize the costs and maximize the benefits? Or does he react to election stimuli in a much less intellectualized manner, operating instead on a generally emotional plane in ways designed (even though he may be unaware of the fact) to maintain his social position and cognitive balance? This question is a subject of continuing debate among political scientists, which is a euphemistic way of saying that no satisfactory answers have as yet presented themselves.[20]

The mutual-mapping framework we have employed to conceptualize the electoral process in our own analysis actually falls somewhere between the two extremes in this debate. On the one hand, by suggesting that voters seek to match the images of available candidates against some more or less clearly determined idealization, we have implied that voters incorporate some judgment of the relative advantages and disadvantages of each alternative into the decision-making process. But at the same time, we have suggested that the judgmental criteria themselves may include such nonrational factors as the subconscious needs of the individual, and that the substance of these judgmental criteria is largely a function of the individual's political milieu (as he sees it) and of his social identifications. So in effect we have argued that voters may make rational types of decisions—weighted evaluations—based

upon nonrational and often unmeasurable criteria.[21] And the aggregate of those individual voter decisions determines not only the
winners and losers among the candidates in question but in the
longer run, the winners and losers in the distribution of political,
economic, social, and psychological resources among the individual
voters as well.

THE CANDIDATE AS PERSUADER

On the basis of our discussion to this point, then, we can summarize the problem that faces a candidate as follows: He (or she) must
attempt to influence, through the issuance of mass communications
and through interpersonal contact between himself and his supporters on the one hand and potential voters on the other, the decisions of a complex set of individuals of differential persuasibility.
He must attempt to reinforce those who support him, to convert or
to deactivate those who oppose him or remain neutral, and to
motivate all his likely supporters to cast votes for him—and at a
particular point in time, election day. To aid him in accomplishing
these goals, he possesses certain resources, including, among
others, time, money, workers, an identification with various social
groups, and some degree of access to various of the mass media.
Although a thorough treatise on political campaigning would require analysis of each of these resources, the last one mentioned
may provide the clearest illustration of the dynamics of campaign
persuasion.

It is, as we have seen, a "given" of the campaign situation that
the voters who will be most open to persuasion during the period
of the campaign are precisely those who are least likely to be
actively involved in electoral politics. These critically important voters are among the least likely to seek out political information, the
least likely to take an interest in either the campaign or its outcome.
And yet, because they hold the balance of power in the election,
these voters must be reached, must be convinced, must be acti-
vated. For to concede the undecided vote is in many instances tan-
tamount to conceding the election itself.

To say that these potential voters are disinterested in the campaign, however, is not to say that they are resistant to its appeals.
To the contrary, while the *resistant* voter actively screens out campaign communication with which he does not wish to come into
contact, the *disinterested* voter tends to be more passive in his avoidance of political propaganda. It is not that he goes out of his way
to avoid campaign information; he simply does not go out of his

way to obtain it. Thus if a candidate can place his messages in media that attract the attention of this low-involvement voter for other reasons, if he can saturate the individual's overall information intake with his political propaganda, he may in fact succeed in accomplishing his purpose. If, in other words, he can catch the voter with his guard down by placing his messages where the voter is likely to happen upon them inadvertently, the candidate may be able to persuade the voter to rally to his support.[22]

Two factors work to the advantage of the candidate in these persuasive attempts. For one thing, it turns out that many low-involvement voters tend to have a relatively low level of formal education, a fact that we should not find especially surprising in view of our discussion of the school and college as agents of socialization.[23] The political knowledge one gains and the politically relevant skills one acquires as one continues his education provide the basis for informed and active participation in the political process. Where these lessons have not been incorporated into an individual's experience, it is quite reasonable to expect a far lower level of political awareness and political activity.

Moreover, individuals with a relatively low level of formal education have been found to rely most heavily on certain kinds of media for both political and other purposes—specifically, those media we earlier described as low in audience participation. This is true in part because the skills and orientations required for the use of high-participation media are acquired principally through the educational process and in part because lower levels of educational attainment tend to relegate such individuals to social situations that restrict their exposure to certain high-participation media.[24] And as a result of these two factors, the informed candidate knows not only whom he must reach, but which media he may use to do so with maximum potential effectiveness.

This good fortune notwithstanding, the candidate is constrained in his attempts to reach low-interest voters by the fact that many individuals, and most certainly those with whom we are concerned here, do not use the mass media solely to seek out campaign information. Quite the reverse: They use the media for a variety of purposes, among which seeking political information of any kind is far from the most important. As a matter of fact, the relative unimportance of political content may be especially pronounced in low-participation media such as television, which are used primarily for entertainment, escape, social contact, and information seeking on nonpolitical subjects.[25] Furthermore, as we noted earlier, all individuals have a limited tolerance for communication of any kind. Surely those who are disinterested in politics will display a still lower tolerance for stimuli that are expressly political. As a consequence, the candidate who wishes to reach low-involvement voters through the use of general-audience, low-participation media must compete for their attention not only with other candidates for the same office but with candidates for other offices, with commercial advertising, with the regular public affairs content of each medium, and even with "Another World," "Family Feud,". and reruns of "I Love Lucy." It thus becomes necessary not only to sell the candidate but to sell the *messages* selling the candidate as well.

Because the candidate must compete with such a wide variety of messages, and because this competition intensifies markedly during the period immediately preceding election day, he may have to resort to attempts to bypass the perceptual screens of the various individual voters. He may be forced by the exigencies of the situation to rely on short-circuiting the individual's evaluation process in the hope that he can motivate the undecided voter to vote for him even in the absence of substantive reasons for doing so. He may, in short, be forced to employ slick, repetitive, avoidance-oriented messages and low-participation media in order to accomplish his electoral goals. In this way, the requirements of the persuasion process may make inevitable a lowering of the quality of effective political dialogue.

IN SUMMARY

In retrospect, each potential voter can be thought of as having a set of predispositions and beliefs about political reality which she (or he) brings to the campaign situation. These predispositions and beliefs are based on the individual's perception of her place in society (her group identifications) as well as other psychological pressures that may be operating. Out of this definition of her own political existence, each individual derives an image of what might constitute an ideal political candidate, one who would meet all of her various needs and expectations.

Within this framework, voters either seek out or are in some other way exposed to a variety of messages regarding the candidates in a given campaign, and each tries to a greater or lesser extent to relate this newly acquired information to her own personal conception of the ideal candidate. She evaluates each message and each candidate image which she receives in terms of such considerations as party identification, group support, issue positions, or personal characteristics. Finally, after a lengthy series of such evaluations which take place over some portion of the campaign period, each voter arrives at a decision as to which candidate most closely approximates her own idealized image. Those voters who are most intensely involved in the campaign issues generally tend to make up their minds rather early in the process—in fact, perhaps before the formal aspects of the campaign even get under way. Those who are rather less interested and less involved, as well as those who are cross-pressured by conflicting beliefs or group identifications, tend to postpone their decisions, either consciously or unconsciously, until closer to election day. Indeed, some of these individuals may be altogether unable or perhaps unwilling to commit themselves one way or the other even at the last moment, when the pressure to do so is most difficult to resist. But sooner or later, most potential voters will resolve whatever conflicts exist and will arrive at an electoral decision.

Viewing this same process from the other side, we have found that campaigners are faced with a closely related problem. For just as each voter must attempt to fit a candidate to personal needs and expectations, to a personal ideal image, each candidate must try to increase the number of needs and expectations, the number of idealized images, with which he (or she) may be perceived as compatible. His positions become more moderate, or at least less clearly delineated, because this enables larger numbers of candidate-seeking voters to live with them. His campaign communication is targeted at low-involvement voters over low-participation media because the competitive advantage in the struggle for attention lies in this direction. And in general, his campaign becomes more and more responsive to the restraints imposed by those whom it must ultimately reach. Thus the informational stimuli presented by the campaign are eventually matched to the cognitive requirements of the voters.

Applying to this mutual-mapping process the perspective that has characterized our earlier discussions, we can identify five key elements in the campaign situation that illustrate the relationship among political stimuli, political attitudes, and political behavior:

1. Political socialization creates the attitudinal foundation that the potential voter brings with him to the campaign situation. Socialization experience helps determine the specific preferences and identifications that the individual will manifest at the outset. (Thereafter, the campaign itself becomes, in a very general sense, an agent of political socialization.)

2. The substance and structure of the individual's attitudes prior to persuasive attempts define, in the aggregate, the informational starting point for the campaign effort. The campaigners must be cognizant of and responsive to the existing attitudes of voters as they plan their strategies of influence.

3. The mechanics of the attitude-change and perceptual screening processes set the psychological rules of the game for persuasive attempts. Only if political campaigners can take advantage of the built-in propensities in the individual's message-reception process can they hope to be effective in their appeals.

4. The political culture sets the social rules of the game for persuasive attempts. While we have not specifically mentioned this element in the present chapter, it should be clear that the more general relationship of the political culture to the transmission and reception of social norms applies quite directly to the area of electoral competition.

5. Finally, the act of voting itself represents one possible behavior that is given impetus by the resolution of all the competing pressures listed above. Both the decision to act and the direction of action arise from the interplay between established attitudes and newly received political stimuli.

Political campaigning, then, indeed provides a useful laboratory in which to illustrate the practical aspects of our notions about attitudes, behavior, and persuasion. For the campaign situation allows us to demonstrate quite effectively just how attitudes serve as a filter—as an interpretive device through which persuasive messages must pass if they are to be successful—and how behavior may be affected as a consequence. The political campaign, however, constitutes only one of many linkages between individual attitude structures and various kinds of political activity. In the following chapter, we shall investigate other such linkages from a rather more general perspective.

SUGGESTIONS FOR FURTHER READING

The literature dealing with political campaigns and voting behavior is probably the most extensive in all of political science, and a complete listing of suggested readings would doubtless exceed the length of this entire chapter. A few books, however, do stand out as being especially worthy of note. In the area of voting behavior these include Bernard R. Berelson, Paul F. Lazarsfeld, and William N. McPhee, *Voting: A Study of Opinion Formation in a Presidential Campaign* (Chicago: University of Chicago Press, 1954); V. O. Key, Jr., *The Responsible Electorate* (Cambridge, Mass: Harvard University Press, Belknap Press, 1966); Angus Campbell, Philip E. Converse, Warren E. Miller, and Donald E. Stokes, *The American Voter* (New York: John Wiley, 1964); and Norman H. Nie, Sidney Verba, and John R. Petrocik, *The Changing American Voter* (Cambridge, Mass.: Harvard University Press, 1976). Each of these books represents a rather different theoretical approach to the phenomenon of voting, and each has provided the impetus for considerable further inquiry.

One of the best collections of research on voting behavior is the volume edited by Edward C. Dreyer and Walter A. Rosenbaum entitled *Political Opinion and Behavior* (3rd ed.; North Scituate, Mass: Duxbury Press, 1976). This anthology brings together a great many findings on electoral politics, but principally those that represent the point of view espoused in *The American Voter*. A similarly valuable and broadly based collection may be found in Richard G. Niemi and Herbert F. Weisberg, eds., *Controversies in American Voting Behavior* (San Francisco: W. H. Freeman, 1976).

The most complete treatment of political campaigning as an influence process may be found in Dan Nimmo, *The Political Persuaders* (Englewood Cliffs, N.J.: Prentice-Hall, 1970). Nimmo offers a social psychological perspective on electioneering that illustrates many of the points raised in the present book.

Finally, for an analysis of partisanship that provides a context for appreciating the broader significance of voting behavior, see Jerome H. Clubb, William H. Flanigan, and Nancy H. Zingale, *Partisan Realignment: Voters, Parties, and Government in American History* (Beverly Hills: Sage, 1980).

NOTES

1. Jarol B. Manheim, "The Effects of Campaign Techniques on Voting Patterns in a Congressional Election" (Ph.D. diss., Northwestern University, August 1971), pp. 9–11.
2. David A. Leuthold, *Electioneering in a Democracy* (New York: John Wiley, 1968), pp. 23 ff. In point of fact, the actual amount of campaign-relevant information which is integrated by the voter into his cognitive structure may be rather limited. Lewis A. Dexter discusses this point in "Candidates Must Make the Issues and Give Them Meaning," *Public Opinion Quarterly* 19 (1955–56): 408–14.

3. For an example of this matching of images, see Roberta S. Sigel, "Effect of Partisanship on the Perception of Political Candidates," *Public Opinion Quarterly* 28 (1964): 483–96. The full range of literature relating to this point is reviewed and evaluated in Dan Nimmo and Robert L. Savage, *Candidates and Their Images: Concepts, Methods, and Findings* (Pacific Palisades, Calif.: Goodyear, 1976).

4. Dan Nimmo, *The Political Persuaders: The Techniques of Modern Election Campaigns* (Englewood Cliffs, N.J.: Prentice-Hall, 1970), pp. 12 ff.

5. The argument that voters respond to the available political stimuli is made with some effect by John Osgood Field and Ronald E. Anderson in "Ideology in the Public's Conceptualization of the 1964 Election," *Public Opinion Quarterly* 33 (1969): 380–98. Experimental evidence leading to a similar conclusion may be found in Donn Byrne, Michael H. Bond, and Michael J. Diamond, "Response to Political Candidates as a Function of Attitude Similarity-Dissimilarity," *Human Relations* 22 (1969): 251–62.

6. An extensive literature developed over some four decades has identified and evaluated a wide variety of sociological and social psychological influences on voting behavior. A few representative titles would include Paul F. Lazarsfeld, Bernard Berelson, and Hazel Gaudet, *The People's Choice* (New York: Duell, Sloan and Pearce, 1944); Angus Campbell, Gerald Gurin, and Warren E. Miller, *The Voter Decides* (Evanston, Ill.: Row, Peterson, 1954); Bernard R. Berelson, Paul F. Lazarsfeld, and William N. McPhee, *Voting: A Study of Opinion Formation in a Presidential Campaign* (Chicago: University of Chicago Press, 1954); Angus Campbell, Philip E. Converse, Warren E. Miller, and Donald E. Stokes, *The American Voter* (New York: John Wiley, 1960); idem, *Elections and the Political Order* (New York: John Wiley, 1966); and Norman H. Nie, Sidney Verba, and John R. Petrocik, *The Changing American Voter* (Cambridge, Mass.: Harvard University Press, 1976).

7. For a related argument on group identification as the basis for rational political action see Arthur S. Goldberg, "Social Determinism and Rationality as Bases of Party Identification," *American Political Science Review* 63 (1969): 5–25. See also Michael Hooper, "The Structure and Measurement of Social Identity," *Public Opinion Quarterly* 40 (1976): 154–64.

8. Gerald M. Pomper, "The Presidential Election," in Gerald M. Pomper et al., *The Election of 1980: Reports and Interpretations* (Chatham, N.J.: Chatham House, 1981), pp. 71–72. In most cases, the groups that define their common interest in alignment with the Republican party tend to be smaller and in a sense more elite than those which align with the Democrats, which is part of the reason for the fact that the Democratic party holds the allegiance of a majority of American voters. At the same time, however, the turnout rate (percentage of those registered actually voting) for Republican identifiers is generally much higher than that for potential Democratic voters, and as a consequence the natural imbalance between the two is frequently redressed at the

polls. The apparent shift toward the Republicans in recent elections among white southerners, Catholics, blue-collar workers, and those with a high school education may signal some realignment of these patterns. For an interesting treatment of related questions see Jerome M. Clubb, William H. Flanigan, and Nancy H. Zingale, *Partisan Realignment: Voters, Parties and Government in American History* (Beverly Hills: Sage, 1980).

9. Samuel A. Kirkpatrick, "Conflicts in Political Attitudes: Behavioral and Dynamic Consequences," in *The Social Psychology of Political Life*, ed. Samuel A. Kirkpatrick and Lawrence K. Pettit (Belmont, Calif.: Duxbury Press, 1972), pp. 342–59; presents an analysis of electoral decision-making in a balance theory framework. Kenneth W. Eckhardt and Gerry Hendershot, in "Dissonance-Congruence and the Perception of Public Opinion," *American Journal of Sociology* 73 (1967): 226–34, provide a discussion of the underlying relationship between personal opinion and the perception of group norms that bears directly on this point.

10. Paul R. Wieck, "McGovern's Jewish Problem," *The New Republic*, 1972, p. 19. Reprinted by permission of *The New Republic*, © 1972 Harrison-Blaine of New Jersey, Inc.

11. Berelson et al., *Voting*, p. 19, passim.

12. David R. Segal, *Society and Politics: Uniformity and Diversity in Modern Democracy* (Glenview, Ill.: Scott, Foresman, 1974), pp. 90–103.

13. Berelson et al., *Voting*, p. 27; and David R. Segal, "Status Inconsistency, Cross Pressures and American Political Behavior," *American Sociological Review* 34 (1969): 352–59. Cf. David L. George, "An Experimental Study of Attitudinal Conflict and Political Involvement in a Voting Context," *Experimental Study of Politics* 1 (1971): 35–64.

14. The differential persuasibility of various voters is summarized by Nimmo, *The Political Persuaders*, pp. 24 f.

15. The term, as well as an argument that electoral victory falls only to the political strategist who successfully claims the ideological middle ground, may be found in Richard M. Scammon and Ben J. Wattenberg, *The Real Majority* (New York: Berkeley, 1970), p. 19 et passim.

16. Nimmo, *The Political Persuaders*, pp. 165 ff.

17. Sigel, "Effect of Partisanship," passim. For related analysis, see Joseph E. McGrath and Marian F. McGrath, "Effects of Partisanship on Perceptions of Political Figures," *Public Opinion Quarterly* 26 (1962): 236–48, and Dan Nimmo and Robert L. Savage, "Political Images and Political Perceptions," *Experimental Study of Politics* 1 (1971): 1–36.

18. Carolyn W. Sherif, Muzafer Sherif, and Roger E. Nebergall, *Attitude and Attitude Change: The Social Judgment–Involvement Approach* (Philadelphia: W. B. Saunders, 1965), pp. 11–17, but especially p. 14, and Nimmo, *The Political Persuaders*, pp. 180–83.

19. The percentage of late deciders is drawn from William H. Flanigan and Nancy H. Zingale, *Political Behavior of the American Electorate* (4th ed.; Boston: Allyn and Bacon, 1979), pp. 170–75. Flanigan and Zingale

argue, however, that the association between time of decision and campaign involvement may be situation-specific.

20. See Goldberg, "Social Determinism and Rationality," passim, for a brief overview of this conflict and an attempt at synthesis. Michael J. Schapiro, in "Rational Political Man: A Synthesis of Economic and Social-Psychological Perspectives," *American Political Science Review* 63 (1969): 1106–19, deals with this problem as well. Two seminal works representative of the rational approach, though differing somewhat in perspective, are Anthony Downs, *An Economic Theory of Democracy* (New York: Harper & Row, 1957), and V. O. Key, Jr., *The Responsible Electorate* (Cambridge: Harvard University Press, Belknap Press, 1966). Note 6 above lists several works representative of the competing sociological and social psychological viewpoints.

21. Goldberg, "Social Determinism and Rationality," makes essentially the same argument though in somewhat different terms.

22. Nimmo, *The Political Persuaders*, pp. 183 ff.

23. Berelson et al., *Voting*, p. 25; and Campbell et al., *The American Voter*, pp. 475–81.

24. Nimmo, *The Political Persuaders*, pp. 114 f.; and Bruce H. Westley and Werner J. Severin, "A Profile of the Daily Newspaper Non-Reader," *Journalism Quarterly* 41 (1964): 45–50.

25. Nimmo, *The Political Persuaders*, pp. 183 ff.

8

Political Activity

A Framework
for Analysis

In the preceding pages we have focused our attention rather narrowly on one or another element in the attitude-behavior matrix. We have considered in some depth the structure and dynamics of attitudes, their cultural context, the ways in which they are acquired, and their importance in electoral politics. In the present chapter we shall attempt to broaden this perspective by presenting a wide-ranging conceptual overview of the whole of political activity in the hope that we may thereby provide the reader with a consistent framework for the reasoned analysis of many varieties of political behavior. For only in the context of such an analytical framework can one acquire a true appreciation of the indissoluble and indispensable relationship between political attitudes and political behavior.

The study of political activity can range from the consideration of a few overt acts such as voting, donating money to political causes, participating in activist groups, or simply talking about politics, to the analysis of all conscious or unconscious political thought and perception: The scope of the phenomenon is limited only by one's choice of definition. Similarly, the impact of political activity may be measured in terms of changes (or perceived changes) in the life situation of the individual, of alterations in the distribution of resources through a society, or of realignments of the political leadership, to name only a few of the more widely regarded outcomes of politics. Very often, however, overly particularistic discussions of one or another aspect of political activity tend to obscure a number of identifiable and recurrent characteristics that may be used to arrive at a more generalized conceptualization of all individual political behavior. Our purpose in the present chapter is to suggest the possible outlines of such a conceptualization.

THE SOURCES OF NONPARTICIPATION IN POLITICS

To begin with, we should recognize that just as there exist varieties of political *activity*, there exist varieties of political *inactivity*; just as there are participants in politics, there are nonparticipants as well. And while most of our discussion here will focus on the positive, or participatory, aspects of political activity, we should say a word at the outset about the negative, or nonparticipatory, aspects so that our later analysis may be understood in its proper context.

No single explanation can account for the adoption by an individual of minimal levels of political involvement. Indeed, political inactivity may derive from any of a large number of highly individualized experiences, some, all, or none of which might be expressly political in nature. Nevertheless, we are able to identify at least three underlying factors pertaining to choice and circumstance which may help us better to understand particular nonactive patterns of behavior. These factors include the ability, the opportunity, and the preference for participation in politics.

Many individuals, for example, may lack the time or the skills requisite for political activity in their particular society. They may, in a very real sense, be unable to engage in politics. A person who holds down two jobs to support a family, for instance, might be less able to become politically active than a well-paid professional worker—not because of any purposeful avoidance of or disinterest in political affairs but simply because he or she has less available leisure time to distribute among nonwork interests. Similarly, a person who is functionally illiterate or physically handicapped or an individual who has not had the opportunity to develop certain group activity skills may be reduced to a role of inactivity—not because of a negative inclination toward politics but because of a fundamental inability either to comprehend or to fully respond to political stimuli. And a person who is geographically isolated from the locus of political activity may be inactive not by choice but as a result of the greater effort required should he or she choose to become a participant. Thus one's ability to participate in politics may be limited by one's occupation, by the extent of one's education, or even by one's physical condition or location.[1]

Alternatively, individuals might engage in politics only to a minimal extent simply because they are not presented with the opportunity for greater participation, and more particularly because they neither possess nor come into contact with politically relevant information.[2] Some people, principally the less affluent, the less educated, and the young, may simply not be exposed to politics very much in the course of their everyday lives and may have a relatively limited storehouse of politically relevant cognitions.[3] And it should be clear from our earlier discussion that in the absence of such external and internal stimuli few individuals are likely to become politically active. Indeed, the paucity of informational stimuli results in a kind of psychopolitical inertia that tends to be reinforced to the extent that an individual's personality and preferences fail to push him or her into initiating political activity. For political involvement requires of an individual a certain degree of gregariousness, a certain willingness and ability to engage in social intercourse, and those who lack either the substantive understanding or the inclination to comply with this requirement may be excluded from the process less by conscious selection than as a matter of course.[4]

Finally, political nonparticipation can result from a variety of affective and cognitive psychological factors, including apathy, anomie, and a low sense of one's political efficacy. As we shall see, each of these attitudinal conditions differs from the absence of an ability or an opportunity to engage in politics in that each reflects a purposeful devaluation—either relative or absolute—of political participation as an attitude object in its own right.

The first of these psychological factors, apathy, refers most simply to an absence of concern with the outcomes of political affairs. The apathetic individual is in effect the end case of the low-involvement political actor of whom we have spoken earlier. He (or she) makes no political judgments, establishes no political preferences, and maintains no stake in the flow of political events. He remains, in other words, politically inert. If he is cynical by nature, he may evolve to a state of alienation; if he is lazy by nature, to a less purposeful state of aloofness. In either event, he will disparage political activity as an undertaking of dubious utility.[5]

Closely related to the apathetic individual, but perhaps less extreme in degree, is the individual who, while not deprecating political activity per se, nevertheless attaches relatively little importance to opportunities for political endeavor. We speak here of that individual who, while not rejecting a role in political life, displays only minimal interest in the process of politics. Thus given a choice between going bowling or viewing a political documentary, such an individual might select the former simply because she enjoys bowling more than she enjoys political documentaries. Given a choice between sleeping late on Sunday morning or attending a campaign rally, such an individual might prefer sleeping in bed to sleeping through the ebb and flow of political oratory. Since for most adults political activity is by and large an elective leisure-time behavior, and since as a consequence it must compete for time with other leisure-time outlets, the disinterested individual may simply assign to her opportunities for political involvement a comparatively low priority. In this way, political abstinence may result less from an overwhelmingly negative view of politics itself than from a willingness to bear political inactivity as an acceptable cost of engaging in some other and more worthwhile behavior.[6]

The second psychological element, *anomie*, refers to a state of mind of an individual who senses that life—or in our case political life—is passing him (or her) by. He feels that he is adrift, that he is unable to anchor himself to the political system, and that the established political life of his society offers him no firm rules appropriate for the guidance of his own personal course. Stating this another way, the understandings of politics conveyed by his society, which is to say its political culture, are no longer accepted by the individual as valid. The symbols of politics no longer seem to relate to the realities of politics as he perceives them. Thus anomie may reflect either disillusionment with or dissociation from the political culture. It represents a breakdown in the psychological and symbolic linkage between the individual and his society, a breakdown that may be learned by the individual (in the socialization sense) or that may result from more basic elements of the individual's personality.[7] In either event, the anomic individual will withdraw from politics because politics itself takes on no meaning.

And finally, the activity of an individual with a *low sense of political efficacy* is likely to remain minimal. The term "sense of political efficacy" refers to one's feeling of her (or his) own political potency, to her beliefs regarding her ability to have an impact upon, if not to manipulate, political events. Thus a person who does not believe that her vote counts may be unlikely to cast it. One who feels that policy makers are unresponsive to her wishes may be disinclined to make those wishes known. The citizen who holds her own understanding of political affairs in low esteem may be unwilling to express herself. And more generally, the individual who, almost regardless of her interest in politics or her acceptance of the importance of political activity, feels that she is unable to influence the forces that affect her political well-being may be expected to display patterns of inactivity, for she may well perceive the potential benefits to be derived from affirmative action as few and insignificant.[8] In some individuals this sense of powerlessness combines with anomie and with a sense of political isolation—a feeling that one's own political preferences differ markedly from those that predominate in one's community—to produce a condition commonly termed *alienation*, in which the individual purposefully rejects political activity and withdraws from political life.[9]

Political nonparticipation, then, is a rather complex phenomenon rooted in both the social and the psychological conditions of any particular individual. Inactivity may be elective, or it may result de facto from related nonpolitical outlooks and orientations. It may be a matter of choice or a matter of circumstance. But whichever is the case, political inactivity has its source in the development and configuration of the social and political attitudes of the individual. And whichever is the case, the breadth and intensity with which political nonparticipation is distributed through a population act, as components of the political culture, to increase or to reduce the freedom of movement of the political leadership of that population. For the more quiescent its citizens, the greater the extent to which they opt for modes of nonparticipation, the greater the number and diversity of viable policy options that are available to a government. And conversely: The more diligent and involved its citizens, the more restricted its choices.

Like the various dimensions of nonparticipation, the more positive aspects of political activity may be seen to derive from the underlying attitude structure of the individual as well. The decision to act and the selection of a particular type of activity reflect the predispositions of the individual—which is to say, his or her attitudes. In order that we may understand this bond between attitude and behavior, however, it will be necessary to employ a rather more complex analytical framework than that we have applied to nonparticipation. In the discussion that follows, therefore, we shall identify and examine at some length three dimensions that may be seen to underlie virtually all instances of affirmative political activity: the *motive* that gives rise to a particular undertaking, the *mode* in which the activity is conducted, and the actual *substantive character* of the behavior in question; or, in reverse order, what is done, how, and to what purpose.

In discussing each of these three dimensions of political participation, we shall present an extended series of matched pairs of alternatives each of which should suggest particular aspects of the more general theme. Thus we may speak of the motive behind a particular activity as being either accidental or purposive, the mode of that behavior as being concrete or symbolic, and the substance of the behavior as being ideological or nonideological. In each instance our purpose is simply to suggest various analytical continua along which one might conceptualize the activity in question. And beyond that, our purpose is to suggest, first, that each of these sets of alternatives has a basis in the attitude structure of the individual, and second, that each represents a way of classifying political activity which can be applied toward achieving a better systematic understanding of many widely differing varieties of political behavior. But while it is hoped that each series of alternatives will prove reasonably comprehensive in suggesting the scope of the dimension in question, these lists should by no means be taken as complete. To the contrary, they are meant only to indicate to the reader some few of the myriad possible ways of organizing and understanding the complexities of political behavior. With that in mind, let us proceed to our analysis of the motives, modes, and substance of political activity.

MOTIVES FOR POLITICAL ACTIVITY

Motivation is the energizing force behind human behavior, the "why" that fuels political as well as other endeavors. Motivation provides the impetus, the psychological equivalent of a kick in the pants, that leads us to engage in political kinds of interaction with our social environment. Motivation, whether acquired through a process of socialization or sensed instinctively, creates within us a need or a desire to become politically involved. Thus motivation must be a key element in the structure of any political behavior. But the unfortunate fact is that at present less is known about the actual nature of motivation than about its importance. Indeed, psychologists, who themselves have several schools of thought on the subject, would be the first to admit that the phenomenon of motivation is highly complex and not yet fully understood in an analytical sense.[10] Nevertheless, we are able to suggest a series of descriptive characteristics that should enable us to identify certain distinctive aspects of the many motives that underlie political activity and to draw from these a strong intuitive sense of the nature and role of political motivation. Let us consider several such aspects.

Accidental vs. Purposive

The first way in which we might differentiate the motives under-lying a series of political acts is to assess the degree to which each act is a result of clear purpose. Here we are in effect asking whether there really exists an identifiable political motive for a par-ticular political act. For example, consider a man who has made a trip to a local shopping center to purchase a pair of shoes at a time of year that happens to coincide with an election campaign period. While walking down the mall with his mind on shoes and his attention fixed on a nearby store window, this individual is politely accosted by a young woman whose outstretched hand offers him an item of political advertising—say, anything from a button to a booklet. Without thinking, reflexively, he reaches out, accepts the proffered propaganda, and perhaps glances at it, noting the candidate's message. As he realizes what has happened, he discards the item—or better yet stuffs it into a coat pocket only to wonder what it is when he goes to discard it at a later time. Once, perhaps twice, the man has engaged in a political act—exposure to campaign communication—though his actions were clearly reflex-ive and devoid of political intent. In such instances, it is not the attitudes of the individual that lead him into political endeavor, but rather the accidents of circumstance.

On the other hand, one can readily imagine a second man who, finding himself in the same situation, notices and actively seeks out the distributors of campaign information in order that he may involve himself in the political process. Indeed, perhaps he chose to shop on this particular day or at this particular shopping center precisely because he anticipated that this sort of opportunity for involvement might present itself. This second individual has performed the same act as the first—exposure to campaign com-munication—but with a significantly greater degree of intent; his *attitudes* have led him into an exchange with the political system. Thus varying degrees of purposefulness may characterize the motivation of a given individual to engage in a variety of political activities.[11]

Directed vs. Undirected

Just as political behavior may be accidental or purposive, it may also be directed at the attainment of some political goal, either spe-cific or general, or it may be independent of such direction. That is, one has the option of engaging in political activity with some ultimate achievement in mind, whether for the immediate future or the longer term, or of politicizing without such an aim in mind. And to the extent that one permits goals or value preferences to lead one into participating, one's activities are guided by his or her underlying attitude structure.[12] The substance of the goals that political activity might be employed to attain covers a wide range, but such goals can generally be conceived of as including the acquisition of some social, political, economic, or psychological advantage, either for oneself, one's community, or one's special-interest group. Thus increasing one's sense of physical or economic security, or obtaining a voice in the policy-making process, or strengthening the military position of one's country, or dealing with economic deprivation—or any of a long list of other ends—can be thought of as giving direction to a given act or set of acts.

We would no doubt expect consistently directed political behavior to be most common among individuals the substance of whose attitudes could be characterized as ideological or programmatic, people who are aware of and adhere to a consistent orientation in their beliefs and attitudes.[13] But we may also find such consistencies among those individuals representing certain personality types (for example, the so-called "authoritarian" and "conservative" personalities) and, of course, among those with mutually reinforcing socialization experiences (consistent lessons learned from a variety of socializing agents).[14] In contrast, we might anticipate an absence of goal direction in the actions of persons whose interest or psychological involvement in politics is relatively low, or whose patterns of thought tend not to be organized along salient political dimensions.[15] Here we might find such vague motives as, "I did it because it seemed the thing to do," or, "It didn't seem to matter much one way or the other, so I did it." Often in such cases the individual in question may in fact have a latent goal, but one that is nonpolitical in nature. "He was such a nice person that I did as he asked." Responses of this sort may reflect attempts to reduce cognitive imbalance by shifting the decision criteria, or they may be directly responsive to perceived communicator characteristics such as credibility. But while such motives are certainly identifiable, they are not substantively political, and they may therefore be differentiated in the present analysis.

Rational vs. Emotional

A third element in the motivation underlying political behavior is the mix of rational thinking and emotional response which gives rise to a particular activity. In the ideal or definitional case of rational behavior, an individual is motivated by a desire to maximize personal advantage and/or minimize disadvantage relative either to some defined goal or, more simply, to her condition immediately prior to initiating the behavior in question. In other words, an individual who is acting for reasons of rationality evaluates her options, ascertains the direction in which her best interests lie, decides which behavior will enable her to move in that direction, and behaves accordingly. She applies her preferences to her perceptions, and proceeds as indicated. In short, she thinks before she acts.

As we have noted earlier (Chapter 7), rational-man models are often applied by political scientists in an attempt to understand and explain voting behavior. In these models, voters are seen as weighing electoral choices in the context of their own needs, and then voting so as to maximize their subsequent positions. While the concept of motivation is often subordinated in these analyses to that of modes or styles of decision making, the linkage is nonetheless significant.

Many political actions, however, are governed less by reason than by emotion or conditioning, though in such instances a subsequent process of "rationalizing" one's behavior may ensue as a form of psychological reinforcement.[16] That is, once an individual has become emotionally committed to a particular action or point of view, he may attempt, as would be predicted by several of the attitude-change theories we mentioned earlier (Chapter 6), to realign his remaining attitudes, beliefs, and perceptions so as to reflect and support his new commitment. Thus if an individual were forced into an act of political violence under intense emotional pressure, he might later develop an extensive rationale supporting the logic of that act. Similarly, one might develop an emotional bond with a charismatic public figure and subsequently construct a set of attitudes that makes this gut response appear "reasonable." In general, such emotions as love, awe, trust, faith, fear, hatred, and outrage frequently provide nonrational or irrational bases for political behavior.

Psychological Need vs. Social Need

Yet another set of alternatives for understanding the impetus to political behavior lies with the locus of arousal, and more particularly with the question of whether the need to act arises from internal or external pressures.[17] Needless to say, considerable overlap exists between the social and psychological conditions of the individual and the resulting pressures for action. Indeed, the substance and the stability of political attitudes are based largely on social experience and social support, respectively. But if we keep that fact in mind, we may still hope to distinguish between those drives that arise principally from internal stimuli such as personality traits or perceptions of cognitive imbalance and those that arise in response to external, presumably social, stimuli. Thus if an individual performs a given act because she feels the need to be honest in all her dealings, or because she feels that she must relate to all authority figures in a certain way, or because she senses that this act is consistent with her attitudes, we may consider her response to have been initiated by internal pressures. If, on the other hand, she responds in order to affect her own position vis-à-vis some other individual or reference group, or to affect the position of that individual or group with relation to still others in the society (or indeed to the society itself), we may then consider her response to have been motivated externally.[18] The distinction we drew between cross-pressuring and status inconsistency in Chapter 7 is a case in point. In essence, then, the difference between responding to internal and to external needs represents a difference in the attitude objects an individual chooses to employ in his or her understanding of a particular political activity.

Initiated by Self vs. Initiated by Others

The fifth element in our analysis arises from the fact that the motivation to act must at some stage include a choice of appropriate behaviors.[19] And the particular set of activities undertaken by an individual who feels himself under either internal or external pressure may have been selected by the individual, or, particularly when external pressure is a factor, it may have been suggested by others to whom he relates. That is, the individual may decide for himself what forms of political activity he will engage in, or he may acquiesce in the decisions of others who serve as opinion or activity leaders. These alternatives are especially important in the context of our earlier discussion, for it we take self-selection to imply greater psychological involvement with one's actions, we may hypothesize that when actions are the result of the individual's evaluation of his situation, his commitment, and his emotional attachment to them, as well as his personal identification with their consequences, they will be of greater significance to him than would be the case with actions determined otherwise.[20] In other words, if an individual has himself consciously served as the predominant force in determining his own actions, we could expect him to be both more interested in those actions themselves and more heavily influenced by their outcomes. Thus self-initiation of political behavior may provide a significantly stronger and more enduring motivation than might an outside impetus.

Manifest vs. Latent

Finally, we should note in this regard that an individual may be either aware or unaware of his own motives. Particularly when he acts unintentionally, without direction, without rationale, or at the suggestion of others, he may be unable to explain why he has chosen a particular behavior.[21] And while we might expect to encounter this phenomenon in situations where the consequences of behavior are minimal—as, for example, when the candidate preferences of low-involvement voters are influenced through low-participation media—neither is it uncommon in situations where the consequences of political action may be somewhat more significant. An example is the individual who, carried along by the momentum of events, finds himself participating in an eruption of mindless mass violence. He may have intended no violence; he may in fact reject violence as a political form. Yet he finds himself swept up in a wave of unthinking behavior. In such instances, where an individual may well be unaware of the forces driving him, we can speak of those forces or motives as being latent. In contrast, when an individual is actively engaged in selecting and directing his own behavior, his motives are raised to the level of consciousness, and we may speak of those motives as being manifest.

Our purpose in this section has not been to provide an analysis of the particular motivations that lead an individual to undertake particular kinds of political activity. The varieties of motivation and the varieties of political activity are far too numerous to permit such an undertaking here. Instead, our purpose has been to suggest some rather general ways in which one might think about *all* motivations and *all* political activities, for in that direction lies a much broader understanding of politics. The objects of motivation may include power, prestige, security, cognitive consistency, rain in Kansas, or any of the other real or imagined values toward which an individual might aspire or with which he or she might otherwise relate. And the styles of political activity are almost as profuse. But regardless of the object of any particular motive and regardless of the substance of the associated behavior, both motive and action may be subjected to analysis in terms of the categories suggested above. In this way, we may hope to find an underlying structure which will enable us to relate political attitudes to political behaviors in a systematic and meaningful fashion.

MODES OF POLITICAL ACTIVITY

The second dimension of political activity with which we shall be concerned is what we might term the mode, or the style, of behavior. The mode of political behavior refers to the types of actions in which we choose to engage.[22] In essence, having investigated why we behave as we do, we must now examine precisely how it is that we behave. The specific acts concerning us here again form a lengthy list: voting, thinking about politics, contributing money to a campaign, expressing a political preference, running for or holding public office, picketing, political assassination, sabotage, acts of war, conciliation, and on and on.[23] The possibilities are manifold, to be sure. But as before, let us focus our examination not on these specific manifestations of political activism, but rather on those characteristics that may allow us some basis of comparison across them all. And to this end, let us once again employ a series of behavioral alternatives that relate variously to the fundamental nature of political actions, their physical manifestations, and the degree to which the individual participates in them. In this way we may be able to indicate certain common elements in a wide variety of political undertakings.

Actual vs. Vicarious

The first question that arises in a consideration of modes of political behavior is whether a given instance of participation in politics is real—in the sense of involving true interpersonal relationships—or whether that participation is simply an act of fantasy. Most simply, one has the option, particularly in this technological age, of entering into actual physical relationships with political reality—by voting, going out and seeing or meeting with public figures, organizing political action groups, and a host of other means—or of experiencing politics largely in one's imagination—as by merely watching election returns on television while believing one has been a part of the process, by fantasizing personal relationships with political leaders, by sympathizing with yet avoiding active participation in political groups, and so forth. One of course does participate in political activity merely by watching, by fantasizing, by sympathizing, or in general by pretending that one is in the thick of things, but it is participation of a different order, of a different quality, than that which demands actual physical involvement.[24] Indeed, if significant numbers of individuals within a given system choose to relate to political life by substitution—as, for example, by merely observing the drama of politics on television—feeling all the while that they are in fact discharging the rights and duties of citizenship, then popular control of that political system may be weakened as a result of reduced vigilance. And over time this effect may be greatly amplified by the decline of real-world experience as a standard against which to evaluate messages received from such agents of vicarious participation as the electronic mass media. Taken at the level of the political culture, then, the aggregate of individual preferences for real versus vicarious political involvement can have significant consequences for the quality of political life in a society.[25]

Concrete vs. Symbolic

Our second set of criteria for differentiating among the modes of political endeavor—that pertaining to the symbolic content of such endeavor—is closely related to the selection of active versus vicarious involvement. For as we noted in the introductory chapter, just as acts of political behavior may be real or imagined, their impact, as determined both by style and by substance, may be tangible or intangible, concrete or symbolic. In the first instance, one might opt for a mode of behavior which pertains to a physical good or service such as money, obedience to laws, or subjugation of oneself to military authority. An example of the second would be adopting a style that coveys a symbolic good or service such as loyalty or patriotism. And of course, a given act can convey both concrete and symbolic values.[26] The point is that one possesses the option to operate in either or both of two distinct political realms, and the combination of the two that is present in any particular political action can provide a meaningful basis for characterizing and understanding that action.

Individual Behavior vs. Group Behavior

A third set of characteristics by which we may categorize political behavior relates to the extent to which that behavior is socially directed. When engaging in political activity, an individual may choose either to act alone or to act in concert with others.[27] That decision may be based upon the exigencies of the situation, upon various personality traits (gregariousness, for example), or upon various attitudinal preferences, including the group identifications of the individual in question. Thus individual perception, inclination, and preference contribute to the selection of behavioral modes here as elsewhere. At the same time, however, we have seen in an earlier chapter that to some extent reliance upon group action is a norm that is peculiar to (and reinforced by) particular political cultures. Thus individual differences notwithstanding, we could expect a citizen of the United States (where the emphasis upon collective action is a central theme of the political culture) to be much more likely than his counterpart in a country such as Italy (where the political culture lacks a group orientation) to prefer a group approach to political activity.[28] In many instances the physical and psychological costs of group activity may be lower than those of individual activity, in part because failure can be rationalized as attaching to the group and can thus be depersonalized, whereas the benefits of collective action may be at least equal to or, in a culture context that supports group action, perhaps even greater than those of individual endeavor.

Once the decision has been made to participate in collective action, the individual must select for himself, a role of leadership or one of subordination. Often this choice is made for him, either by the circumstances that led him to choose collective action (e.g., the prior existence of a relevant political group) or by the preferences of others who share his interest in group action and who, by exercise of their own personal prerogatives, thrust either him or themselves into positions of leadership. This selection process may be further influenced by a collective determination of the requisites for leadership and by the distribution of free time, leadership skills, personality traits, preferences, and other resources among the membership or potential membership of the group in question.[29] The psychological costs of leadership are probably somewhat greater than those of following, particularly since the leader cannot easily dissociate himself from unsuccessful group action, but the personal rewards of successful leadership may be commensurately greater as well.

The nature of group activity itself can have a significant influence on the quality of the participation of its individual members. For example, a group that is tightly organized in its approach to political action can structure and direct the activities of its members in order to maximize efforts to attain group goals, while a group that is more loosely organized leaves more room for individual variation in terms of both the amount and the type of political participation. Typical of the former might be Common Cause, the so-called citizens' lobby, which regularly attempts to mobilize its membership for specific purposes ("tasks"); while the latter might be typified by ad hoc community-action groups whose memberships share common goals but exhibit little systematic structure and exercise minimal control over members' actions. Still a third option may be found in affiliation with a group that seeks a broad base of support for a relatively small group of active participants. One such group is Public Citizen, Inc., Ralph Nader's coordinating organization, which seeks public support for the efforts of a few consumer advocates. Association with a group of this type is neither very demanding nor very costly in terms of precluding behavioral options. To summarize, then, individuals may accept or reject collective political action, and in the event that they opt for a group approach the structure of the particular group with which they choose to associate may have a significant impact upon the nature and scope of their political participation.

Systematic vs. Random

Whether a person engages in individual or in group activity, a further characteristic of his or her mode of political participation is the degree to which that participation itself is organized. Here we are interested not in isolated acts of political behavior that an individual might carry out, but rather in the relationship (if any) among many different acts. In rather general terms, we may think of multiple acts of political behavior as displaying greater or lesser degrees of coherence and consistency that allow us to speak of "patterns" of behavior. The greater the coherence and consistency of an individual's various political actions, the more justified we are in referring to them as systematic (and, incidentally, the better able we are to predict them accurately), whereas the limiting case in the opposite direction would be pure randomness and total unpredictability.

We can identify at least three different but closely related factors that influence the organization of political action by a given individual. The first of these is the extent to which political behavior reflects an associated and tightly organized attitude cluster of the type we discussed in Chapter 2. Where the attitudes that give rise to an individual's political activity are consistent, salient, and consciously held, and where the relationship between these attitudes and the available behavioral options is clear to the individual (conation), we can expect such attitudes to provide systematic guidance to the choice of political actions. Where such attitude clusters are more loosely organized, or where the particular attitudes in question fail to meet the other standards we have set forth, less systematic behavior may result.[30]

The second factor that may influence the organization of political activity is in a sense a special case of the first. Here we refer to the extent to which any set of political activities is planned as opposed to resulting from impulse. By definition, the existence of a plan, a framework for action, indicates systematic behavior, or at least premeditation. Since a plan is simply a linkage of the various elements of a whole one to another, an individual who behaves according to a plan must have at least some perception of the whole at the outset and must have derived his or her plan from a relatively organized evaluation of the situation and the alternatives. In contrast, impulsive behavior need only be as consistent as the emotions that give rise to the impulse or the stimuli that activate those emotions.[31]

Implicit in the above analysis is the third factor influencing the extent of systematic behavior—the role performed by goals. For if an individual has a particular goal in mind, then all actions that are instrumental to achieving that goal will be systematic, while actions that are either ancillary or extraneous to achievement of the goal are at least potentially random. That is to say, if a given action is directed toward some identifiable purpose, it will fit into a pattern with all other actions directed toward that same end; but where political action is without clear direction or purpose, it may prove to be random (though it may also result from a pattern of personality traits which has not been considered by the observer in the search for goal orientation).

Overt vs. Covert

Viewed from yet another perspective, the mode of political participation may be described as more or less open, more or less concealed. Particularly when an individual is acting contrary to what she perceives to be the dominant views of her peers or her community, she may prefer private rather than public forms of political action such as membership in a secret organization or writing anonymous political letters. Clearly, covert political activity of this sort offers fewer options than does overt activity, and in certain circumstances there exists a risk that discovery may magnify the apparent differences between the individual and his reference group. Thus with the possible exception of those individuals who adopt covert political behavior for reasons of personality (shyness, uncertainty), we might expect to find only those individuals who are relatively highly politicized engaging in clandestine forms of participation. Where the views of the individual are consonant with those of her peers or her community, however, and where personality factors do not lead her to seek anonymity, a more open approach to political activity may prove not only more likely but more desirable for the individual as well, for such activity often carries with it a variety of social rewards.[32]

Involving vs. Noninvolving

Underlying much of our discussion of modes of participation to this point has been one factor that deserves to be brought to the fore—namely, the willingness of the individual to become actively and personally involved in the political process. Clearly it is possible to be active in politics and yet not "involved" in the sense we used the term in Chapter 6. One may, for example, be a follower of cultural patterns and group initiatives, a steady participant and perhaps a "model citizen," and may yet remain aloof from the process. One may be an intellectual political activist and yet remain emotionally uncommitted, above the fray. Indeed, we have seen one consequence of this lack of psychological involvement earlier in our discussion of elections and campaigning. The point that should be emphasized here, however, is that the meaning that the individual herself attaches to her own participation in politics and the degree to which she internalizes her experience (relates it to her attitude structure) may be largely dependent upon her feelings of involvement—of investing a part of her own psychological well-being—in her activities. Only to the extent that this investment of self is undertaken will the mode of political participation assume personal significance.

Active vs. Passive

Very closely related to the notion of personal involvement in political activity is our final consideration regarding the modes of political behavior—the extent to which one is willing to engage actively in such endeavors. Generally speaking, the level of political activity assumed by an individual may be viewed in qualitative, quantitative, or temporal terms.[33] Qualitatively, an individual may choose to put her best efforts into her political activity, or she may prefer to coast. She may strive for excellence or perfection in her behavior, or she may satisfy herself with an indifferent performance. When an individual is highly emotionally involved in her participation, as when she becomes a fervent advocate for some candidate or political movement, she is more likely to concentrate her efforts than when her concern is less intensely personalized. At the same time, we may expect an individual who is either highly motivated or highly politicized to put forth a maximal *quantitative* effort as well: We may, in other words, expect her to do more. People will not only perform better but they will perform more frequently when they are stimulated in this manner.

Along these same lines, individuals differ in how they choose to distribute the time during which they engage in political activities. Without carrying the analogy between political participation and illness too far, let us borrow from medical science the notions of "acute" and "chronic" to describe the alternatives.[34] On the one hand, an individual may choose to concentrate his political activity in short and possibly (though not necessarily) intensive bursts, moving in and out of politics as the mood strikes him. The political participation of such an individual could be described as an *acute* phenomenon, one confined to relatively limited and more or less clearly delineated periods of time. The marginal voter who becomes interested in politics shortly before a presidential election, perhaps casts his ballot or even campaigns for a candidate, and then returns to political hybernation for another four years would exemplify acute political participation. In contrast to this style or mode of behavior, an individual might choose to participate in politics more or less continuously over an extended period of time. And even though the level of activity assumed by such an individual might at no time exceed the peak levels of activity achieved by the acute participant—it could in fact be considerably lower—his cumulative participation over time might be far greater.[35] Maintaining such a consistent level of political activity, no matter how high or how low the level, can be described as a *chronic* mode of political participation. Thus in selecting a style of political behavior, the individual may distribute the quality, number, and timing of his efforts as he sees fit, and in analyzing his behavior we may employ these same categories for explanatory purposes.

These, then, are several criteria we might use to differentiate among a variety of political styles. These modal characteristics may be seen to underlie many different types of political endeavor, and in many cases to provide an important link between the substance of the political activity, on the one hand, and the personality and attitudes of the individual on the other.

THE SUBSTANCE OF POLITICAL ACTIVITY

Thus far in our discussion, we have focused on what might be termed the procedural aspects of political participation, the mechanics of how and why an individual acts in a particular situation. In this context, we have investigated both the choice of political action in general and the selection of particular behavioral tactics. Yet no analysis of political activity would be complete that did not include some effort to understand not only the form but the substance of participation. For as we suggested in our introductory chapter, we must be able to ascertain not only the mechanics of political behavior but its meaning as well, both for the individual who engages in particular activities and for the political system within which he or she operates. We must be able to assess the symbolic aspects of political actions as well as their physical manifestations. It is to this task that we turn in the remainder of the present chapter, again with an eye toward generalization and broadly applicable description, and again with the aid of several illustrative sets of alternatives.

Functional vs. Dysfunctional

We may begin this final phase of our analysis by considering those situations in which an individual directs personal activities toward some goal. It should be clear that in any such instance, any particular action might either facilitate or impede the attainment of the goal in question. Thus not only may the motivation for a particular act be (for example) rational or nonrational, directed or undirected, and not only may the mode of that act be systematic or random, but in particular situations both the symbolic and real content of the act itself may prove either functional or dysfunctional to the individual performing that act. For instance, the act of voting in an election in the United States, which may be viewed as a symbolic statement of one's willingness to accept and abide by the processes of a democratic political system, might be functional for an individual who seeks the goal of maintaining a stable democracy. But that same act would most assuredly impede progress toward the alternative goal of overthrowing the existing political order. Alternatively, some would argue that voting in an election in the

Soviet Union serves to legitimize a nondemocratic system, while withholding one's vote might in some small way help to bring on true democracy.[36] Thus the same act can be functional for one person or under one set of circumstances and dysfunctional for another person or under different circumstances. There is nothing intrinsic in the act itself which makes it equally potent or equally valuable in all cases. Rather, it is the combination of the individual, his or her goals, the act, and the circumstance that determines the functional value of any given instance of political behavior.

Satisfying vs. Unsatisfying

Almost regardless of its functional aspects, however, an act of political behavior may prove more or less satisfying to the individual who performs it, for satisfaction is a product not only of the reasoned goals of an individual but of his emotional state as well. Depending on whether he seeks rational or emotional ends, or whether he simply values participation itself, an individual may feel more or less pleased with himself as a result of engaging in any particular activity.[37] If one votes for a candidate whom he perceives only as the lesser of two evils, for example, he may derive little pleasure from his actions; and should that candidate win election, the individual may feel little gratification and little sense of personal accomplishment. If one is acting out of clear preference, on the other hand, his act (voting) has the potential of providing great satisfaction. Thus the election of a candidate whom one actively favors and supports can prove a source of elation, of system affect, and of a sense of political efficacy. Success, in fact, becomes an important consideration here, for an individual is naturally more satisfied when he can regard his actions as having measured up to whatever standards of accomplishment he has established for himself than he is when he senses failure. It may be an absence of just such personally satisfying experiences in the socialization of particular individuals that leads them to withdraw from political life.

Partisan vs. Nonpartisan

Yet another element in the substance or meaning of a political act, again based in the attitude structure of the individual, is the degree of partisanship which is associated with that act. The term *partisanship* is used rather broadly here to include not only those activities of an individual which arise from and/or relate to his identification with a political party, but more generally to those which result from or relate to his association with any kind of political group. Thus an action taken in behalf of an interest group attempting to influence a political party is in this view considered equally as partisan as an activity undertaken in behalf of the party itself. In other words, it is the relative importance of *group considerations* in the decision-making process leading to a given behavior that concerns us here. The substance of a political activity can be determined by or in behalf of a group to serve the presumed common good; or it can be determined by or in behalf of the individual himself, in which case its impact may accrue more directly to his benefit. One may accept and aspire to group goals and judge one's actions accordingly, or one may accept and aspire to one's own goals and apply a rather different standard, one that suggests alternative meanings for particular activities.[38] Thus a person might consciously act in concert with partisan or group goals—as when she writes letters to various public officials at the suggestion of some interest group—or she may act independently and write similar letters on her own initiative and for her own reasons. While each behavior is physically identical, each may be construed rather differently: The meaning of each behavior varies according to the context in which it is perceived.

Ideological vs. Nonideological

Just as the degree of partisanship underlying political acts may vary, the ideological content of those acts is also subject to fluctuation. An individual may, for instance, select behaviors for either well-thought-out ideological reasons or for emotionally demanded ideological reasons, as a nonideological yet reasoned response to the exigencies of a particular situation, or as a nonideological yet emotional response to particular circumstances. And as the motivation for a particular action varies, the meaning of that action for the individual may vary correspondingly. Some evidence indicates that the degree of ideological content of political behavior may itself be a response principally to the available political stimuli rather than to some internal living driving force. That is to say, ideological content may often be at least as much a function of externally controlled selective exposure as of internally directed selective perception. For example, voters in the 1964 presidential contest between Johnson and Goldwater, which offered relatively more and clearer ideological cues than do most elections in the United States, were apparently more likely to view that electoral situation in ideological terms than are most American voters in most presidential elections.[39] At the same time, the number of Americans who maintain systems of beliefs consistently structured according to what might be considered ideological patterns remains relatively low (according to one estimate, the proportion is below the 10 percent level).[40] Ideological substance in political activity, then, may be peculiar to a given situation rather than simply to a particular individual, although it remains a significant element in the meanings that will attach to the activity in question.

Licit vs. Illicit

Viewed from yet another perspective, that of the society as a whole, the substance of political activity may be seen to lie either within or outside the bounds of acceptable behavior established by that society and incorporated into its political culture. Licit (socially acceptable) behavior may be legal (voting) or extralegal (thinking about politics), but in either case the individual who engages in such behavior generally feels free to adopt an overt mode. Indeed, as we have suggested earlier, political activity that has been sanctioned by one's society tends to be both easier and more socially rewarding than that which is proscribed. Illicit behavior, on the other hand, is subject to both legal and social restraints, and is therefore quite likely to be covert in mode. Examples of illicit political activity include acts of sabotage and participation in an outlawed and/or unpopular party or political movement.

Continuative vs. Disruptive

Along the same lines, political activity may serve either to maintain or to disrupt the existing political order or the relationship of the individual to that order (his or her adherence to the political culture). This is, by engaging in a particular action one may advance either the status of the political system itself or one's role in it (at the symbolic level, for example, the act of voting accomplishes both); or one may lessen either the effectiveness of the system or the strength of the bonds tying him to it (as by openly rejecting the dominant structure of political myths). In either event, the effect of the behavior upon the system becomes an important part of its meaning. One popular theory contends that system-disruptive behavior comes about when an individual or group reaches a high level of what is termed *relative deprivation*. In simplified terms, this argument holds that there exists in people's minds a threshold of dissatisfaction, and that when an individual perceives his own social, political, or economic goals as realistically beyond reach, he is pushed by the force of his perception toward, and ultimately across, that threshold: He is drawn into a pattern of behavior that seeks to disrupt the status quo, which is seen as working to his disadvantage. Basically, then, this theory views disruptive behavior as a function of psychological pressures.[41]

Supportive vs. Demanding

Finally, and again from the perspective of the whole society, any particular political action on the part of an individual *may* have the effect of either providing support (in a sense, "fuel") for the political system or placing demands upon it. Such activities as paying taxes, voting in elections, and serving in the armed forces provide the political system with the physical, symbolic, and human resources that it requires in order to function effectively. In contrast, such acts as petitioning for particular allocations of goods and services (a school or a traffic light, for instance), lobbying for a particular set of laws or regulations, and demonstrating for the very right to participate in the political process constitute demands upon the system, pressures that require some response by others within the system.[42] Thus the relationship between the individual and the political system is a two-way relationship involving both give and take, and any particular action may be representative of one or the other. As a result, in assessing the meaning of any political act we must view that act in the larger social context as well as in personal psychological terms. For the substance of individual political action in a given instance must be understood not only as an isolated act of an isolated individual but as a linkage between that individual and his political environment as well.

IN SUMMARY

This final dichotomy concludes our analysis of the particulars of motive, mode, and substance in political action. The more general problem of understanding political behavior, however, requires further comment. For if one point emerges from our discussion of these three dimensions of political participation, it must be that the quality of individual political activity is inseparably bound to the attitudinal propensities and personality configurations of the individual. The affective associations (value and preference structures) and the beliefs that an individual brings to a particular situation interact with the stimuli provided by the situation itself to guide him or her into various patterns of behavior. And on the cutting edge of this interaction we find the third element in the attitudinal equation. For we can see now that the evaluation of behavioral alternatives we earlier labeled conation is a complex process indeed, one that involves the intertwining of unique combinations of personal preferences and characteristics with complicated situational stimuli. And we can further see that by structuring as they do an individual's responses to behavioral stimuli, attitudes truly serve as the building blocks of political behavior.

SUGGESTIONS FOR FURTHER READING

The topic of political participation is treated at some length by Robert E. Lane in *Political Life* (New York: Free Press, 1959) and by Seymour Martin Lipset in *Political Man* (Garden City, N.Y.: Doubleday, 1960). Both works bring together the results of a number of empirical studies of various aspects of political participation and suggest frameworks within which these results may be understood. Many of these same results and others as well are presented in near-encyclopedic form in Lester W. Milbrath and M. L. Goel, *Political Participation: How and Why Do People Get Involved in Politics* (2nd ed.; Chicago: Rand McNally, 1977).

Several case studies of the factors that motivate particular individuals to participate in politics are presented in a most interesting collection, edited by Robert Paul Wolff, entitled *Styles of Political Action in America* (New York: Random House, 1972). The articles in this book are invariably well written and collectively they suggest some intriguing conclusions regarding the relationship between personality and socialization factors and individual political involvement. Robert S. Gilmour and Robert B. Lamb offer an analysis of nonparticipation in *Political Alienation in Contemporary America* (New York: St. Martin's, 1975). And the protagonist in Jerzy Kosinski's novel *Being There* (New York: Harcourt Brace Jovanovich, 1971) provides a rather unique example of an individual who has lived in a condition of political isolation for much of his life and suddenly finds himself thrust into a more active role.

Finally, no review of literature in this area can exclude Sidney Verba and Norman Nie's *Participation in America: Political Democracy and Social Equality* (New York: Harper & Row, 1972), a seminal empirical treatment of the characteristics, correlates, and consequences of political activity.

NOTES

1. Robert E. Lane suggests the occupational sources of such time and skill differences in *Political Life* (New York: Free Press, 1959), pp. 331–34; the educational factors bearing on participation are summarized by Gabriel A. Almond and Sidney Verba in *The Civic Culture* (Princeton: Princeton University Press, 1963), pp. 379–87. Some of the physical restrictions on participation are suggested in Lester W. Milbrath and M. L. Goel, *Political Participation* (2nd ed.; Chicago: Rand McNally, 1977), p. 124.

2. Paul Allen Beck and M. Kent Jennings suggest this is in part a function of the times. "Political Periods and Political Participation," *American Political Science Review* 73 (1979): 737–50.

3. Norval D. Glenn, "The Distribution of Political Knowledge in the United States," in *Political Attitudes and Public Opinion*, ed. Dan D. Nimmo and Charles M. Bonjean (New York: David McKay, 1972), pp. 273–83. Cf. Philip E. Converse, "Information Flow and the Stability of Partisan Attitudes," *Public Opinion Quarterly* 26 (1962): 578–99. A variant of this notion is treated in Dale C. Nelson, "Ethnicity and Socioeconomic Status as Sources of Participation: The Case for Ethnic Political Culture," *American Political Science Review* 73 (1979): 1024–38.

4. Lester W. Milbrath and Walter Klein, "Personality Correlates of Political Participation," *Acta Sociologica* 6, fasc. 1–2 (1962): 53–66.

5. Angus Campbell describes some of the correlates of apathy in the context of a more general discussion of nonparticipation. "The Passive Citizen," *Acta Sociologica* 6, fasc. 1–2 (1962): 9–21. See also Paul H. Mussen and Anne B. Wyszynski, "Personality and Political Participation," *Human Relations* 5 (1952): 65–82.

6. Virtually all analyses of political interest to date have been concerned with the relationship between interest and participation in electoral politics in particular. For examples see Bernard R. Berelson, Paul F. Lazarsfeld, and William N. McPhee, *Voting: A Study of Opinion Formation in a Presidential Campaign* (Chicago: University of Chicago Press, 1954), passim; Lane, *Political Life*, pp. 143–46; and Angus Campbell, Philip E. Converse, Warren E. Miller, and Donald E. Stokes, *The American Voter* (New York: John Wiley, 1960), pp. 102 f.

7. Herbert McClosky and John H. Schaar, "Psychological Dimensions of Anomy," *American Sociological Review* 30 (1965): 14–40. Some definitional difficulties are discussed in Dennis R. Eckart and Roger Durand, "The Effect of Context in Measuring Anomia," *Public Opinion Quarterly* 39 (1975): 199–206.

8. Lane, *Political Life*, pp. 149–55; Campbell et al., *The American Voter*, pp. 103–5; and Almond and Verba, *The Civic Culture*, chap. 7. For a related definitional analysis, see Edward N. Muller, "Cross-National Dimensions of Political Competence," *American Political Science Review* 64 (1970): 792–809. See also Robert Weissberg, "Political Efficacy and Political Illusion," *Journal of Politics* 37 (1975): 469–87.

9. Ada W. Finifter, "Dimensions of Political Alienation," *American Political Science Review* 64 (1970): 389–410. Joel D. Aberbach argues that the behavioral implications of political alienation may be a function of the particular stimuli available in a given situation. "Alienation and Political Behavior," *American Political Science Review* 63 (1969): 86–99.

10. For a discussion of this point and a catalog of conceptual approaches to motivation, see James Deese, *Principles of Psychology* (Boston: Allyn & Bacon, 1964), pp. 54–83. It is a topic to which we shall return in the next chapter.

11. Richard E. Dawson and Kenneth Prewitt provide a discussion of this dichotomy and its applications to the socialization process in *Political Socialization* (Boston: Little, Brown, 1969), p. 64.

12. Talcott Parsons et al., "Some Fundamental Categories of the Theory of Action: A General Statement," in *Toward a General Theory of Action*, ed. Talcott Parsons and Edward A. Shils (New York: Harper & Row, 1962), pp. 4–6.

13. For analysis of this point with regard to voting behavior, see V. O. Key, Jr., *The Responsible Electorate* (Cambridge, Mass.: Harvard University Press, Belknap Press, 1966), and Peter B. Natchez and Irvin C. Bupp, "Candidates, Issues, and Voters," *Public Policy* 17 (1968): 409–37.

14. See, for example, Theodor W. Adorno, Else Frenkel-Brunswik, Daniel J. Levinson, and R. Nevitt Sanford, *The Authoritarian Personality* (New York: Harper, 1950), and Glenn D. Wilson, ed., *The Psychology of Conservatism* (London: Academic Press, 1973).

15. Berelson et al., *Voting*, pp. 284 f.

16. Talcott Parsons and Edward A. Shils, "Values, Motives, and Systems of Action," in Parsons and Shils, *Toward a General Theory of Action*, pp. 135 f. Lane discusses the role of emotion in determining political participation in *Political Life*, chap. 10.

17. Lester Milbrath, *Political Participation* (Chicago: Rand McNally, 1965), p. 10. This discussion was eliminated from the revised edition of the book.

18. Robert E. Lane and David O. Sears suggest that the distinction between rationality-emotion and psychological need–social need is both valid and functional. *Public Opinion* (Englewood Cliffs, N.J.: Prentice-Hall, 1964), pp. 81 f.

19. Deese, *Principles of Psychology*, p. 67.

20. Milbrath, *Political Participation*, p. 10.

21. Lane and Sears, *Public Opinion*, p. 74.

22. The appropriateness of our concern with a modal dimension in political participation is suggested by Sidney Verba and Norman H. Nie in *Participation in America: Political Democracy and Social Equality* (New York: Harper & Row, 1972), especially chaps. 3 and 4, and by Verba, Nie, and Jae-On Kim in *The Modes of Democratic Participation: A Cross-National Comparison*, Sage Professional Paper in Comparative Politics no. 01–013 (Beverly Hills, Calif.: Sage Publications, 1971), pp. 7–19.

23. For an analysis of various system-supportive modes of participation,

see Milbrath and Goel, *Political Participation*, pp. 10–24.

24. Kurt Lang and Gladys Engel Lang, *Politics and Television* (Chicago: Quadrangle Books, 1968), p. 20, and Dan Nimmo, *The Political Persuaders: The Techniques of Modern Election Campaigns* (Englewood Cliffs, N.J.: Prentice-Hall, 1970), pp. 186–91.

25. What is interesting here is that attitudes formed through such vicarious involvement may be especially susceptible to manipulation. See Russell H. Fazio and Mark P. Zanna, "Attitudinal Qualities Relating to the Strength of the Attitude-Behavior Relationship," *Journal of Experimental Social Psychology* 14 (1978): 398–408.

26. For the application of this argument to the electoral process, see Murray Edelman, *The Symbolic Uses of Politics* (Urbana: University of Illinois Press, 1964), pp. 2 f. The importance of symbols in participation more generally is discussed by Roger W. Cobb and Charles D. Elder in *Participation in American Politics: The Dynamics of Agenda-Building* (Boston: Allyn and Bacon, 1972), chap. 8.

27. Milbrath, *Political Participation*, p. 13.

28. Almond and Verba, *The Civic Culture*, p. 191.

29. In this context, Stephen V. Monsma offers an interesting analysis of those who claim group leadership at the electoral level in "Potential Leaders and Democratic Values," *Public Opinion Quarterly* 35 (1971): 350–57.

30. This is implicit in the arguments of Martin Fishbein, "The Relationships Between Beliefs, Attitudes, and Behavior," in *Cognitive Consistency: Motivational Antecedents and Behavioral Consequents*, ed. Shel Feldman (New York: Academic Press, 1966), pp. 200–23.

31. The latter point is certainly clear in the work of Herbert E. Krugman on low-involvement learning. Krugman in fact argues that behavior can operate independently of intent under certain circumstances. "The Impact of Television Advertising: Learning Without Involvement," *Public Opinion Quarterly* 29 (1965): 349–56.

32. This represents an extension of the conceptualization set forth by Milbrath, *Political Participation*, p. 10. Cf. Lane, *Political Life*, pp. 337–40.

33. Milbrath, *Political Participation*, p. 9.

34. This conceptualization differs somewhat from Milbrath's "Episodic versus Continuous" dichotomy (*Political Participation*, p. 11) in that it emphasizes volition rather than circumstance.

35. For an interesting analysis of substantive differences between partisans adopting acute and chronic modes of behavior see David Nexon, "Asymmetry in the Political System: Occasional Activists in the Republican and Democratic Parties, 1956–1964," *American Political Science Review* 65 (1971): 716–30.

36. For an interesting commentary on this point see Jerome M. Gilison, "Soviet Elections as a Measure of Dissent: The Missing One Percent," *American Political Science Review* 62 (1968): 814–26.

37. Henry A. Murray, "Toward a Classification of Interaction," in Parsons and Shils, *Toward a General Theory of Action*, pp. 455–57.

38. Lane, *Political Life*, p. 190; Lane and Sears, *Public Opinion*, pp. 8 f.; and Verba, Nie, and Kim, *Modes of Democratic Participation*, pp. 16 f.

39. John Osgood Field and Ronald E. Anderson, "Ideology in the Public's Conceptualization of the 1964 Election," *Public Opinion Quarterly* 33 (1969): 380–98.

40. Philip E. Converse, "The Nature of Belief Systems in Mass Publics," in *Ideology and Discontent*, ed. David E. Apter (Glencoe, Ill.: Free Press, 1964), pp. 206–31. For a variety of views on this point, consult the sources cited in Chapter 2, note 14.

41. For the most comprehensive statement of this notion; see Ted Robert Gurr, *Why Men Rebel* (Princeton: Princeton University Press, 1970). Samuel Long offers evidence that such notions may have limited utility. See "Personality and Political Alienation among White and Black Youth: A Test of the Social Deprivation Model," *Journal of Politics* 40 (1978): 433–57.

42. David Easton, *A Systems Analysis of Political Life* (New York: John Wiley, 1965), chapters 3–15, but especially pp. 37–56, 153–70. Milbrath and Goel, *Political Participation*, pp. 9–10, refer to these respectively as inputs and outtakes.

The Body Politic

Physiological Bases of Political Behavior

Over the past several chapters we have attempted to make clear both the nature and the significance of individual political attitudes. We have described the structural characteristics of these psychological predispositions; considered their relationship with the underlying dynamics of personality; analyzed the mechanisms of attitude change and the strategies and tactics of persuasion; placed the political attitudes and orientations of the individual into a social and cultural context and traced their development through time; observed the interaction between individuals and political stimuli in the real-world laboratory of the political campaign; and, finally, extended our analysis to some more general comments on the underlying dimensions of political activity. We have, in short, presented an outline of the complex relationship by which politically relevant attitudes guide political perception and influence political behavior.

But the thought may have occurred to you as you perused the lengthy discussion that has brought us to this point that all these attitudes we have been talking about have one rather disturbing characteristic in common, one that we have thus far neglected to mention. For none of us—not you and surely not I—has ever actually seen one of these mythical beasts upon whom we have spent so many words; none of us has ever come face to face with an *attitude*. Rather, we have *inferred* not only the characteristics but the existence of these critically important psychological states on the basis of their apparent explanatory powers. We have, in essence, guessed—aided immeasurably by scientific observations of human behavior and by some fairly rigorous logic—that such things as attitudes must exist. For attitudes as we have conceptualized them here offer what seems to be a persuasive and comprehensive tool for explaining systematic variations in the political behavior of the individual.

Inference of this type is not uncommon in science or social science, and while it does have its dangers, it often provides valuable insights that are later supported by hard evidence. Much of the theory of atomic physics, for instance, was developed in a similar fashion, and many astronomical discoveries have resulted from precisely this kind of educated guessing as to where, based upon analyses of known and observable phenomena, some as-yet-undetected heavenly body must lie. These notable successes notwithstanding, a word of caution is most assuredly in order.

Science, it would seem, is much like a culture in its own right. Just as a culture has certain accepted patterns of behavior and certain taboos, for example, just as a culture adopts certain dominant values, science endorses at any particular period in history certain perspectives on natural or social phenomena. Just as a culture constrains its constituent members to certain patterns of perception, science restricts the direction of discovery in which its adherents are encouraged to move. Thus there exists at any particular moment in history what amounts to a dominant scientific ideology, a set of professional norms and expectations, generally termed the "scientific method," that guide the conduct of inquiry and may even go so far as to preclude the asking of certain questions or predetermine investigative outcomes.[1]

In times past, for example, natural phenomena not readily understood by what we today would consider the relatively unsophisticated scientific minds of the period were frequently attributed to the whims and fancies of invisible forces that existed in the superstitions and religions of earlier cultures. After all, it was reasoned, these so-called demons *must* exist, since no other possible explanations could be devised for certain observations. Reality demanded elucidation, and as long as demonology could provide reasons and mechanisms for all known events, science was incapable of ignorance. No one, of course—hysterical reports of the contrary notwithstanding—ever actually saw a demon. But their existence was both scientifically and politically useful, and demons endured as a dominant ideological force in scientific thought for centuries.[2]

I mention this because we, in our infinitely greater wisdom and
sophistication, may be making a similar error today in our reliance
upon the explanatory powers of attitudes. Admittedly, it is entirely
possible, and *probably quite likely*, that some phenomenon resembling what we have called an attitude does occur naturally—does in
fact exist beyond the paper-and-pencil tests we generally use to
measure it.[3] Thus we must press our inquiry based on attitude
theory just as hard and as far as it will carry us; we must take full
advantage of our available interpretive devices. But we must also
be prepared to acknowledge the possibility that an attitude is simply an artifact of our search for an attitude—that it exists, in essence, only because we design tests to measure it. We must be willing to admit the possibility that we may not yet possess the key to
understanding political and other forms of human behavior. We
must at the least remain open to the suggestion that attitudes may
be little more than an intellectual placebo whose perceived explanatory power has proven adequate to deflect our curiosity in the
short run, but whose intuitive appeal may decline as we acquire
ever-greater amounts of empirical evidence.

But how else might we explain the systematic variations in
observed political behavior that attitudes account for so handily?
What, if anything, could replace, or more probably supplement,
attitudes as the intermediary between stimulus and response? A bit
of history suggests one direction in which we might focus our
inquiry.[4] In medieval times, the tombs of kings and queens were
frequently adorned with two images, one of the deceased monarch
in a death pose and another of the ruler alive and fully potent.
Such persons were said to have two distinct selves: a body mortal,
which suffered the same needs and afflictions as did those of less
regal lineage; and a body politic, which carried forward the rights
and obligations of sovereignty from one mortal repository to the
next. To the extent that such representations were attempts by the
ruling elites of the period to institutionalize political power and
leadership by emphasizing their continuity, they were important
sources of legitimacy and stability for the political systems that
used them. But to the extent that they reflected a genuine theory
of the relationship between the individual and the polity, they
were, quite simply, mistaken. For it is not possible to separate the
mortal being from the political actor; they are one and the same.

Put most starkly, people are animals. This fundamental fact, at
once recognized and rejected by those medieval potentates, must
in the final analysis be the basis of all political behavior. Somewhere in the physiological makeup of the human being, in the

structure or chemistry of life, there must exist an explanation of the motivations for, and styles of, the political and other behaviors we have seen describing. And it follows from this that if we are to understand fully why and how an individual behaves relative to the political system, we cannot exclude from investigation the physiological characteristics of the human body that constitute the gears and wheels of mental and physical action. If we are to understand why and how people behave *toward* anything, politics included, we must consider the mechanisms by which they behave *at all*. It is here that the answers to at least some of our questions may well be found.

THE PHYSIOLOGY OF BEHAVIOR: STRUCTURES

It would be nice to claim that the stuff of life is fully understood, that we have in hand the master key that opens all the doors of self-knowledge and reveals the most secret of phenomena, the processes of human thought. It would be nice, but alas, it is not so. To the contrary, the mechanisms of human action, like those of attitudes, are neither fully nor in some cases even well understood, and sometimes it seems that the more we learn, the less we know. Nevertheless, science has accumulated substantial knowledge about how our bodies work, how we receive, process, and respond to information from our environment. And that knowledge can go a long way toward both increasing our understanding of political behavior and helping us appreciate the essentiality of the link between physical and psychological processes. Let us consider in some detail these basic characteristics and functions, these substrata of human psychology and behavior, so that we may achieve a more rounded perspective on the ties between people and politics.

The most important structural element of the human body is the *cell*. Cells consist of an outer surface, or membrane, that serves as a filter to let certain chemical substances into the cell and keep others out; a main body where nutrients are converted into energy through chemical processes; and a nucleus that, using genetic information, determines the function of the cell, the particular task it performs for the body. There are two chemicals in the nucleus, one called *deoxyribonucleic acid* (DNA) and the other *ribonucleic acid* (RNA), which help to integrate and guide the cell as a functioning biological system. DNA stores the genetic determinants of cell function, while RNA carries this information from the nucleus to the cell body where it controls the chemical processes taking place.

The basic material that makes up a cell is called *protoplasm*. Depending on the cell, this protoplasm consists of between 60 and 90 percent water. Because much of the activity of cells is electrochemical in nature, this water is very important, for it allows the other chemicals present to be dissolved and to distribute themselves uniformly around the cell. These other chemicals, including acids, bases, and salts, have electrical properties that allow the cells to function. Indeed, all the actions of cells and groups of cells (glands, organs, and the like) arise from electrical and chemical reactions.

Some of these chemical constituents are more important than others to our understanding of the essentially psychological processes we are most interested in here. Proteins are a case in point. *Proteins* are large and complex molecules that provide the structural material for cell development. They can be split into smaller substituent molecules, called amino acids, approximately forty of which have already been identified. The multitude of different combinations of these amino acids helps to account for the variety of different cell structures found in the body and, as we shall see, may be central to an explanation of how the brain remembers past experiences. Closely related to proteins are *enzymes*, which facilitate and increase the speed of chemical reactions within cells. Some functions of enzymes are so specialized that there may exist a unique enzyme for every type of chemical reaction that occurs within us.[5] The third class of related chemicals is the hormones. *Hormones* are secreted by the endocrine glands to regulate the pace of internal chemical reactions.[6]

The human body consists of many different types of cells, but for our purposes two are of particular interest. The first are the *receptors*, cells that specialize in receiving physical energy from outside the organism in the form of heat, light, pressure, or chemical exchanges and converting this energy into electrochemical reactions that are transmitted to other cells. Thus the eyes respond to light, the membranes in the ears to changes in the surrounding air pressure, the skin to warmth, the nose to chemical traces (called *pheromones*) emitted by substances in the environment, and the taste buds to chemicals in the materials we place in our mouths. These outside stimuli generate reactions within the cells with which they come into contact, and it is these reactions, or *sensations*, that make the body aware of and responsive to its environment. But it is the sensations, the electrochemical messages, not the stimuli themselves, to which other cells ultimately react. It is not the combination of black marks on white paper that move toward your brain as you read this book, but rather the vast array of electrochemical signals directed there by the receptors in your eyes as they are struck by the physical (and, one hopes, intellectual) light reflected off the printed page.

By what mechanism are these signals carried? This is where the second type of cells, the so-called *conductors*, comes in. Cells whose task is to carry electrochemical energy from the receptors to the brain (and elsewhere) are called *neurons*, or nerve cells. They consist of a main cell body, termed a *soma*, a nucleus, and some rather weblike and spindly projections on either end called *dendrites* and *axons*. Neurons occur in long chains rather like wires which connect the receptors with other areas of the body, most notably the brain. These chains are arranged such that the dendrite of a given cell receives an electrical charge from the preceding cell, passes it through the cell body utilizing the chemical properties we mentioned earlier, and issues a charge through the axon where it is sent out in the direction of the next cell in the chain, all within the tiniest fraction of a second. The process is then repeated to completion. A portion of such a chain is illustrated in simplified form in Figure 9.1. The dendrites, which conduct energy toward the cell body, are typically quite short, but the axons, which conduct energy away, may be quite long, in some instances as much as several feet. It is important to note, too, that nerve cells do not generally come into direct contact with one another. Instead, they are separated by a gap, called a *synapse*. When an electrical charge arrives at the synapse, it does not jump the gap, like the charge in an automobile spark plug; rather, it causes the secretion of chemicals called neurohumors (literally, nerve fluids) or *neurotransmitters*, which in turn cause electrochemical changes in the membrane of the adjacent cell creating, in effect, a new charge. The process is then repeated along the length of the chain.

This conduction process is not instantaneous, since each phase of transmission requires secretion of and then reaction to neurotransmitters at each synapse, as well as electrochemical reactions to carry the charge along the length of each cell; nor is it always completed, since the charge transmitted may be insufficiently strong to progress through the entire length of a given nerve-cell chain. Moreover, the transmission of a series of charges may be interrupted by what amounts to the overexcitation of a particular cell (and its consequent inability to continue receiving electrical charges), and that of a single charge by the presence of hormones or other chemicals in the neurons or the synapses that inhibit the flow. Nevertheless, the process is generally quick and efficient in conveying information from the receptors to the remainder of the organism.[7]

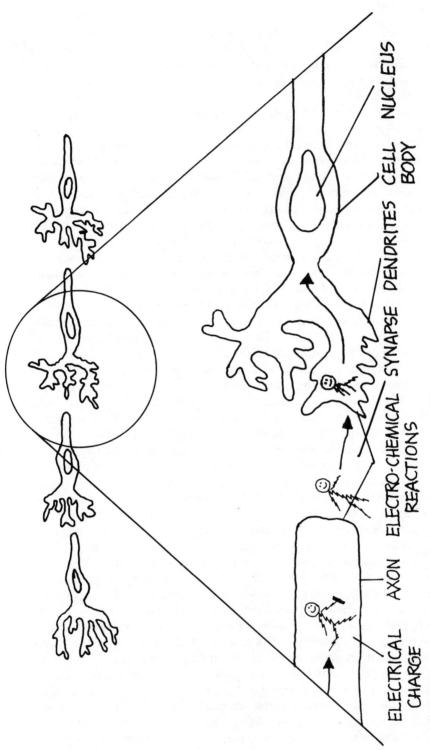

ELECTRICAL AXON ELECTRO-CHEMICAL SYNAPSE DENDRITES CELL NUCLEUS
CHARGE   REACTIONS   BODY

FIGURE 9.1 Relaying an Electrical Charge along a Neuron Chain.

Most of the sensory messages that would interest us in our study of political attitudes and behavior eventually reach the brain, which has been described as "a gelatinous three-pound lump of fat, connective tissue, spinal fluid, veins, and nerve cells—the last generating some twenty-five watts of total power."[8] The human brain contains about 100 billion cells, about a tenth of which are neurons. Each neuron contains some 20 million molecules of RNA, and each molecule of RNA is capable of generating any of 100,000 proteins depending on its DNA-programmed instructions. Because of the multitude of end points on the dendrites and axons of each cell and the sharing of synaptic spaces, each neuron has the potential to interact with between 60,000 and 300,000 others. It is the selection of pathways through this neural maze, guided by the chemical activity we have already described, that determines a person's receipt of and response to information arriving from the receptors.[9]

THE PHYSIOLOGY OF BEHAVIOR: PROCESSES

The brain is a highly complex organ, much more so than we have suggested here, and it performs a wide variety of functions, not the least of which involves the issuing of messages through "motor nerves" that drive the muscles of the body and determine its physical actions. But students of political behavior are more interested in a different set of brain functions, those involving such psychological phenomena as memory, learning, attention, motivation, and emotion. Each of these has arisen in our earlier discussion; each has a physiological basis in the structure and functioning of the brain (or, as we noted in Chapter 3, of the autonomic nervous system), though not necessarily one that is well understood at the present time; and each is worthy of note.

The memory function provides a good starting point for this portion of our discussion because it has been a factor in so many of the arguments we have made in earlier chapters, because it derives most clearly from the physical processes we are focusing on now, and because it helps to put the other functions in perspective. The most widely accepted theories of memory describe it as a two-stage process. In the first stage, short-term memories are generated by neurobiological processes that themselves have short lifetimes, as, for example, the electrical activity we described earlier. In effect, electrical charges moving along a neuron chain set up a temporary pathway that is preserved for some period of time by the recycling charges themselves. This procedure is somewhat analogous to the "do loop" in computer programming, a set of instructions that causes a computer to repeat a series of operations over and over until some escape threshold is reached. In the case of short-term memory, the loop is believed to be created by the formation of chemical traces that define the relevant neural pathway. The escape threshold, which is to say, forgetting the information, may be a function of simply removing the stimulus to recall. Thus it is possible to remember the telephone number of a casual acquaintance long enough to dial it, but it may be impossible to recall it later.

In instances where stimuli are especially strong or are repeated frequently (as, for example, in experiments involving behavioral conditioning), or where, for reasons suggested in Chapter 3, the essential needs or well-being of the person in question are involved, more permanent transformations may follow. These may take the form of protein growth along the neural pathway, which, in a sense, sets it in biological concrete and assures retention of the information, changes in the chemical constituents of the membranes of the affected neurons that assure the continued facilitation of the electrical flow, and, ultimately, micro-anatomical changes in the synapses that effectively lock in the information. The result of this more extensive series of metabolic reactions is long-term memory, a physical alteration in the functional relationships among brain cells.[10]

Learning, the second of the functions we shall examine and another that has recurred often in our earlier discussion, is most simply thought of as the creation of memories, whether short-term (as in the case of the portions of this text you will recall vividly until two hours before taking an examination) or long-term (as in those you will recall vividly forever after taking that examination). In general, learning takes one of three forms. The first, *habituation*, involves reducing one's response to outside stimuli of a continuing nature. Thus people who live in cities, near airports, or in college dormitories become accustomed (habituated) to relatively high levels of background noise and are able to carry on their normal daily activities including sleep (or perhaps even studying) without interruption. They are no longer "conscious" of the noise. Should someone call attention to the noise level, however, others will become more aware of it; if constant reminders are presented, the noise itself can become unbearable. This phenomenon is characteristic of the second type of learning, *sensitization*. Such patterns of learning are common in politics. People who are accustomed to tolerating some degree of injustice or inequity (which no political system can escape entirely), for example, even at their own expense, will remain quiescent unless their leaders sensitize them to the extant conditions. As William James put it, "habit alone" is the greatest barrier to revolution. And it was sensitization of precisely the type we are describing that characterized much of the social upheaval in the United States during the 1960s and early '70s. First civil rights leaders, and later antiwar and other activist leaders, forced people to acknowledge and respond to conditions most had simply regarded as the "givens" of political life. The result was the learning by a great many Americans of lessons that still influence our social and political behavior today.

Finally, learning can take the form of an ability on the part of an individual to associate two events with one another because they take place at the same time or share some other evident relationship. It is this *associative learning*, which we discussed in considerable detail in Chapter 3, that provides the basis for many of the higher-order psychological and behavioral activities we have treated in this book.[11]

Such learning, of course, is a relatively high order psychological process in its own right, and the degree of its development in humans is one of our most important distinguishing characteristics. One theory of brain structure, called the *triune brain model*, suggests that the structural elements of our brains reflect three stages of evolutionary development. The first, or primitive component, contains the neural machinery necessary for life (e.g., that which regulates the heart rate, circulation, and respiration). It is, according to the theory, the seat of emotion and the various basic drives that so interest personologists working in the psychoanalytic tradition. The second, or limbic component, evolved more than 150 million years ago and added the capacity for low-level associative learning, memory, and differentiated emotion. The third and most recent component, the neo-cortex, adds the ability for abstract reasoning to the more basic attributes and provides the capability for much more complex learning. In humans, all three of these systems continue to function simultaneously and may compete for control over particular preferences or behaviors (or at least may offer competing explanations for them). For instance, does an individual prefer a reduction in taxes because he or she will therefore have more money for personal use ("primitive" selfishness), because smaller government is less constraining and therefore better government ("limbic" association), or because an econometric model predicts an increase in real economic growth if taxes are reduced ("neo-cortical" rationalization)? Each response reflects learning, but learning of a very different kind.[12]

As is the case with attitudes, however, one difficulty with measuring learning, or for that matter memory, is that we cannot observe it directly; we can only infer that it has or has not occurred by observing the presence or absence of behavioral responses that we assume to be associated with it. Thus your instructor can only infer the degree to which you have learned the material in this book from your contribution to class discussions, your performance on an examination, or less directly still from the knowing smiles and nods you subtly display as others discuss this information. Yet as every student has argued at one time or another, these indicators may be inadequate or misleading. Quiet students learn just as do loquacious ones, and one or another test may not succeed in eliciting the information acquired. Moreover, the occurrence of a learning-related behavior requires not only the prior creation of the relevant memory trace but also the coordination of motivational, sensory, and motor mechanisms to (1) make the initial connection to the appropriate memory, (2) identify the "appropriate" response, and (3) initiate and carry out that response. Only if one is willing to assume optimal conditions in each of these regards can behavior provide evidence of learning.[13]

Undeterred by these constraints, physiological and social psychologists have developed numerous theories of how learning occurs. The social-psychological processes described in these theories are discussed elsewhere in this book (Chapters 3 and 5). By and large, they relate to the characteristics of an individual and of that individual's relationship with his or her environment that enhance the strength or potency of external stimuli (or increase the motivation to internalize them) and thereby increase the likelihood of creating memories. The physiological theories of learning, on the other hand, emphasize both the transformation of individual cell structures to incorporate learned information and the patterning of intercellular relationships toward the same end. Most agree that learning requires a more or less permanent change in neural function, which is simply to say that it entails a physical process (as opposed, for example, to a spiritual process) and that this process probably involves systematic electrophysical or anatomic reactions at selected synapses that provide storage for and access to information by reducing their electrical or chemical resistance. Whether that information is stored in electrical or anatomical form, as suggested by studies showing impaired learning and recall to be associated with brain lesions (cuts in the neural chains),[14] or chemical form, as suggested by research showing that certain learning can apparently be transferred from one animal to another by drawing protein from the brain of the former and injecting it into that of the latter,[15] as well as the precise location where such storage takes place, are matters of rather more debate.[16] (Note the importance of several such processes in our description of memory.) Nor has any research to date dealt definitively with the more difficult question of selectivity, with the explanation of how information is not only selectively stored but is selectively and appropriately accessed for subsequent use.

The so-called anatomical theories of learning[17] hold that the passage of excitation (electrical charges) through a neuron chain causes certain neighboring cells to extend their respective dendrites and axons toward one another, to grow together, and in the process to reduce the size of the synapse between them and concomitantly its resistance. Through processes we need not describe here, the network of cells in the brain ultimately closes the loop by directing the electrical impulse back into the chain at some point, causing it to recycle. In time, the elements of the loop become fused, and the information is learned.

Molecular theories of learning,[18] on the other hand, build on the notion that the function of a cell is determined by the type of proteins it produces and the rate at which it produces them. These theories generally argue that excitation of a cell may cause to be generated a unique protein template, an enduring chemical structure within the cell that is selectively sensitive to the particular impulse that led to its creation. In some theories these structures are seen as providing connections between adjacent cells, or alternatively as altering the chemistry of the neurotransmitters to facilitate the flow of impulses across certain synapses. In part because the technology for examining them is relatively new, these theories are generally less fully developed than others, but they are attracting substantial interest.[19]

The principal arguments of the anatomical and molecular theories of learning and memory are illustrated in Figure 9.2. In Figure 9.2(*a*), which represents the anatomical theories, adjacent axons and dendrites grow toward one another, reach out as it were, creating a path of least resistance for electrical charges. In Figure 9.2(*b*), representing the molecular theories, proteins are generated that form a bridge across the synapse and facilitate the flow of energy. Although the relative importance of these two processes is open to debate, proponents of both agree that ultimately a physical

(a) Anatomical Theories: Growing Together.

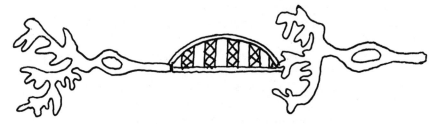

(b) Molecular Theories: Bridging the Synapse.

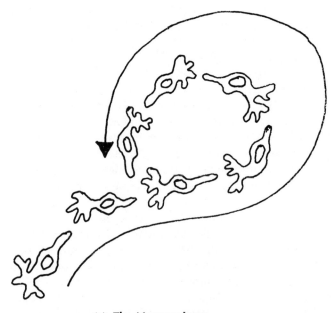

(c) The Memory Loop.

FIGURE 9.2   Theories of Memory.

linkage or loop is formed, as illustrated in Figure 9.2(*c*), to "lock in" the information in question.

Attention, our third psychological function, is generally regarded as having three components.[20] The first is *alertness*, or the general receptivity of an individual to incoming information. The second is the *selection* of some particular bit of information from a larger array of available stimuli, whether because of the contextual characteristics of the information itself (e.g., its prominence in the environment) or because of some internally generated set of selection criteria. The third is the degree of *conscious effort* put forward by a person in seeking information. We have, of course, already examined the social aspects of these components of attention (see Chapter 6), so we shall focus here on their physiological characteristics.

Alertness is one of several bodily functions that might be classified as indicators of performance; the more alert a person is, the better he or she is performing. More particularly, alertness refers to the effectiveness of performance of the body's receptor cells. To some extent, this effectiveness has a temporal component, indeed a daily cycle, such that most people are most alert early in the day and less so as the day progresses, with a new cycle beginning around four a.m. That hour also corresponds with the maximum level of certain hormones (adrenal cortical steroids) that other evidence suggests are related to variation in the sensory detection threshold in such a way that as the level of such hormones increases, the sensitivity of the receptors to stimulation decreases.[21] In other words, these hormones inhibit the effectiveness of the body's receptors, and alertness is greatest at the times of day when they are at their lowest levels.[22] When alertness is made a conscious task rather than a passive function (PAY ATTENTION!), other correlates observed in a number of studies include systematic changes in the electrical activity of the brain, deceleration of the heart rate, inhibition of psychomotor activity (reduction of irrelevant movement), inhibition of certain spinal reflexes, and a decrease in the rate of eyeblinking.[23]

Selectivity of attentiveness, the second component, amounts to filtering information as it arrives either at the receptors on the body's periphery (i.e., refusing to receive it) or in the central nervous system or the brain after the information has been received (i.e., refusing to acknowledge it). Most students of the subject agree that the latter is more probably the case, that all information is received by the individual but that the passage of certain messages is facilitated while that of others is inhibited. One theory holds that molecular channels (a fancy way of describing protein linkages) operate near the synapses in the neural chains to release substances that arouse or make more sensitive particular chains while leaving others relatively dormant.[24] As with other similar notions, however, the mechanisms of selectively are not yet well defined.

Conscious effort at attention, the third component, appears to arise from the same areas of the brain that are most important in controlling the primary sensory systems (eyes, ears, and the like). One possible mechanism by which conscious attention works is through the activation of a neural pathway from the inside out, which is to say as a product of neural activity rather than a cause of it. What this amounts to is making a reservation for the incoming information and assuring its safe arrival even if this means that other information will be diverted or its passage impeded. For all its billions of cells, the human brain has a distinctly limited information-processing capability. Other things being equal, the relative strength of an outside stimulus, the sensitivity of the receptors, the electrochemical status of the neural chains, the chemical components of the cells involved, and the luck of the draw combine to determine which information is fully processed. This view of purposeful attention suggests that the process can be made less random and be more readily determined by the individual in question through a systematic physiological preparation of the receiving network to accept particular kinds of information.[25]

At the physiological level, motivation, the fourth psychological process we shall consider, is best understood as a contributing factor in both alertness and overt behavior. Motivation is that mechanism or set of mechanisms that leads a person to do something (as opposed to doing nothing, i.e., lying in a lump and staring vacantly into space). And the most fundamental thing that a person can do is to act to preserve his or her safety or comfort. At the physiological level, one way to define safety and comfort is in terms of maintaining a level of sensory input to the brain that is at once high enough to stimulate some minimal level of neural activity but not so high as to disrupt normal neural function. In other words, the electrochemical system of the body tends toward a state of moderate activity. In this view, the absence of sufficient stimulation to maintain that activity leads one to become more active. In effect, when we are bored, we look for things to do (though the concept of boredom assumes a level of awareness of this equilibrium seeking that need not be present). On the other hand, when the level of stimulation rises high, we act to reduce that level to a more tolerable range. When we become hungry enough or thirsty enough, we eat or drink; when we see too many commercials for political candidates, we stop watching; and this action has the effect of reducing the level of stimulation. The source of stimuli that threaten the preferred state may be either external or internal to the organism itself. External stimuli enter the system in the manner we have described earlier. Internal stimuli may become known through receptor cells located within the body, most notably in the major organs, and connected to the autonomic nervous system; or they may take the form of changes in body chemistry such as the volume of fluids (thirst), the level of blood sugar (hunger), or the secretion of particular hormones that affect neural activity.

An extension of this framework helps account for the selection of particular behaviors in particular circumstances. Except in the case of certain chemical changes, stimulation is traceable to identifiable sensory inputs. That being true, the body is able to recognize and localize the source, or at least the nature, of any imbalance it senses, and to respond to the sensation so as to restore the requisite balance. In the case of chemical changes, other regulatory mechanisms seem to be at work that have the same effect. As the needs of the organism are met, the stimulation of arousal, or more activity, is replaced by the stimulation of inhibition, by an alternative set of electrochemical impulses that lead to a decrease in behavior. Recent research suggests that two proteins in the brain, dopamine and endorphin, respectively provide the alternative driving forces toward enhanced stimulation and quiescence. At this level, then, motivation is a biological drive not only for self-preservation, but for body-system stability as well.[26]

Closely related to motivation is the final psychological phenomenon we shall discuss: emotion. In the most basic sense, emotion-arousing phenomena are those that have special meaning for the individual, whether that meaning be fear for one's life, love for one's country, or surprise at some unexpected occurrence, to name but three. Exposure to all such stimuli is accompanied by a more or less standard combination of physiological events typically including increases in the pulse and respiratory rates and in blood pressure, increases in perspiration followed by associated decreases in skin temperature, and increased electrical potential in the muscles. The stronger the stimulus, the greater the physiological reaction.

These indicators are useful for telling us when emotionality occurs, but they do not tell us what the basis for emotion is, of what it consists. There are some apparent differences in the particular combinations of physiological indicators that correspond with different types of emotions and with positive and negative feelings (e.g., the diameter of the pupil of the eye increases with exposure to positive stimuli and decreases with exposure to negative ones), but these observations have yet to be fully explained.[27] One promising theory that has implications for memory, learning, attention, motivation, and emotion alike revolves around the two proteins mentioned above, dopamine and endorphin. In this view, the production of these and related chemical substances is related to the level of pain or pleasure felt by the body. A person associates these feelings with particular experiences (recall the notion of classical conditioning) and learns from those experiences in the context of the particular feeling in question. The result is affective (judgmental or evaluative) recall ("I'd better watch out. The last time this happened to me it was painful"), which influences the selection of behaviors.[28]

PHYSIOLOGY AND PERSONALITY: DIMENSIONS OF DIFFERENCE

We can see some similar factors at work when we consider the biological bases of personality, or more particularly of differences in personality across individuals. Each of us has a unique physiological makeup and a unique genetic history, the combination of which generates an individualized pattern of behavior. We know, for instance, that people can vary in the size, shape, and performance of their various body systems. Endocrine glands, for example, can vary as much as six- to tenfold in size from one person to the next, and the thickness of the adrenal cortex, the source location of a number of important hormones, can vary as much. Indeed, secretions of these chemical agents themselves, whose importance in determining behavior we have already noted, can vary over a sevenfold range and still be considered "normal."[29] When one considers that similar variation is common in the skeletal, muscular, circulatory, and nervous systems of the body, the potential for individuation becomes apparent.

What is the source of these differences across individuals? To a significant extent, it is genetic in character. Recall from our discussion a bit earlier that the functioning of individual cells and, by extension, of organs, glands, and the like is controlled by chemical instructions emanating from the DNA in the nucleus of each cell. This DNA is the carrier of genetic information that derives from the parents of the person in question and that can be traced back through the generations. What is transmitted through this process, then, is not individual behaviors or even patterns of behavior; rather, it is types of physical differences that can be related to behavior in any of three ways.

The first such relationship, termed *susceptibility*, refers to the differential impact of a given experience on different types of people. For example, a person whose physiology was such that he or she was generally quite emotional or at least manifested emotion intensively when it occurred might react very differently than might a physiologically more subdued person to news of the death of a political leader. In such a case, the differing genetic makeup of the two individuals, translated into differences in physiological function, would lead in turn to differing reactions to, and probably qualitatively different learning from and memories of, the same external event. In this instance, then, genetic factors are said to influence the *reaction to experience*.

The second relationship between behavior and physiology is called *differential exposure* (as distinct from *selective* exposure, which we discussed in Chapter 6) and refers to the fact that precisely because they differ physically in terms of both internal functioning and external appearance, people. will have differing experiences. Such factors as the timing of puberty, the degree of physical attractiveness, the rate and function of one's metabolism, and the like are genetically determined; and they can in turn influence the selection and quality of interaction with one's peers, the development of self-confidence or interpersonal anxiety, and other psychosocial characteristics with long-term implications.[30] So in this instance, the *selection and quality of experience* are said to be influenced by genetic factors.

The third and final relationship of this type is *differential capability*, a recognition that heredity influences behavior by imposing differing limits on such abilities as intellectual, athletic, or musical prowess. Irrespective of any behavioral opportunities that might be available to individuals or any amount of effort that might be expended, people have limits. And because not everyone has the same limits, not everyone can have the political acumen of a Barbara Jordan, the physical coordination of a George Brett, or the rhythmic and tonal instincts of an Aaron Copland. Differences in capacity necessarily affect the way an individual experiences the world by influencing the kinds of things he or she does and the degree of success with which they are accomplished. These experiences subsequently influence the individual's self-concept, his or her sense of innate ability, and probably have an impact on motivation as well.

Putting all of this together, we can see that genetic makeup and experience, or, to use the more popular phrase, heredity and environment, interact with one another to impose certain patterns on human behavior. Physical differences and associated behavioral tendencies with clear genetic origins can lead to different social experiences and learning; these differing experiences and learning tend to reinforce already existing genetic differences. The result, presumably, is a long-term set of dispositions that constitute, or at least contribute to, one's personality.[31]

PHYSIOLOGY AND BEHAVIOR: YOU ARE WHAT YOU SECRETE?

To this point we have examined the structures and components of human physiology that must inevitably lie at the roots of political and other behaviors, and we have examined the associated characteristics of several higher-order psychological processes that help form a bridge between the physiological and social aspects of behavior. What remains is to suggest more directly where this bridge leads, or in other words, how our knowledge of physiology can help us understand that set of human behaviors and interactions we have termed "politics." To accomplish this task we must think of the political behavior of the individual as occurring on one of three levels, which we shall label *stimulus-specific behavior*, *mid-range behavior*, and *stimulus-nonspecific behavior*.

Stimulus-specific behavior is that which involves particular and generally isolated responses to particular and generally isolated stimuli.[32] A typical finding of research on such behavior might be that such things as the rate of eyeblinking, the temperature or electrical conductivity of the skin, heart rate, and pupil dilation indicate that people are attentive to particular themes or styles of presentation in political advertising, that they are more alert when one candidate speaks in a debate than another, or that they are emotionally involved in the graphic portrayal of violence or sexual activity in film.[33] In general, these studies point to patterns of arousal that help us evaluate the impact of classes of external stimuli (e.g., to identify such characteristics of the information leading to arousal as its novelty or repetition) on a person's psychophysiological equilibrium.

Stimulus-nonspecific behavior is that which involves broad classes of associated physiological responses where the impetus is often internal to the actor in question and where that person may or may not differentiate among the external objects of his or her behavior. Stress, fatigue, aggression, anger, and impatience, among other states, have physiological components that govern not only the specific actions we undertake (which may in these instances be influenced mostly indirectly) but the classes of actions we might select from (an angry person will adopt different types of behavior than will one who is not angered), the style of action we might adopt (passive or aggressive, for example), the quality of our performance (fatigue tends to impair our ability to function effectively, stress to enhance it, at least to a point), and even our sensitivity to outside stimuli (fatigue makes us less sensitive, which is to say raises our threshold of receptivity, while stress appears to have quite the opposite effect). Here we are describing gross characteristics of behavior that are likely to apply in a more or less generalized way to whatever particular stimuli a person encounters at the time they are extant but that are not necessarily initiated directly in response to those stimuli.[34] The so-called final-exam syndrome, in which stress produces changes in the efficiency of cognitive function and in sensitivity (perhaps "irritability" is a better word here), is a case in point, and represents a pattern that is also found among political leaders making decisions in times of crisis.[35]

What remains is that vast array of mundane decision making and implementation that we see operating in day-to-day political life, which we have termed mid-range behavior. Reading the newspaper, talking politics, thinking about issues, dealing with bureaucracies, selecting among candidates—these and a host of other activites fall into this category. For one thing, they are more complex activities than those we have described as stimulus-specific behaviors. They involve multiple stimuli from a variety of sources and might be thought of as aggregates of large numbers of individual behaviors, yet they are generally accompanied by what students of stimulus-specific behavior would regard as background or base levels of physiological activity. There is, in short, nothing remarkable about the physiology of doing these things; the body functions within normal tolerances. Indeed, these behaviors and others like them help define the very concept of normality. Moreover, precisely because these activities are generally traceable and substantively related to one or more sets of internal or external stimuli that have no especially noteworthy characteristics, such stimulus-nonspecific behavioral conditions as stress or fatigue, though they may very well influence the style or effectiveness with which daily activities are performed, do not offer any general explanation for the selection or conduct of them. These factors are neither specific nor comprehensive enough to do so.

We are left, then, without any clear explanation for these mid-range activities. We know they are processed physiologically in essentially the way we have described here, though because our description underemphasizes the incredible number of neurons and neuron chains, their processing is a bit more complicated than we have indicated. We know as well that they are influenced by, and in this way express, moods, emotions, and the like, but only in very general ways. Beyond that, the state of our knowledge does not permit us to specify with great precision exactly how they work.

The key to this understanding undoubtedly lies in discovering more about the essentially psychological functions we discussed earlier; memory, learning, attention, motivation, and emotion. For these are the functions that provide the link not only between stimulus-specific and stimulus-nonspecific behaviors but between the mechanical aspects of human physiology and the social and political environment in which we interact with one another. It is this environment that provides the opportunities for behavior, as well as the associated external rewards and sanctions that help to shape motivations. It is this environment that generates the experiences that become the stuff of learning and recall. It is this environment in which the human organism must define and preserve its safety and well-being. Politics, like society more generally, provides emotional attachments and behavioral cues, channels for behavior and a context of physical and psychological conditions that give rise to it. In the end, then, while it is true that we cannot fully understand the individual's social behavior unless we understand his or her physiological makeup, it is equally true that physiological perspectives are of limited utility in the absence of social and political understanding.[36] Therein lies the integral concept of this book.

SUGGESTIONS FOR FURTHER READING

The best sources for a functional overview of physiological psychology are Sebastian P. Grossman, *Essentials of Physiological Psychology* (New York: John Wiley, 1973); and Thomas S. Brown and Patricia M. Wallace, *Physiological Psychology* (New York: Academic Press, 1980). Grossman's earlier book, *Textbook of Physiological Psychology* (New York: John Wiley, 1967), offers a more technical but equally broadly based introduction to the literature in this field, though the rapid technological and theoretical advances of recent years may detract from its timeliness. A more recent, albeit more selective, review of this literature and of recent developments in the area may be found in Michael S. Gazzaniga and Colin Blakemore, eds., *Handbook of Psychobiology* (New York: Academic Press, 1975).

Political scientists have begun working on related questions only recently, and the literature in our own discipline is not yet fully developed. Examples of the directions being pursued may be found in Thomas L. Thorson, *Biopolitics* (New York: Holt, Rinehart and Winston, 1970), an essentially philosophical treatise; Lionel Tiger, *Men in Groups* (London: Thomas Nelson and Sons, 1969), written from an anthropological perspective; and Gerald W. Hopple, *Political Psychology and Biopolitics: Assessing and Predicting Elite Behavior in Foreign Policy Crises* (Boulder, Co.: Westview Press, 1980), a study of elites based in part on psychophysiological factors. Two relatively general books of interest are Albert Somit, ed., *Biology and Politics: Recent Explorations* (The Hague: Mouton, 1976), a collection of papers delivered at a recent conference on the subject; and Thomas C. Wiegele, *Biopolitics: Search for a More Human Political Science* (Boulder, Co.: Westview Press, 1979), which provides an overview of the directions and potential significance of biopolitical analysis.

NOTES

1. Thomas Kuhn, *The Structure of Scientific Revolutions* (Chicago: University of Chicago Press, 1962).
2. The significance of demonology in early science is suggested throughout the eight volumes of Lynn Thorndike's *History of Magic and Experimental Science* (New York: Columbia University Press, 1929–58).
3. David J. Hanson, in "Relationship between Methods and Findings in Attitude-Behavior Research," *Psychology* 17 (1980): 11–13, suggests otherwise.
4. A second possible explanation, with which we shall not deal here, rejects the notion that internal dynamics are independent factors in political or other behavior. A concise statement of this so-called behavioristic approach may be found in B. F. Skinner, *Beyond Freedom and Dignity* (New York: Alfred A. Knopf, 1971). An illustrative critique of the theory of cognitive dissonance (one of the balance theories of attitude change) from this perspective is offered by Daryl J. Bem in "Self-Perception: An Alternative Interpretation of Cognitive Dissonance Phenomena," *Psychological Review* 74 (1967): 183–200.
5. Sebastian P. Grossman, *Essentials of Physiological Psychology* (New York: John Wiley, 1973), pp. 12–14.
6. Ibid., pp. 166–67; and Joel Greenberg, "The Brain: Holding the Secrets of Behavior," *Science News* 114 (1978): 362.
7. Grossman, *Essentials*, pp. 16–24; and Thomas S. Brown and Patricia M. Wallace, *Physiological Psychology* (New York: Academic Press, 1980), pp. 10–44.
8. Lawrence S. Burns, "Anatomy of a Brain," *Harper's* 251 (1975): 6.
9. Michael Aron, "The World of the Brain," *Harper's* 251 (1975) 4.

10. Dan Entingh et al., "Biochemical Approaches to the Biological Basis of Memory," in *Handbook of Psychobiology*, ed. Michael S. Gazziniga and Colin Blakemore (New York: Academic Press, 1975), pp. 202–4.
11. Brown and Wallace, *Physiological Psychology*, pp. 454–55.
12. Paul D. MacLean, *A Triune Concept of the Brain and Behavior* (Toronto: University of Toronto Press, 1973), pp. 6–60; and Carl Sagan, *The Dragons of Eden: Speculations on the Evolution of Human Intelligence* (New York: Random House, 1977), chap. 3. For a related discussion see Albert Bandura, *Social Learning Theory* (Englewood Cliffs, N.J.: Prentice-Hall, 1977), pp. 72–74. The theory itself squares nicely with some central arguments of the psychoanalytic approach to personality.
13. Grossman, *Essentials*, pp. 377–78.
14. A classic analysis in this tradition, though not in the end an encouraging one, is K. S. Lashley, "In Search of the Engram," *Symposia of the Society of Experimental Biology* 4 (1950): 454–82.
15. See, for example, the summary of research in James Y. Dyal, "Transfer of Behavioral Bias: Reality and Specificity," in *Chemical Transfer of Learned Information*, ed. Ejnar J. Fjerdingstad (Amsterdam: North-Holland, 1971), pp. 219–63.
16. Grossman, *Essentials*, pp. 371, 471.
17. Examples include D. O. Hebb, *The Organization of Behavior: A Neurophysiological Theory* (New York: John Wiley, 1949); and P. M. Milner, "The Cell Assembly: Mark II," *Psychological Review* 64 (1957): 242–52.
18. See especially T. K. Landauer, "Two Hypotheses Concerning the Biochemical Bases of Memory," *Psychological Review* 71 (1964): 167–79; and E. Roberts, "The Synapse as a Biochemical Self-Organizing Cybernetic Unit," in *Molecular Basis of Some Aspects of Mental Activity*, ed. O. Walaas (London: Academic Press, 1966), 1: 37–82.
19. Grossman, *Essentials*, pp. 474–80; and G. Berlucchi and H. A. Buchtel, "Some Trends in Neurological Study of Learning," in *Handbook of Psychobiology*, ed. Michael S. Gazzaniga and Colin Blakemore (New York: Academic Press, 1975), pp. 483–88.
20. For interesting research on the relationship between attention and learning, see Karl H. Pribram, Roberta U. Day, and Victor S. Johnson, "Selective Attention: Distinctive Brain Electrical Patterns Produced by Differential Reinforcement in Monkey and Man," in *Behavior Control and Modification of Physiological Activity*, ed. David I. Mostofsky (Englewood Cliffs, N.J.: Prentice-Hall, 1976), pp. 81–114.
21. A variety of such cycles and their relationships with cycles in the physical environment are discussed in Gay Gaer Luce, *Biological Rhythms in Human and Animal Physiology* (New York: Dover, 1971). See especially chap. 4.
22. R. I. Henkin, "The Neuroendocrine Control of Perception," in *Perception and Its Disorders*, Research Publication ARNMD 48 (1970), pp. 54–107, as cited in Michael I. Posner, "Psychobiology of Attention," in *Handbook of Psychobiology*, ed. Michael S. Gazzaniga and Colin Blakemore (New York: Academic Press, 1975), p. 448.

23. Posner, "Psychobiology of Attention," pp. 448–53.
24. Gerhard D. Wasserman, *Neurobiological Theory of Psychological Phenomena* (Baltimore: University Park Press, 1978), pp. 35–37.
25. Posner, "Psychobiology of Attention," pp. 468–69.
26. Grossman, *Essentials*, pp. 363–70; and Larry Stein and James D. Belluzzi as quoted in Joel Greenberg, "Memory Research: An Era of 'Good Feeling,'" *Science News* 114 (1978): 364–65.
27. Grossman, *Essentials*, pp. 276–81; and Brown and Wallace, *Physiological Psychology*, pp. 243–55.
28. Greenberg, "Memory Research," pp. 364–65.
29. For a collection of literature relating personality to this notion of normality as a biological central tendency rather than as a subjective state, see R. A. Prentky, ed., *The Biological Aspects of Normal Personality* (Lancaster, England: MTP Press, 1979).
30. One interesting avenue of theory and research of this type is reviewed by Seymour Fisher and Sidney E. Cleveland in *Body Image and Personality* (2nd rev. ed.; New York: Dover, 1968).
31. Jerry S. Wiggins, K. Edward Renner, Gerald L. Clore, and Richard J. Rose, *Principles of Personality* (Reading, Mass.: Addison-Wesley, 1976), pp. 18–32; and Ervin Staub, "The Nature and Study of Human Personality," in *Personality: Basic Aspects and Current Research*, ed. Ervin Staub (Englewood Cliffs, N.J.: Prentice-Hall, 1980), pp. 11–12. For an interesting extension of the same argument to collective political behavior, see Fred H. Willhoite, Jr., "Evolution and Collective Intolerance," *Journal of Politics* 39 (1977): 667–84.
32. The methodology and rationale of such studies is treated in Bernard Tursky, Milton Lodge, and David Cross, "A Bio-Behavioral Framework for the Analysis of Political Behavior," in *Biology and Politics: Recent Explorations*, ed. Albert Somit (The Hague: Mouton, 1976), pp. 59–96.
33. One such study typical of many is Meredith Watts and David Sumi, "Attitudes and Physiological Response to Audiovisual Display of Aggressive Social Behavior" (paper presented at the annual meeting of the Midwest Political Science Association, Chicago, 1976).
34. Brown and Wallace, *Physiological Psychology*, pp. 245–46.
35. See Oli Holsti, "Foreign Policy Decision Makers Viewed Psychologically: 'Cognitive Process' Approaches," in *In Search of Global Patterns*, ed. James N. Rosenau (New York: Free Press, 1976).
36. A similar argument is set forth in Glendon Schubert's "Politics as a Life Science: How and Why the Impact of Modern Biology Will Revolutionize the Study of Political Behavior," in *Biology and Politics: Recent Explorations*, ed. Albert Somit (The Hague: Mouton, 1976), pp. 155–96, and is neatly, albeit only partially, illustrated in Schubert's "A Biocultural Model of Judicial Activism and Restraint" (unpublished paper, University of Hawaii, 1980.)

10

Some Concluding Remarks

The key to understanding the ideas presented in this book is simply to realize that no one of them stands alone, that none of the characteristics or processes we have described here exists or operates in isolation. To the contrary, it is the continuous interaction among them all that culminates in political behavior. This is as true of a tired, frightened president or prime minister deciding upon war as it is of a confused, disappointed voter casting a ballot; as true of a charismatic leader rousing his or her followers from apathy as of two friends talking politics over coffee. In each instance, biological, physiological, psychological, and sociological events combine to produce political action.

In Chapter 1 we spoke of politics as encompassing all thoughts, actions, attitudes, and events that relate to objects perceived to have political meaning; and we suggested, for example, that political thinking was merely thinking applied to political objects, political learning was learning similarly applied, and so forth. By this point, the significance of this notion should be clear. If we wish to understand what makes people behave as they do politically, we must understand, first, what makes them behave as they do in general (irrespective of the objects of their action), and second, what there is about political objects or politics per se that leads to the specific behaviors we are most interested in. In our discussions of physiology, attitude structure and change, personality, learning, and the modes and motives of participation, for example, we have emphasized the former, while our examination of political culture, political socialization, persuasion, competition, and the substance of participation has focused more directly on the latter. None of these discussions, however, can be offered as a sole, or even as the principal, explanation of political behavior in its own right.

People are indeed animals, as we observed in Chapter 9, and their biological antecedents and imperatives and bodily functions do help to structure their behaviors; but those behaviors are far too complex to be accounted for so simply. Rather, heredity produces physical characteristics that provide a stage, and perhaps some direction, for psychological activity. In its turn, personality both reflects these biological and physiological attributes and guides more specialized psychological functions. The seeming correspondence between the three stages of development (primitive, limbic, and neo-cortical) in the triune model of the brain and the Freudian tripartite conceptualization of personality (id, ego, and superego), for example, tantalizingly suggests a linkage of the first type; the association between personality characteristics and attitudes is apparent in both the functional and the social-judgment–involvement approaches to attitude change. Similarly, attitudes derive from but also help structure the socialization process (consider the operation of the perceptual screen), a political culture represents an aggregation of individual beliefs and preferences while acculturation of each individual to it helps shape those very phenomena, and patterns of participation both reflect and give rise to individual and cultural values and perceptions. The key in every instance is interaction.[1]

Nor does this series of exchanges and interminglings take place in a vacuum. It takes place in a context, and more particularly in a political context provided by events; by the attributes of particular social and physical locations and political structures; and by the actions of other individuals, groups, and systems. Such variables as the availability and type of food in a given area can affect physiological function and, in line with the "hierarchy of needs" notion, personality alike, while the degree of openness of the political system has a direct effect on perceptions and participatory styles. War, or the threat of war, with its accompanying stress and deprivation can be felt at all levels of analysis, while the mere perception of relative deprivation can lead to frustration and in turn to violence. Put most simply, people learn from and react to their environment. And this learning and reaction takes place at all levels from instinctive self-preservation to calculated political decision.

The processes and attributes we have described here at such length are universal. Leaders and followers, activists and inactives, we all have them. But to say that they are universal is not to say that they are uniformly distributed among us. Leaders and followers act as people, as do activists and inactives, and in that there is continuity; yet these types of individuals act differently from one another. Some, after all, have become leaders; others have not. Some have chosen to involve themselves actively in politics; others have not. Whether as a result of genetic selection (e.g., giving rise to differences in physical attractiveness that advantage one individual over another), personality differences (e.g., the degree of aggressiveness), differing socialization patterns (e.g., the number or type of efficacy-arousing experiences), the degree of adherence to the political culture or to other widely shared belief systems, or even the differential distribution of physical values (e.g., wealth), to name but a few, individuals differ from one another along these dimensions.

But that, of course, is precisely the point. Individuals do differ along these dimensions, and the dimensions themselves do have explanatory power. People think and behave in the ways we have described, and differences in the degree to which one or another individual manifests a characteristic or the way in which he or she engages in or is acted on by a process are useful in explaining why and how politics works. If this assertion is valid, and the evidence we have developed here strongly indicates that it is, then we have in hand a powerful analytical tool indeed. For it is the primary benefit of conceptualizing political behavior as we have that such notions in fact provide a meaningful basis for furthering our understanding of political reality.

In conclusion (and as a final defense), let me assert once more that this book has been intended not as a gospel on political behavior but as a primer, a mere introduction. Behind every issue I have raised here lies a complex body of research and theory that is more far-reaching than these few brief pages could possibly suggest and a quantity and quality of scientific endeavor to which an introductory volume could never do proper service. Accordingly, the judicious reader should regard the various propositions advanced here not as pronouncements but as possibilities, not as signboards to be read and filed in memory, but as paints with which to design still more sophisticated conceptualizations. Wisdom, after all, is a question, not an answer.

NOTES

1. John Wahlke extends this notion of "levels of analysis" to elites, institutions, and systems in "Pre-Behavioralism in Political Science," *American Political Science Review* 73 (1979): 9–31.

Index

DATE DUE

			Printed In USA

HIGHSMITH #45230